# Grace

## Purpose of the Devotions

The purpose of the Devotions from Oakdale is to encourage you, the reader and prepare you for your daily walk with the Lord. To share with you that God gives us GRACE. It is shared with us in 1 Peter 3:18 "Rather, you must grow in grace and knowledge of our Lord and Savior Jesus Christ."

What a great way to begin each day with the ONE who has given His life for you and me. He is waiting to share it with you if you will invite Him in.

While you are reading, I am in Oakdale allowing God to speak to me and through me His promises so I can pass them on to you, the reader. I pray for you and hope you will build new friendships and open new ministries through sharing the devotions from Oakdale.

## Don't Forget Jesus!
*Greg*

PRESENTATION PAGE

PRESENTED TO

_____

FROM

_____

DATE

_____

Also by
Gregory A. Smith

The Don't Forgets
of
Life

# Devotions
## FROM
# OAKDALE

## A 365 DAY DEVOTIONAL

## GREGORY A. SMITH

PRIMIX
PUBLISHING
THE WRITE CHOICE

Primix Publishing
East Brunswick Office Evolution
1 Tower Center Boulevard, Ste 1510
East Brunswick, NJ 08816
www.primixpublishing.com
Phone: 1-800-538-5788

Published by Primix Publishing: 12/18/2024

ISBN: 979-8-89194-350-6(sc)
ISBN: 979-8-89194-351-3(hc)
ISBN: 979-8-89194-352-0(e)

Library of Congress Control Number: 2024922087

# CONTENTS

Contact us
Or
Share with us

# DEDICATION

To Cheri, the love of my life.

Thank you for loving me unconditionally and encouraging
me to be the best I can be. Your affection, kindness,
friendship and our soulful spirit make each day for
me full of joy. You pour into me each and every day
from 160 miles away while I am here at Oakdale.

I respect you, believe in you and look forward
to the great adventure ahead of us spending our
lives together for the rest of our days.

To Bekah, Betsy and Mollie Catherine

My beautiful daughters, I am so proud of each of you.
You each have provided me with many 'Don't Forgets'
in my life and I love each of you from the bottom of
my heart and am very proud to be your Dad.

To my parents, Don and Marilyn Smith

To you both, I am so thankful for the strong Christian
example that you have instilled in me throughout my life.
Your strong Godly beliefs and your daily lifestyle has been
lived out and has provided freshness to me as your son, to your
grandchildren as well as your great grandchildren. Thank you
for your prayers and encouragement that always inspires me.

To my friends at Oakdale

You have added so much inspiration, friendship and insights into a new future. Thank you, Art, Bryan, T.J., Brad, Hector, Wayne, Arnold, J.D., Victor and David. You all gave me a safe place to land. To the Prayer Circle group, thank you as well.

Bible Verse

Psalm 91:4 'He will cover you with His feathers.

He will shelter you with His wings. His faithful
promises are your armor and protection.'

# ACKNOWLEDGMENTS

My oldest daughter, Bekah, is one of the main reasons this devotional project took place. As things were sinking in that I was headed to Federal Prison in Oakdale, she recommended that I write devotions and send them to her. She would input them into an app and then once I exited Oakdale upon completion of my sentence, she would put together a book. Thank you, Bekah for encouraging me to start the project.

It all started three days before self-surrendering at Oakdale and then 205 days later, the 365 devotions were completed. God has blessed me through this entire project.

To Ron Smith, I wish to thank him for his talented touch upon the front cover design, the coin design as well as a very special place in my heart as one of my closest friends. My best man and friend to partner with along this walk to inspire others. Thank you, my brother, in Christ!

Last but not least. My everything in thanks to my beautiful wife, Cheri. You have blessed me in so many ways through this project. From mailing you devotions, making corrections and typing each one of the devotions to build the project we now have in completed form, Devotions from Oakdale. Day in and day out, your encouragement from 160 miles away transpired from Day 1 to Day 205. I am thankful for all you have done along the way and I just want you to know that you are amazing. I love you!

# INTRODUCTION

## 3 DAYS AND COUNTING....

As I write this introduction, the book of devotions is completed and waiting for you, the reader to saddle up and join me for the adventure. I am excited for you to be a part of a daily walk that has been a very exciting experience for me and for those involved. So, here we go.

We begin forty-eight hours prior to arriving at Oakdale Federal Correction Institute in Oakdale, Louisiana.

January 3, 2021 - 48 hours until I report and I am awakening to a beautiful sun-filled morning with ice on my windshield and windows fogged to the max. I am so thankful for the life I have in Christ and I am looking forward to what God will reveal to me as we begin the Devotions from Oakdale.

My approved items are ready which include first and foremost my Bible, God's Word, my sword, glasses, my Don't Forget coin, 12 Grace tickets from my sweet sister Donna Kay, my handbook for Oakdale, tennis shoes, 12 photos, Chuck Swindoll's book 'Meet Me in The Library,' my most comfortable tattered blue jeans, and my shirt that I will wear, imprinted Fearfully and Wonderfully made in honor of my grandson Landrum.

A lot of unknowns ahead of me on a minute-by-minute basis in Federal Correctional Institute that will soon become my temporary home for a short while.

As I write this 48-hour post, I am leaving behind a wife of 3 ½ months, 3 beautiful daughters, 7 totally awesome grandkids, 2 wonderful parents and 3 siblings that love their brother with all of their heart. My sister, Donna Kay wrote to me and shared the following promise that I will end on today; 'My grace is sufficient for you, my power is made perfect in weakness.' II Corinthians 12:9

Look unto Jesus and Don't Forget! See you in Oakdale.

January 4,2021 - 24 hours until I report and I am looking out at a beautiful sunrise this morning. I am so thankful to be alive and know that even though I am 24 hours away from stepping into a new and different life at Oakdale, I am at peace.

At peace with God my Creator, at peace with my family members, and at peace with my fellow workers. My parents have been my rock for so many years and they continue to be the same even up until the day before my departure.

Today I am reminded by the verse "I can do all things through Christ which strengthens me." The word ALL is so important and need to have great emphasis placed upon it. God sent His Son for ALL who will believe upon His name, trust Him, and follow Him.

Will you walk alongside me as we walk alongside Christ as I enter Oakdale?

January 5, 2021 – reporting day. Well, the day has arrived after nearly 33 months. Today my family will have a mid-morning brunch with me and then a final 30-minute drive to Oakdale.

Today is a day of hope for me. I hope my family stays strong and I will be strong. I hope my friends stay strong and know that God is still God even during tough times. I hope for world health during a very trying COVID-19 pandemic. I hope that the grace tickets my sister has given me continue to remind me of the unending grace of God, I will need them. I hope that I will be able to continue in leadership roles wherever I am and whatever I do.

Today begins a new journey, a new road to walk into a new environment, a new temporary home. Trusting God with me as we begin a new walk in a new season. Same God, same miracles, same grace, same love and the same hope. Welcome to Oakdale........

Isaiah 41:10, 13 "So do not fear, for I am with you, do not be dismayed, for I am your God. I will strengthen you and help you; I will uphold you with my righteous right hand. For I am the Lord your God who takes hold of your right hand and says to you, DO NOT FEAR: I will help you."

JESUS:

Servant

Humble

Hope

Kindness

Love

Forgiveness

Joy

Patience

Strength

Teacher

Prayer Warrior

Son

DEVOTIONS FROM OAKDALE

# TRUST

SCRIPTURE: Proverbs 3:5-6

WRITER: King Solomon

KEY WORDS: TRUST, SEEK, SHOW, ALL, WILL

Proverbs 3:5-6 'Trust in the Lord with all your heart, do not depend on your own understanding. Seek His will in all you do, and He will show you which path to take.

In dealing with the Christian walk, it always begins with trust. We have to place our trust in God/Christ to initiate acceptance of Jesus dying for our sins. Secondly, we have to be fully committed as the verse says 'all your heart,' not just a portion of it. The verse then goes on to tell us not to depend on our own understanding because we are not smart enough or good enough on our own.

That is why seeking Christ each and every day in all that we do is truly following the will of God. Ultimately, He will show you His direction for your life each day.

PRAYER: Heavenly Father, please help us to know that when we trust in You and seek Your will. You are there for us and will help us go in the right direction. We ask safety for family and friends and the love I pray over each one of them.  AMEN

DON'T FORGET!

# JOY IN LIVING

SCRIPTURE: Philippians 1:2-11

WRITER: Paul—his letter to the Philippians along with Timothy

Philippians 1: v.2 'May God our Father and the Lord Jesus Christ give you grace and peace.' V.3 'Every time I think of you, I give thanks to my God.'

Today Paul offers prayer and thanksgiving for the church, leaders and deacons along with the people in Philippi.

PRAYER: Thank You, God for Your grace, it is sufficient.

Don't Forget

# DON'T WORRY

SCRIPTURE: Philippians 4:6

WRITER: Paul

Philippians 4:6 'Don't worry about anything; instead, pray about everything. Tell God what you need, and thank Him for all he has done.'

We have to go back to verses 4 and 5 to see that Paul uses the word "always" be full of joy in the Lord. I say it again – rejoice! Let everyone see that you are considerate in all you do. Remember, the Lord is coming soon.

There are a lot of things to unfold in these 3 verses. Paul is exclaiming that we are not to worry about things going on in this life, but to be full of joy and rejoice.

Being in prison myself I can relate to what Paul is saying and I am blessed to have a loving family praying for me and encouraging me not to worry that they are protected while I am away on this mission trip with Christ.


DON'T FORGET!

P.S. Everyone is important!

# ENDURANCE

SCRIPTURES: Hebrews 12:1; Psalm 136:1

WRITERS: Hebrews-unknown; Psalm-David

Hebrew 12:1 'Therefore, since we are surrounded by such a huge crowd of witnesses to the life of faith, let us strip off every weight that slows us down, especially the sin that so easily trips us up. And let us run with endurance the race that God has set before us.'

Psalm 136:1 Give thanks to the Lord, for He is good! His faithful love endures forever.

God calls us to bring everything to Him and place it at His feet. He has already paid the price for our sins and desires to be in constant communication with us. However, the choice is ours and we must keep our lives free of sin so we can endure and impact others around us.

Lastly, we need to be thankful to God because He is good. He is faithful and just and will forgive us of any unrighteousness if we call upon Him. (1 John 1:9)

PRAYER: Lord, we pray today for the endurance needed to run this race of life. We are sinners saved by your grace and we love You with all our hearts. AMEN

DON'T FORGET!

# RUN

SCRIPTURE: Proverbs 4:12-13; I Corinthians 9:24-27

WRITER: Proverbs—King Solomon; I Corinthians—Paul

Proverbs 4:12-13 'When you walk, you won't be held back; when you run, you won't stumble. Take hold of my instructions; don't let them go, guard them, for they are the key to life.'

I Corinthians 9:24-27 Don't you realize that in a race everyone runs, but only one person gets the prize? So, run to win! All athletes are disciplined in their training. They do it to win a prize that will fade away, but we do it for an eternal prize. So, I run with purpose in every step. I am not just shadowboxing. I discipline my body like an athlete, training it to do what it should. Otherwise, I fear that after preaching to others I myself might be disqualified.

Welcome to the topic of running in the Christian walk, no pun intended. We have two different writers tapping on the same idea of always giving your all, not holding back and counting on and trusting Christ to make sure you finish the task and do not stumble. Paul goes deep to the finish line speaking of the athlete and the rigorous training that he or she goes through just to be physically fit not to miss the mark. A question is asked of who gets the prize and a very quick answer follows with the challenge to run to win. We need the same discipline in training in our daily Christian walk. If we don't, we will run the risk of stumbling. So, let me encourage you today to discipline yourself daily. Keep your eyes on Christ and always run the race to win the prize of Christ.

PRAYER: Father, may you direct each of our steps to always follow You and seek You in the race of life. AMEN

DON'T FORGET!

# INTEGRITY

SCRIPTURES: Psalm 119:1-2; Proverbs 10:9

WRITERS: Psalm—David; Proverbs—Solomon

DEFINITION: integrity—honesty; without compromise or corruption

Psalm 119:1-2 'Joyful are people of integrity, who follow the instruction of the Lord.' Joyful are those who obey His laws and search from Him with all their hearts.'

Proverbs 10:9 'People with integrity walk safely, but those who follow crooked paths will be exposed.'

Honesty, with compromise or corruption are all good topics to discuss when someone wants to depict integrity. To live with integrity is to live your life with the best of intentions and with honesty.

I remember my PawPaw early in my life taking me to a local drugstore. While in the store, he noticed that someone had dropped a $5 dollar bill on the floor. My PawPaw, not making a big deal of it put it in his pocket then went to find the manager and turned in the money as lost. By the way, he made a huge impression on his grandson and that has been 50 years ago. Amazing how something so small could have such a large impact on me and how I live my life today.

I can't say I have not made mistakes in my life in the area of integrity because I have. But that is why I am thankful that Jesus died on the cross for my sins and sees them no more.

I also experienced finding money in a store while with one of my daughters. So, I went through the same process of returning it to the store manager. Always strive to do the right thing. That continues to build integrity just as Christ would want.

PRAYER: Lord God, You call us to a high standard of integrity. Help us not to miss the mark and to bring honor and glory to You. AMEN

DON'T FORGET!

# HELPER

SCRIPTURES: Psalm 70:5; Psalm 115:7; Hebrews 13:6

WRITERS: Psalm—David; Hebrews—Unknown

Psalm 70:5 'But as for me, I am poor and needy; please hurry to my aid, O God you are my helper and my savior, O Lord, do not delay.'

Psalm 115:9 'O Israel, trust the Lord! He is your helper and your shield.'

Hebrews 13:6 'So we can say with confidence, The Lord is my helper, so I will have no fear. What can mere people do to me?'

DEFINITION: helper—one who gives aid

You know as soon as I finished writing the definition of Helper, I truly recognize that God sent his son Jesus to give us aid all of the time. We recognize in the scripture from Psalm 70:5, the request is one of pleading. Hurry, don't wait, I need you. Then in Psalm 115:9 the request and command from the writer is to trust the Lord, exclamation point. I am truly thankful that the Lord is our helper and shield and no doubt, whatever we are going through in this life, we can say with confidence that we have no fear.

We are living in times of a pandemic with many life changes going on around us from Zoom meetings to social distancing along with many other struggles. Don't forget that the one who created you and me is the greatest helper we could ever have. Trust Him today.

Prayer: Lord God, thank you that You are our helper. Help us to lean on you and bring everything to your feet and surrender all we have to You. To God be the glory for the great things He does for us. AMEN

DON'T FORGET!

# YESTERDAY, TODAY
# AND FOREVER

SCRIPTURE: Hebrews 13:8-9

WRITER: unknown

Hebrews 13:8-9 'Jesus Christ is the same yesterday, today and forever. So, do not be attracted by strange new ideas. Your strength comes from God's grace, not from rules about food, which don't help those who follow him.'

I have fallen back on and quoted this verse 8 of Hebrews for as long as I can remember. You know that when you step back and take it all in, it really makes sense. Our Lord and Savior Jesus Christ is the SAME yesterday, today and forever. That is a terrific promise that you and I can hold onto as believers. Verse 9 tells us to stay on point towards Him and not to be pulled away by outside interests.

Our world is facing so many different things when people have life choices in careers, colleges, relationships, religion and many more. Ultimately, as that verse says, Jesus Christ will not change and He will give you the gift of salvation if you will just call upon his name and trust him. My aim and goal in writing Devotions from Oakdale is to glorify God, encourage you the reader and ultimately lead the unsaved to Jesus Christ. Will you make a decision to follow him for a first time or perhaps re-commit your life? We all have times when we take steps backward in our walk. That is okay because Jesus is there to hear our prayers. Trust Him today.

PRAYER: Dear God, In an ever-changing world, we need You! Cover us, protect us like You did yesterday and like You are doing today. We thank You and praise You. AMEN

DON'T FORGET!

# IMPROVING YOUR SERVE

SCRIPTURES: Romans 12:7-8; Galatians 5:13; 1 Timothy 5:10

WRITERS: Romans—Paul; Galations—Paul; 1 Timothy—Paul

Romans 12:7-8 'If your gift is serving others, serve them well. If you are a teacher, teach well. If your gift is to encourage others, be encouraging. If it is giving, give generously. If God has given you leadership ability, take the responsibility seriously. And if you have a gift of showing kindness to others, do it gladly.'

For me, 'Improving Your Serve' came at a fairly early age of 24 or 25. Our new Pastor, Brother Mark Sutton, shared a book with me by Chuck Swindoll that changed how I looked at myself and others around me. I have shared with him over the last 25 years in serving beside him, how much that book touched my life. Brother Mark was always about serving, but more importantly, improving that serve. Think about the word improve for a moment. It means to give more, do more and always striving to get better. What has God placed on your heart that you would like to improve on? Maybe strengthening your marriage, your relationships with your family, friends or most importantly, your relationship with God.

Sometimes when we strive to improve something, we have to recognize that something is lacking or missing in the equation. The title today is Improving your serve. Your means you. Let me encourage you to work on you and be the best you can be in improving how we serve others. People are hurting, they are lonely and missing a special touch. Reach out to someone today that needs you. This will help you improve your serve.

PRAYER—Heavenly Father, today I am thankful for Brother Mark Sutton who always encouraged me to improve my serve, lead from my heart and do everything unconditionally. Today, I am especially thankful for my family, friends and loved ones. May they seek ways to improve their serve daily. AMEN

## DON'T FORGET!

# SERVING OTHERS

SCRIPTURES: 1 Timothy 4:6; Zechariah 3:8; 1 Corinthians 16:18

WRITER: I Timothy—Paul ; Zachariah

DEFINITION: servant--to meet the needs of and subject one's will to that of another

1 Timothy 4:6 'If you explain these things to the brothers and sisters, Timothy, you will be a worthy servant of Jesus Christ, one who is nourished by the message of faith and the good teaching you have followed.'

Zachariah 3:8 'Soon I am going to bring my servant, the Branch.'

1 Corinthians 16:18 'They have been a wonderful encouragement to me, as they have been to you. You must show your appreciation to all who serve so well.'

I love this topic and when I look at verse 18 'to all who serve so well,' one person comes to mind and it is my great friend, brother in Christ and co-worker, Dave Baker. His name has to be considered in the definition of serving others just because that is what he does. My writing today in no way allows me to hit on everything I know and see that this guy has done over the years for other people but he sure reminds me of my PawPaw, Aubrey Boswell. They have a lot of similarities. They both are active walkers, woodworkers, 'savers of wood' is a great term, entrepreneur, giver, difference maker, teacher, humorist just to name a few. Most of all, I call him a trusted friend. So here is a short list of tasks completed to serve others well-

1) Worked alongside me for the past 18 months with a smile and a willing heart.
2) Mowing someone's yard just because and he doesn't like yard work-funny huh!!
3) Remaking a piece of broken furniture structurally sound again and can you do it by tomorrow?

4) He along with his wife Jeri making cookies and lots of them for the crew daily.
5) Blowing the gutters and someone's roof just to make it look good-he doesn't always have stable footing though!
6) Making rolling pins, tissue box covers, cutting boards and beautiful bowls all from tree jobs completed-Impeccable design and craftsmanship. Thanks Dave.
7) Donating to others that are in need and thinking nothing of it.
8) Always having an 'all in' attitude.
9) Preparing and teaching God's word to his Sunday School group. His home table has his library and preparation materials so he can deliver God's word.

PRAYER: Dear God in Heaven, thank You for blessing me and my family with Dave Baker! What a servant of God and a man on a mission to always do more and does not want any credit. I am thankful today for such a friend. May I be the same to those I am around. AMEN

DON'T FORGET!

# DIFFERENCE MAKER

SCRIPTURE: Galatians 6:7-9

WRITER: Paul

Galations 6:7-9 'A man reaps what he sows. The one who sows to please his sinful nature, from that nature will reap destruction; the one who sows to please the spirit, from the spirit will reap eternal life. Let us not become weary in doing good, for at the proper time we will reap a harvest if we do not give up.'

Arnold Palmer, the King of Golf legend comes to mind of a man that was one of the all-time greatest golfers, a successful business partner and owner, but most of all a Christian man that was truly a difference maker. Some of his accomplishments were: Palmer Golf Academy, Latrobe Pennsylvania as a neighbor and friend, Bay Hill Golf Resort, Pebble Beach, a strong work ethic, belief in himself to win and always a firm handshake with whomever he met. Accomplishments are not always projects that generate income. They are also a personal touch in someone's life along with the character that God provides. Arnold Palmer always exhibited those traits and I know why my PawPaw looked up to him so much and I now see why my PawPaw was the man he became. I am very thankful that the Arnold Palmer character was passed on to me by such a wonderful example like my PawPaw. I still have handwritten notes from my PawPaw that encourage me to be a good son, a good student and teammate. These two men are 'standouts' to me in the category of being a difference maker. Are you a difference maker? Are you touching people in ways that I have described today that cause you to go the extra mile…to be kind, patient and not judgmental? Will you join me today and think who you can make a difference with today?

PRAYER: Heavenly Father, thank You for Godly men like Arnold Palmer and my PawPaw who did things because they were the right things. Also, because their attitude was that of Jesus. A pure desire to please God in all they did. AMEN

DON'T FORGET!

# "ALL IN" ATTITUDE

SCRIPTURES: Philippians 2:5; 1 Peter 3:8; 1 Peter 4:1

WRITER: Paul

KEY WORD "ALL IN" – Committed, teamwork, a mental position with regard to a fact or state; a feeling or emotion toward a fact or state

Philippians 2:5 'You must have the same attitude that Christ Jesus had.'

1 Peter 3:8 'Finally, all of you should be of one mind. Sympathize with each other. Love each other as brothers and sisters. Be tenderhearted, and keep a humble attitude.'

1 Peter 4:1 'So then, since Christ suffered physical pain, you must arm yourselves with the same attitude he had and be ready to suffer too. For if you have suffered physically for Christ, you have finished with sin.'

When you hear someone tell you that they are 'all in', what you believe is that they are committed to the cause that you have placed before them. It is a full commitment that they will not back down from until they see everything to completion. The definition above speaks about 'mental' which means that the mind has surveyed and decided to say yes.

An 'all in' attitude is like that of Jesus Christ which is one of kindness, meekness, patience and the list continues.

Think of some positive projects that either you have had placed on your heart like preparing a loaf of bread for a home bound widow or widower, participating in a function that honors our service men and women or perhaps serving the homeless in a shelter or camp. It is your choice today. Will you commit to be 'all in' and make a difference and also, bring someone along with you.

PRAYER: Lord Jesus, thank you for being 'all in' for me and everyone else that You gave Your precious life for on Calvary's cross. I am thankful for Your unfailing love each and every day. AMEN

DON'T FORGET!

# PEACE THAT PASSES ALL UNDERSTANDING

SCRIPTURE: Psalm 23:2; Galatians 5:22; 2 Timothy 2:22

WRITERS: Psalm—David; Galatians—Paul; 2 Timothy—Paul

Psalm 23:2 'He lets me rest in green meadows; He leads me beside peaceful streams'

Galatians 5:22 'But the Holy Spirit produces this kind of fruit in our lives: love, joy, peace, patience, kindness, goodness, faithfulness, gentleness and self-control. There is no law against these things.'

2 Timothy 2:22 'Run away from anything that stimulates youthful lusts, instead pursue righteous living, faithfulness, love and peace. Enjoy the companionship of those who call on the Lord with pure hearts.'

'Peace that passes all understanding.' When you read and meditate on these focus verses today, it is hard not to just fall into a very severe picture of what God does for us on a daily basis. I want and need the peace of God in what I am experiencing each and every day here in Oakdale. My writings are from my prison cell #49, yet when I look out of my 2' x 7' window with bars across them, I see multiple crosses just like those of Jesus died on for you and me. At night, I have an illuminated flood light that beams right into my cell that I think is 8000 lumens it is so bright. Again, another great reminder to this writer that I am blessed beyond measure, highly favored and loved by many. I also see beyond the prison fencing, thick wooded areas of oaks and pine trees that are outside the penitentiary property. Are you at peace in your life or are you struggling with things that bring you down and weigh heavy on your shoulders? Pray that God will help you to find peace you need to also be able to strengthen and comfort those around you.

PRAYER: Dear God, I pray for peace for everyone reading and studying these devotions from Oakdale. We all have opportunities to our left and to our right. Help us to be mindful of how powerful it is to be able to share peace with others. AMEN

DON'T FORGET!

# DETERMINATION

SCRIPTURES: Proverbs 4:23; Ecclesiastes 11:6

WRITERS: Proverbs—King Solomon; Ecclesiastes—Qoheleth, King Solomon

Proverbs 4:23 'Guard your heart above all else; for it determines the cause of your life.'

Ecclesiastes 11:6 'Plant your seed in the morning and keep busy all afternoon, for you don't know if profit will come from one activity or another or maybe both.'

DEFINITION: determination—to decide; resolve, having a can-do attitude, pushing forward in an effort; things that one may determine to accomplish; succeed in business, finish a race, win an award, get married, have children, win someone to Christ. Interact with other people, make new friends, love others an provide joy to their life

It comes to my mind not to settle for status quo. We have all heard, 'where there is a will, there is a way.' You have many choices in the lineup of the day. When to set the alarm to get up, what to prepare for breakfast, sack lunches to get ready for the kids, what you will do with your daily schedule and then perhaps what the evening meal or plans will be based on your family situation. I hope and pray that you have determination to succeed and to accomplish because we all need it in our fast-paced world.

Step back for a minute and look at Proverbs 4:23, 'guard your heart ABOVE all else, it determines the course of your life.' We need to protect what God has given us. He also says that we need to be planters planting a positive seed here and a positive seed there and God will bring about the profits.

Think about the two or three things that are on your to do list today that you are determined to accomplish. Do them with all you heart, soul, and mind and God will bless you.

PRAYER: Lord God Redeemer, thank You for determination.

You were determined to send Jesus to this world to live among us, perform miracles, accept everyone and then die a terrible death to save us of our sins. Please help us to have a strong determination in how we live our lives. AMEN

DON'T FORGET!

# MIRACLES

SCRIPTURES: Mark 6:2; Galatians 3:5; Luke 23:8

WRITERS: Mark—Mark; Galatians—Paul; Luke—Luke

DEFINITION: miracle—an extraordinary event manifesting divine intervention in human affairs

Mark 6:2 'The next sabbath he began teaching in the synagogue and many who heard him were amazed. They said, 'Where did he get all this wisdom and the power to perform miracles?'

Galatians 3:5 'I ask you again, does God give you the Holy Spirit and work miracles among you because you obey the law? Of course not! It is because you believe the message you heard about Christ.'

Luke 2:7 'She gave birth to her first-born son. She wrapped him snugly in strips of cloth and laid him in a manger, because there was no lodging in the inn.'

We are looking at miracles today. What an honor it is to speak of miracles. As we see in Luke 2:7, the greatest miracle of all, the birth of our Lord and Savior, Jesus Christ. When we read the definition of miracle and see the words, 'extraordinary, divine intervention' both taking part in human affairs, that pretty much says it all. When we look through the Bible, we see many miracles that Jesus performed…the feeding of the 5,000, walking on water, turning water into wine, and raising Lazarus from the dead… just to name a few.

How about you today? Can you think of any miracles that occurred in your life you need to thank God for again? Maybe a new marriage, a new son or daughter, a new career, a new medical prognosis stating that the cancer is gone, a relationship reestablished, or perhaps prayers that you have been offering that have now been answered?

PRAYER: Dear Righteous One, You make all miracles take place in your timing, big or small. We thank You for being a righteous God and providing the greatest miracle, that of giving your Son Jesus to die on the cross for our sins. AMEN

DON'T FORGET!

# EAGLES

SCRIPTURES: Isaiah 40:31; Revelation 4:7

WRITERS: Isaiah—Isaiah; Revelation—John

Isaiah 40:31 'But those who trust in the Lord will find new strength. They will soar high on wings like eagles. They will walk and not faint.'

Revelation 4:7 'The first of these living beings was like a lion; the second was like an ox; the third had a human face; and the fourth was like an eagle in flight.'

What words come to mind when you hear the word 'Eagle?' Unique, strength of talons, size, wing span, domination, powers of light.

I associate the eagle with the United States of America and the freedom that we have in this great country. An eagle is skilled to be able to attack its prey to nourish itself along with its nest of eaglets. My high school mascot where I grew up was an eagle. One of my mentors, John Franks, had eagles posted on his driveway columns at this home. So, I guess you see by now that I love eagles.

When we look at scripture, we see in Isaiah that trusting in the Lord allows us to have the paralleled strength of that of an eagle. We will soar high and we will not grow weary because our trust is in him.

Lastly, in Revelation, John speaks that in the end, life is not about us. It is all about God. Every earthly thing will fade away. That clearly defines the awesome nature of God. Are you prepared today for that day? Mount up like an eagle and soar with a life in Christ.

PRAYER—Lord God, thank You that we have strength in You no matter what we come up against in this life. May we always yield to You in all we do. AMEN

DON'T FORGET!

# REDEMPTION

SCRIPTURE: Ruth 3:1-2

WRITER: Samuel the Prophet

DEFINITION: redeem—to buy back; to save by payment of a ransom; to free from the consequences of sin. One who frees or delivers another from difficulty, danger or bondage, usually by the payment of a ransom price

Ruth 3:1-2: 'One day Naomi said to Ruth,' My daughter, it's time that I found a permanent home for you, so that you will be provided for. Boaz is a close relative of ours, and he's been very kind by letting you gather grain with his young women. Tonight, he will be winnowing barley at the threshing floor.'

Well, well, well. This topic definitely has me today since I am in prison and definitely fit the description of bondage. I am in quarantine right now due to COVID-19 protocol and will remain between 14 and 28 days. I reside within a 10' X 7' solid wall cell thankfully with a 2' X 7' window that looks out to a heavily wooded area. However, and I mean a big however, this is temporary and I am reminded of Isaiah 41:10 that states 'so do not fear, Greg, for I am with you; do not be dismayed for I am your God. I will strengthen you and help you; I will uphold you with my righteous right hand.' Thank You Jesus. Jesus is our kinsman redeemer who came to redeem me and you so that we might trust in him and receive the gift of eternal life through him. It is through believing in him that we have eternal life. Help us to share this good word today.

PRAYER: Heavenly Father, continue to help us draw nearer to You each and every day. Thank You for redeeming us from eternal separation and torment. Use us today. AMEN

DON'T FORGET!

# DEFENDER

SCRIPTURE: Psalm 68:5; Proverbs 22:23; Jude 1:3

WRITERS: Psalm 68—David; Proverbs—Solomon; Jude—Jude

DEFINITION: defender—one who guards and protects, to maintain and support in the face of argument or hostile criticism, to drive danger away from

Psalm 68:5 'Father to the fatherless, defender of widows, this is God whose dwelling place is holy.'

Proverbs 22:23 'For the Lord is their defender. He will ruin anyone who ruins them.'

Jude 1:3 'Dear friends, I had been eagerly planning to write to you about the salvation we all share. But now I find that I must write about something else, urging you to defend the faith that God has entrusted one for all time to his holy people.'

I believe DEFEND is a terrific topic for us today because who in this world defends us better than our Heavenly Father? We are called to be a defender of widows, protecting them and also entrusting with the ability to defend the faith.

Colossians 3:2 states 'set your mind on things above, Greg, not earthly things.' We need our focus on God all the time so we can defend when we need to on his behalf.

PRAYER: Heavenly Father, I pray for Your wisdom today as I strive to defend my faith to those around me. AMEN

## DON'T FORGET!

# ABUNDANCE

SCRIPTURE: John 16:24; Matthew 13:12

WRITERS: John—John; Matthew—Matthew

DEFINITION: abundance—great quantity, affluence, more than ample, great plenty

John 16:24 'You haven't done this before. Ask, using my name, and you will receive, and you will have abundant joy.'

Matthew 13:12 'To those who listen to my teaching, more understanding will be given and they will have an abundance of knowledge. But for those who are not listening, even what little understanding they have will be taken away from them.'

To receive more than expected is always a nice thing. Both writers in today's readings show that if we trust and ask in Jesus' name, we will receive plenty of joy in our life. When we are in God's word and striving to apply ourselves, we will gain abundant knowledge. However, if we stray and don't listen and pay attention, we will be given a lesser amount, no doubt, we always appreciate more in this life we live so be thankful with what you are blessed with today.

PRAYER: Father God, thank You that You always bless us abundantly. I pray that we will examine ourselves to be in a right relationship with You. AMEN

DON'T FORGET!

# LORD'S PRAYER

SCRIPTURE: Psalm 23

WRITER: David

I have been looking forward to this particular chapter. It is one of my favorites in the Bible. This particular chapter is probably used in more hospitals and prison cells because it provides hope for one's life. 'The Lord is my shepherd; I have all that I need.' I guess we can really stop there. Enough said, we only need Jesus in our life and daily walk. He will give us rest when we need it and will guide us beside peaceful and restful waters that He created. While we are walking through, we will encounter dark days, challenges, financial loss, grieving time spent in the dark valleys. He tells us hey, I am with you, by your side. Six strong verses of promise, protection and peace. Blessings and goodness will pursue us for our entire life and then for eternity if we will seek him.

We all need a shepherd in our life. Could you give me a name of a local shepherd that you might recommend? Sometimes we float on our own thinking that we are in charge and we can do things ourself. We know that failure lurks around the corner sometimes and we should not go it alone.

- God leads us to the rest that we need
- He leads us through discipline for restoration
- He takes us through darkness with his presence

Walk with confidence today with the Good Shepherd. John 14:6 says, 'I am THE way, THE truth, and THE life. No one comes to the Father except through me.'

Do you know the Shepherd today? If not, invite him into your heart. (see plan of salvation on back inside cover).

PRAYER: Dear God, Thank You for John 10:11. 'I am the good shepherd; the good shepherd lays down his life for his sheep. AMEN

## DON'T FORGET!

# DON'T FORGET 'WINK' MOMENTS!

SCRIPTURES: Isaiah 43:19; James 1:23; Proverbs 17:17

WRITERS: Isaiah—Isaiah; James—James; Proverbs—Solomon

DEFINITION OF DON'T FORGET MOMENTS: These are some of my own that I have been blessed with over the years—completion of my first book 'The Don't Forgets of Life', special times with my PawPaw and my parents, true friendship that is genuine and you know it will last.

I remember one of my favorite 'wink' moments came with my youngest daughter. We started out giving allowance to the girls for no other reason than to teach them to tithe 10% to God. So, with the oldest daughter it went like, Okay, I'm getting $5.00 so .50 cents will go in my envelope for church. A few years later with the middle daughter it was about the same. All were willing to give as commanded in the Bible. Malachi 3:10 'Bring all the tithes into the storehouse so there will be enough food in my temple. If you do, says the Lord of Heaven's Armies, 'I will open the windows of heaven for you.' So, I hand the four one-dollar bills and four quarters to the youngest daughter just waiting for her to figure out the math and give two quarters as her 10% into her envelope. All of a sudden, a wink moment! She slides $3.00 of her $5.00 allowance into her envelope. My heart sunk thinking my little girl would nearly give it all when all of a sudden, my wife looks at me and said 'Whatcha gonna do now big boy?' as to say 'Check!'

I remember my dad using the same principles with me and my siblings. I once told my dad that 2 quarters would buy some extra ICEEs at the store.

I am very proud of my daughters and the way in which they model the Christian life and their walk with the Lord.

PRAYER: Mighty God, thank You for the 'wink' gifts that have always come about in my life for 61 years. Even as I praise You from a prison cell, I am thankful for all You do for me. I know You are with me always. AMEN

DON'T FORGET!

# EARNESTLY

SCRIPTURES: II Chronicles 15:15; James 5:16; Colossians 4:12

WRITERS: II Chronicles—Ezra; James—James; Colossians—Paul

II Chronicles 15:15 'All in Judah were happy about this covenant, for they had entered into it with all their heart. They earnestly sought-after God, and they found him.'

James 5:16 'Confess your sins to each other and pray for each other so that you may be healed. The earnest prayer of a righteous person has great power and produces wonderful results.'

DEFINITION: earnestly—in a manner that is intense and serious, fervently; a serious state of mind

In Colossians 4:12, we see Epaphras, a servant of Christ Jesus, sending greetings and earnestly praying and asking God to make those in his following strong and perfect. We are talking about reaching to others and letting them know that they were important.

Sometimes we have situations within a family or with a friend where a relationship has been damaged and Paul lays the ground work for restoration.

Lastly, James says confess your sins to each other and pray for one another and this will bring about healing. An earnest prayer is the key to having successful results.

Is there a relationship with a family member or friend that you need to earnestly approach? If so, allow God to move your heart and choose to forgive.

PRAYER: Great Forgiver, Holy One, Lord help us daily to earnestly seek out those that we need to make things right with because You command us to. AMEN

## DON'T FORGET!

# HARVEST

SCRIPTURE: John 4:35-36; Galations 6:9

WRITERS: John—John; Galations—Paul

John 4:35-36 'You know the saying, four months between planting and harvest. But I say, wake up and look around. The fields are ripe for harvest. The harvesters are paid good wages, and the fruit they harvest is people brought to eternal life.'

Galations 6:9 'So let's not get tired of doing what is good. At just the right time, we will reap a harvest of blessings if we don't give up.'

We are no doubt speaking about a spiritual harvest when we look at both passages. When I think of a harvest in Louisiana, I think of a cotton crop. At the first of the season, you see the farmer out on his huge John Deere tractor turning the soil and preparing it for seed. Then he prays for sunshine and rain, enough to grow the crop and provide for a big harvest. Financially speaking, a farmer's profit is to provide for his family, reinvest in his equipment, his storage, his insurance, his fertilizer and of course any help he has hired. There is a lot that goes into bringing about a harvest. The same is true about investing in the lives of those we meet as we plant the seed of the gospel and pray for them. Developing relationships and community is about pouring into one another and not getting tired of doing it. Everyone reaps a blessing when we trust God to bring it about.

PRAYER: Father God, the fields are ripe for the harvest. Help us to do our part when sometimes we simply need to plant seed and allow You to water. AMEN

## DON'T FORGET!

# JUDGING

SCRIPTURE: John 5:30; James 4:12

WRITERS: John—John; James—James

John 5:30 'I can do nothing on my own. I judge as God tells me. Therefore, my judgement is just, because I will carry out the will of the one who sent me, not my own will.'

James 4:12 'God alone, who gave the law, is the Judge. He alone has the power to save or to destroy. So, what right do you have to judge your neighbor?'

Condemnation on someone is just not right. God speaks about judging and how in James 4:12, 'God alone' is the judge. I am guilty myself of having brought judgement against people because of the clothes they were wearing or the car they were driving. You get the picture; the list can go on for days. I experienced this when my indictment occurred and frankly between what I thought was close associates and friends. I learned better. I learned the hard way. My 33 months after my indictment I was working 6 and 7 day workweeks just to survive financially. I found that I was more or less pretty much by myself. I did it. I brought it on myself and I am paying the price which is my life on hold from my family, friends and loved ones. We just can't judge. It is hurtful, painful and not a quality that Almighty God wants in us.

PRAYER: Father God, thank You for forgiveness, it heals the heart. AMEN

DON'T FORGET!

# ONE OF THE TWELVE

SCRIPTURE: Matthew 10:1

WRITER: Unknown

Matthew 10:1 'Jesus called his twelve disciples together and gave them authority to cast out evil and to heal every kind of disease and illness.'

The list of the twelve is as follows:

- John
- Simon (called Peter)
- Andrew (Peter's brother)
- James (son of Zebedee)
- Philip
- Bartholomew
- Thomas
- Matthew (the tax collector)
- James (son of Alphaeus)
- Thaddaeus
- Simon (the zealot)
- Judas Iscariot (who later betrayed Jesus)

Without the list above printed for you, could you name all of the Disciples? I missed some because I took my little self-help test. I missed Thaddaeus and Bartholomew. What a list! If you had polled people in the areas that Jesus walked and worked, the list would have been different. Look at the list which is made up of ordinary people. Those ordinary people would ultimately change the world.

I have some questions that I want you to ponder for a few minutes. They are questions that I have often asked myself. So, here goes.

- What would it have been like to serve and be asked by the Master, Jesus to follow Him?
- How would you feel being told to go into the cities with no money, no gold, no silver or coins? Total faith, total trust? Basically, it is up to you to make it happen.

- How would you feel with Jesus providing you all the power you needed to do what he had called you to do?
- You are a new disciple for the King, how will you handle unbelievers, those that were not interested?

Now that you have had time to ponder and answer the questions, did you notice that it is really not that different for us today. It is all about faith and trust. God gives us the tools we need. We know the world is a difficult place but God prepares us.

Jesus knew we would not be perfect and failure would exist in our lives. It happened to the disciples. Be real in what you do each and every day and God will bless the situation.

PRAYER: Dear God, thank You for the encouragement in life to reach others for You and for the kingdom. Help us to disciple those You place in our path. AMEN

DON'T FORGET!

# CHOSEN

SCRIPTURES: I Peter 2:9

EXAMPLES: Deacon, Pastor, Teacher, Leader, Boss, Athletic participant, Husband, Wife, Friend

I Peter 2:9 'But you are not like that, for you are a chosen people. You are royal priests, a holy nation.'

We as Christians were not chosen because we are worthy. We were simply chosen because God loves us. John 3:16 sets that out very clear 'God so loved the world that he gave His only begotten son that whosoever believes in him shall not perish but have everlasting life.' What a great promise!

Being chosen is a good feeling and it makes you feel as if you have a lot of self-worth because you have been picked. Save that thought. Deuteronomy 7:6-8 addresses that God did not choose us because we were numerous among nations, we were the smallest at that. God is faithful to keep His promises and being chosen is a great example of that.

PRAYER: Heavenly Father, we are thankful that we are a chosen people. You had a choice and You chose us. You knew we would sin against You and You still gave Your life as ransom for many. Thank You Lord! AMEN

DON'T FORGET!

# STRONG GRANDPARENTS

SCRIPTURE: II Timothy 1:5

WRITER: Paul

II Timothy 1:5 'I remember your genuine faith, for you share the faith that first filled your grandmother and your mother, Eunice. And I know that same faith continues strong in you.'

Timothy grew in his faith due to a mother and grandmother that poured into him and nurtured his life through love and care. We are told never to be fearful or timid in sharing our faith. Paul in turn tells us to have power, love and self-discipline. We are also told to be ready to suffer because of our beliefs. So, be strong.

Wow, I am intrigued just to see the word grandparent. My PawPaw and MeeMee were always steadfast in their walk and their beliefs. My MeeMee would instruct me in a Godly fashion and then remind me, kiddingly, that she had her wet Kleenex ready if I didn't fully understand! I am laughing because she would point that finger. My PawPaw, on the other hand, would be quiet and reserved with his witness being his actions. I now am enjoying the benefits of having 7 grandchildren. Thankfully my three daughters are great moms and therefore I have not had to pull out the wet Kleenex, as of yet!

Let me challenge you today if your grandparents are still living to give them a call or go see them before it is too late. They are wise and deserve your time.

PRAYER: Lord Jesus, thank You for Godly grandparents around the world that want to help their kids and love on their grandchildren. May You bless them today. AMEN

DON'T FORGET!

# CHALLENGES

You don't really hear the word challenge a lot in the Bible. However, there are plenty of other words that mirror challenge like obstacles, adversity, making the most of things. You and I at some point have seen where obstacles become opportunities and that is where we will focus a few minutes today.

QUESTION—What are three of your greatest challenges facing you today? How will you handle those challenges? How long have you been faced with these challenges?

Psalm 31:14-15 'But I am trusting you, O Lord, saying, 'You are my God!' My future is in your hands. Rescue me from those who hunt me down relentlessly.'

The great Norman Vincent Peale is one of my favorite authors and he writes, 'We all have difficulties at some point in our lives. What matters is how we handle them. And what we do with them depends upon whether we know the power we have over them. In the 21$^{st}$ chapter of Matthew we read: 'Jesus said to them, 'if you have faith and don't doubt, I promise that you can do what I did to this tree. And you will be able to do even more. You can tell this mountain to get up and jump into the sea, and it will. If you have faith when you pray, you will be given whatever you ask for.'

PRAYER: Faithful God, when we think about challenges, You overcame the greatest challenge of giving Your life for us as sinners. Help us to always have faith and look to You. AMEN

DON'T FORGET!

# HARD WORKER

SCRIPTURE: II Timothy 2:15-16

WRITER: Paul

SETTING: Paul is in a dark, damp Roman prison cell as he writes

II Timothy 2:15-16 'Work had so you can present yourself to God and receive his approval. Be a good worker, one who does not need to be ashamed and who correctly explains the word of truth. Avoid worthless, foolish talk that only leads to more godless behavior.'

Here we see Paul writing again to Timothy who was a young leader and trying to provide him with encouragement in the face of challenges and difficulties. Paul is at the end of his ministry and making sure he would carry his legacy. This is why we see earlier in I Timothy 1:18 for Timothy to 'fight the good fight.'

Today we are focusing on the "hard worker" concept. Paul was a hard worker and with those he discipled like Timothy, he instilled the trait of being prepared.

Think today about how we present ourselves to God each day. Are we really giving it our all to represent our Lord and Savior? Are we using our talents to the fullest or are we holding back?

Let me encourage you today to work hard in all areas of your life. Always striving for excellence and truly impacting everyone we come in contact with each day. Sometimes we only get one opportunity to touch someone. Make it count today.

PRAYER: Heavenly Father, thank you for work. More importantly, Your work that we desire to do to honor you. May we be pleasing in Your sight. AMEN

## DON'T FORGET!

# CHARACTER

SCRIPTURE: Romans 5:3-35

WRITER: Paul

Romans 5:3-5 'We can rejoice, too, when we run into problems and trials, for we know that they help us develop endurance. And endurance develops strength of character and character strengthens our confident hope of salvation. And this hope will not lead to disappointment. For we know how dearly God loves us, because He has given us the Holy Spirit to fill our hearts with His love.'

ENDURANCE---STRENGTH---CHARACTER---HOPE OF SALVATION

I will be the first to share with you that it is very hard to understand how we rejoice not IF we run into problems but WHEN. Also, not just problems either, we need to add into the equation some trials. God gives us encouragement that it will fast develop endurance. Endurance means we are able to withstand, suffer and persevere through the problems and trials we encounter. Paul clearly states a number of times to get ready because it was coming.

What kind of trials are we speaking of here? Well, let us give it a go here...

- Marriage and Family
- Job or Career
- Friendships
- Gossip
- Judgement
- Cancer
- Loss of a loved one
- Accident
- Unforeseen financial difficulties
- Job Advancement
- Foreclosure
- Heartache

Well, just a few to get us thinking. We have or will encounter challenges that will build our character. Don't try to do it yourself. Turn it over to God and let Him carry the load. He IS stronger than we are.

PRAYER: Mighty God with the utmost character, we praise You today for who You are and thank You that You help us build character through the events of our life. You are good. AMEN

DON'T FORGET!

# PRAYER

SCRIPTURES: Colossians 4:2; John 10:10; II Corinthians 12:9-10

Colossians 4:2 'Devote yourselves to prayer with an alert mind and a thankful heart.'

John 10:10 'The thief's purpose is to steal, and kill and destroy. My purpose is to give them a rich and satisfying life.'

II Corinthians 12:9-10 'Each time he said, 'My grace is all you need. My power works best in weakness.'

I remember years ago teaching a couples class at church and having it on my heart to ask each person to hand over two things that morning that would really get them thinking as well as asking you to do the same. Ready? Give me your Bible and your prayer life. I guess you are saying….are you crazy? What are you thinking? Well, today our topic is prayer and I want to know how moved your heart is to be protective about what you have. Colossians 4:2 says DEVOTE yourselves to prayer with what, an alert mind, as in be sharp when praying to our God and be thankful. As for our Bible, how in the world would you be able to study, meditate and research if you did not have it? The devil wants and thrives off of keeping us from it.

In the end, grace is all we need today.

PRAYER: Father God, thank You for Your word and prayer, and for hearing our hearts, our desires, our longings, our petitions and our praises. AMEN

DON'T FORGET!

# FEAR

SCRIPTURES: Isaiah 41:10; Hebrews 13:6,8

WRITERS: Isaiah—Isaiah; Hebrews—Unknown

Isaiah 41:10 'Don't be afraid, for I am with you. Don't be discouraged, for I am your God. I will strengthen you and help you. I will hold you up with my victorious right hand.'

Hebrews 13:6 'So we can say with confidence, The Lord is my helper, so I will have no fear. What can mere people do to me?'

Hebrews 13:8 'Jesus Christ is the same yesterday, today and forever.'

DEFINITION: fear—to be afraid or apprehensive, dread or alarm in facing danger

Have you ever been afraid of anything in your life? Are there things you are afraid of today? God says not to be afraid of anything you are encountering. He tells us not to be discouraged because he is with us. Aren't we thankful that God gives us just the right amount of strength when we need it?

Are you facing health fears? We each probably know someone who they or their family have been affected by the COVID pandemic. The Lord is our helper and therefore we should not live in fear.

I added Hebrews 13:8 for the reassurance to us all that Jesus Christ is the same always. Trust Him today.

PRAYER: Lord Jesus, Great Creator, we adore You and thank You that we do not have to live in fear anymore. We have You to turn to in all we do. AMEN

DON'T FORGET!

# HIDDEN IN GALATIANS

SCRIPTURE: Galatians 5:16, 22-23

WRITER: Paul

Galatians 5: 16 'So I say, let the Holy Spirit guide your lives. Then you won't be doing what your sinful nature craves.' Vs. 22-23 'But the Holy Spirit produces this kind of fruit in our lives: love, joy, peace, patience, kindness, goodness, faithfulness, gentleness and self-control. There is no law against these things.'

As I was being processed into Oakdale as a federal prisoner, I had some unique 'Grace' moments occur. Especially the first day, when peace came to me like a hidden treasure, while under tough conditions with unknown feelings. As we approached the main entrance at Oakdale, we looked left where a new church is being planted and there were three crosses facing us. Grace ticket #1 used right then and there. While being processed once I entered in, I was held in a cell to give up my civilian clothes for the clothing of the quarantine unit. While changing clothes, I looked down and there was a Jesus stamp on the floor looking up at me. Grace ticket #2 used right then and there. After getting dressed I was handed back my personal items that I could take in with me. My Bible, reading glasses, and my silicone wedding band. Grace ticket #3 about to hit. I then made a long walk with Bible in hand to my quarantine area. Once I entered, within 15 seconds, I met Sean. Sean is an orderly who is a Christian and has served me my entire time of quarantine with toiletry items, fruit, an extra t-shirt, etc. Lastly, Grace ticket #4 was a surprise when I went to read my Bible that night. I had stuck an actual Grace ticket in Galatians as a reminder that God's grace would cover me in anything I did. My Grace ticket was given to Sean yesterday for all he has done for me. Now it was time for me to pass it on.

PRAYER: Dear God, help us each day to recognize Your grace and to be able to pass it on to others. AMEN

## DON'T FORGET!

# INTEREST IN OTHERS

SCRIPTURES: Philippians 2:3-5

WRITER: Paul

Philippians 2:3-5 'Don't be selfish; don't try to impress others. Be humble, thinking of others as better than yourselves. Don't look out only for your own interests, but take an interest in others too. You must have the same attitude that Jesus had.'

I have a great example of taking an interest in others, my father. He will offer for someone at the grocery store, a restaurant or just walking into a church service to let them go ahead of him. He is full of humility and trying to put others first. And, on top of that, he is going to offer you a "Don't Forget Jesus" coin for you to pocket. Speaking of those coins, my family has been blessed over the last 15 years to put over 77,000 coins out in circulation to pass on the great news of Jesus.

Our passage today instructs us not to be selfish and worried about what people will think about us. God's word says He will meet our needs and that's why we need to step back and see what opportunities God has in front of us. Having a Godly attitude is always a key in serving others.

PRAYER: Dear Lord, help us today to be open to serve others without agendas of our own. May what we do be pleasing unto You. AMEN

## DON'T FORGET!

# COURAGE

SCRIPTURES: I Chronicles 28:20; Joshua 1:9; Hebrews 3:6

WRITERS: I Chronicles—Ezra; Joshua—Joshua; Hebrews—Unknown

DEFINITION: courage—mental or moral strength, being brave

I Chronicles 28:20 'Then David continued, be strong and courageous and do the work. Don't be afraid or discouraged, for the Lord God, my God, is with you. He will not fail you or forsake you.'

Joshua 1:9 'This is my command—be strong and courageous! Do not be afraid or discouraged. For the Lord your God is with you wherever you go.'

Hebrews 3:6 'But Christ, as the Son, is in charge of God's entire house. And we are God's house, if we keep our courage and remain confident in our hope in Christ.'

Well, when we look at the definition of courage and see that it is mental strength, moral strength and being brave, I believe it!

God's word is very clear about being strong and courageous. It is a command which tells us to know that He is with us and for us, to not be afraid.

Do you have fears in your own life that you are facing at this time? Maybe you don't know which way to turn. Trust God and turn all things over to him so he can take control and help you. He loves you and me and longs to hear our requests. Have courage today my friend.

PRAYER: Lord Jesus, we come to You asking for the courage we need each and every day to make it and make it big in your eyes. Sometimes we are afraid and just need your assurance that we have You right there with us. AMEN

DON'T FORGET!

# LOVER OF YOUR SOUL

SCRIPTURES: Ephesians 3:17-19; Psalm 63:1

WRITERS: Ephesians—Paul; Psalm—David

Ephesians 3:17-19 'Then Christ will make His home in your hearts as you trust in Him. Your roots will grow down into God's love and keep you strong and may you have the power to understand, as all God's people should, how wide, how long, how high, and how deep his love is. May you experience the love of Christ, though it is too great to understand fully. Then you will be made complete with all the fullness of life and power that comes from God.'

Psalm 63:1 'O God, You are my God; I earnestly search for You.'

As we think about our soul today, it is very clear in the scriptures that Christ wants to take up living in our hearts. How do we know that He wants to do what you ask? John 3:16 is a great reminder that Jesus, the lover of our soul, gave his life loving us so much that a price was paid to free us of our sins. It's unbelievable for that much love to be shown to us!

Stop for a moment and thank God for just making so many provisions for us and our families. Also, thank Him for His wonderful grace and mercy in our life.

Ephesians 3:17-19 is a prayer that you can pray anytime you have discouragement in your life. God will help to bless that prayer and give you direction for your life.

PRAYER: Lord God, thank You for Your word, Your promise within and for being the lover of our souls. AMEN

DON'T FORGET!

# THE MAN IN THE ARENA

TITUS 1:9 'He must have a strong belief in the trustworthy message he was taught, then he will be able to encourage others with wholesome teaching and show those who oppose it where they are wrong.'

"It is not the critic who counts; not the man who points out how the strong man stumbles, or where the doer of deeds could have done them better. The credit belongs to the man who is actually in the arena, whose face is marred by dust and sweat and blood; who strives valiantly; who errs, who comes short again and again, because there is no effort without error and short coming; but who does actually strive to do the deeds; who knows great enthusiasms, the great devotions; who spends himself in a worthy cause; who at best knows in the end the triumph of high achievement, and who at the worst, if he fails, at least fails while doing greatly, so that his place shall never be with those cold and timid souls who neither know victory or defeat."

THEODORE ROOSEVELT, APRIL 23, 1910

PRAYER: Heavenly Father, as we are in the arena, help us to be strong. Also, give us the encouragement that we need to reach others that need your Son Jesus. Father, thank You for how important life is and how precious time is here on earth. AMEN

DON'T FORGET!

DEVOTIONS FROM OAKDALE

# TIME

SCRIPTURES: Proverbs 10:4-5, Psalm 62:8

WRITERS: Proverbs—Solomon; Psalm 62—David

Proverbs 10:4-5 'Lazy people are soon poor; hard workers get rich. A wise youth harvests in the summer, but one who sleeps during harvest is a disgrace.'

Psalm 62:8 'O my people, trust in Him at all times. Pour out your heart to Him, for God is our refuge.'

Do you make good use of your time each and every day? With the pandemic going on I know for a lot of families with children that are school age, things have changed dramatically. Everyone from teachers, administrators, restaurant owners, churches and just everyday sole proprietor business owners now have to be so careful with their time.

Draw a big circle and jump right in the middle of it. Let's play a quick game. Where does your time go on a daily basis from the time the alarm goes off until you go to bed. Probably something like this, perhaps:

1. Computer time
2. Cell Phone time
3. Shower and prepare for work
4. Meals
5. Errands and shopping
6. Meetings
7. Conference calls - zoom
8. Exercise
9. Check on loved ones
10. Cooking or dining out

This is a brief list, just to name a few, but......where did you make time for Bible study, prayer time, daily reading of scriptures, etc. I know you are saying, Brother Greg, that is a lot of things to do! Check out our verses. Trust in God at all times – God is there. Work hard but work smart.

PRAYER: Lord Jesus, we are definitely in unusual times and we need your clock management for our busy lives as well as balance. AMEN

DON'T FORGET!

# NAMES OF JESUS – PRAYING THROUGH THE NAMES OF JESUS BY TONY EVANS

Dear Reader, as we start Day 2 of the second 40 Days from Oakdale, my heart is moved as I write the Names of Jesus. My eyes are flooding with tears of joy as I honor my Lord and Savior, Jesus Christ. You may do the same. I hope you are filled with the Holy Spirit as you read today.

- In Genesis, He is the creator God.
- In Exodus, He is the redeemer.
- In Leviticus, He is your sanctification.
- In Numbers, He is your guide.
- In Deuteronomy, He is your teacher.
- In Joshua, He is the mighty conqueror.
- In Judges, He gives victory over enemies.
- In Ruth, He is your kinsman, your lover, your redeemer.
- In I Samuel, He is the root of Jesse.
- In II Samuel, He is the Son of David.
- In I and II Samuel, He is the King of Kings and Lord of Lords.
- In I and II Chronicles, He is your intercessor and Great High Priest.
- In Ezra, He is your temple, your house of worship.
- In Nehemiah, He is your mighty wall, protecting you from your enemies.
- In Ester, He stands in the gap to deliver you from your enemies.
- In Job, He is the arbitrator who not only understands your struggles but also has the power to do something about them.
- In Psalms, He is your song and your reason to sing.
- In Proverbs, He is your wisdom, helping you make sense of life and live it successfully.
- In Ecclesiastes, He is your purpose, delivering you from vanity.
- In the Song of Solomon, He is your lover, your Rose of Sharon.
- In Isaiah, He is the wonderful Counselor, mighty

God, eternal Father and prince of Peace. In short, he is everything you need.

- In Jeremiah, He is the balm of Gilead, the soothing salve for your soul.
- In Lamentations, He is the ever faithful one upon whom you can depend.
- In Ezekiel, He is the one who assures that dry, dead bones will come alive again.
- In Daniel, He is the ancient of days, the everlasting God who never runs out of time.
- In Hosea, He is your faithful lover, always beckoning you to come back – even when you have abandoned Him.
- In Joel, He is your refuge, keeping you safe in times of trouble.
- In Amos, He is the husbandman, the one you can depend of to stand by your side.
- In Obadiah, He is the Lord of the Kingdom.
- In Jonah, He is your salvation, bringing you back within His will.
- In Micah, He is the judge of the nations.
- In Nahum, He is the jealous God.
- In Habakkuk, He is the Holy One.
- In Zephaniah, He is the witness.
- In Haggai, He overthrows the enemies.
- In Zachariah, He is the Lord of Hosts.
- In Malachi, He is the messenger of the covenant.
- In Matthew, He is the King of the Jews.
- In Mark, He is the servant.
- In Luke, He is the Son of Man, feeling what you feel.
- In John, He is the Son of God.
- In Acts, He is the Savior of the world.
- In Romans, He is the righteousness of God.
- In I Corinthians, He is the rock that followed Israel.
- In II Corinthians, He is the triumphant one, giving victory.
- In Galations, He is your liberty; He sets you free.
- In Ephesians, He is the Head of the church.
- In Philippians, He is your joy.
- In Colossians, He is your completeness.
- In I Thessalonians, He is your hope.
- In II Thessalonians, He is your glory.
- In I Timothy, He is your faith.

- In II Timothy, He is your stability.
- In Titus, He is God your Savior.
- In Philemon, He is your benefactor.
- In Hebrews, He is your perfection.
- In James, He is power behind your faith.
- In I Peter, He is your example.
- In II Peter, He is your purity.
- In I John, He is your life.
- In II John, He is your pattern.
- In III John, He is your motivation.
- In Jude, He is the foundation of your faith.
- In Revelation, He is your coming king.

Friends, there is something awesome about the names of Jesus.

PRAYER: Holy Father, we glorify your names today! AMEN

DON'T FORGET!

# FAITH

Facts About Faith from Paul David Tripp

SCRIPTURE: Habakkuk 2:4 'The righteous shall live by his faith.'

## FACTS

- Faith is something that shatters you and rebuilds you
- Faith is a transaction of your heart that will radically alter the way you live your life
- Faith is abandoning your own righteousness and entrusting the hope of your soul, in this life and the one to come, to the righteousness of another
- Faith is the willingness to confess, without excuse or shifting the blame, sins that you once denied and hid
- Faith is abandoning your own wisdom and feeding your heart on the wisdom of God
- Faith is giving up on your delusions of control and resting in God's sovereign authority
- Faith is admitting your weaknesses and crying out for the strength that only God can give
- Faith is refusing to be a glory thief any longer and living for the greater glory of God
- Faith is taking up your cross, dying to yourself, and committing yourself to live as a disciple of Jesus
- Faith is letting the cross of Jesus Christ and his empty tomb define your identity and your hope
- Faith is much more than a one-time decision; it is a lifestyle lived with the presence, promises and call of God always in view
- Faith is important because it is the only pathway to finding and receiving God's greatest gift, his grace in the person of his son Jesus

PRAYER: Heavenly Father, thank you for such a powerful word, definition, way of living in faith. We praise You that through faith in You, we find You.   AMEN

DON'T FORGET!

# LOVE—From The Don't Forgets of Life 2011
## by Greg Smith

SCRIPTURE: John 3:16

What is love? What does the word 'love' mean to you? Love is something so powerful that it could change the face of the world. It is said that love makes the world go round.

Here are a few examples:

- A nice gesture to show someone you care
- A simple kind word of encouragement
- An act above all acts – giving your all for someone
- Something special at an unexpected time
- Something unconditional

Perhaps you have some of your own that you can think of. Love is powerful, soulful, moving and in some instances helps one through difficult and challenging times.

Is there someone you need to take a minute and call so you can tell them you love them? Don't put it off and regret it later.

Don't forget that the ultimate act of love was given when Jesus Christ gave of his life on the cross. Don't forget, that is true love.

PRAYER: Dear God, help us to show love towards others today. Perhaps someone that is down, lonely or just needing a friend. We thank You. AMEN

DON'T FORGET!

# FREEDOM

SCRIPTURES: Psalm 119:45; II Corinthians 3:17; Ephesians 1:7

WRITERS: Psalm 119—David; II Corinthians—Paul; Ephesians—Paul

DEFINITION: freedom—independence, liberty, ease of movement, a right

Psalm 119:45 'I will walk in freedom, for I have devoted myself to your commandments.'

II Corinthians 3:17 'For the Lord is the Spirit, and wherever the Spirit of the Lord is, there is freedom.'

Ephesians 1:7 'He is so rich in kindness and grace that he purchased our freedom with the blood of the son and forgave our sins.'

I always think of my PawPaw, my Uncle John, and my Dad when I think about freedom. My PawPaw was shot in the calf in the Korean War, my Uncle John was a frogman UDT-Special Forces and my Dad was in the Army Reserve. All representing our great country and committing to give their lives in the line of duty. That is the ultimate unconditional gift of a lifetime here on earth. It is with great honor that I wish to say thank you to all of the men and women and their families that are currently serving or have served in our branches of armed forces. You exude Patriotism.

I can think of another example that we have of being free. Jesus went to the cross and paid for our sins. In Ephesians 1:7, we see that Christ purchased our freedom with his own blood. We now walk in freedom because of his love. Will you devote yourself today and commit to reach out to those that you are friends with and of course family and loved ones? The day is coming near, don't put it off.

PRAYER: Dear Lord, we have just witnessed a new President being sworn into office that will help provide freedom for the citizens of this great country. So much is going on that we need You and depend on You. Please bless our land.  AMEN

DON'T FORGET!

# OBEDIENCE

SCRIPTURE: Luke 5:10-11; Luke 1:38; Mark 1:19-20

WRITERS: Luke and Mark

DEFINITION: obedience—an act of obeying, submissive to authority, willing to obey

Luke 5:10-11 'His partners James and John, the sons of Zebedee, were also amazed Jesus replied to Simon 'Don't be afraid.' From now on you will fish for people.'

Luke 1:38 'Mary responded, 'I am the Lord's servant. May everything you have said about me come true.' And the angel left her.'

Mark 1:19-20 'A little farther up the shore Jesus saw Zebedee's sons James and John, in a boat repairing their nets. He called them at once, and they also followed him, leaving their father, Zebedee, in the boat with the hired men.

'FOLLOW ME!' That means no matter the circumstances, location or situation, let's go now. Accounts in both Luke and Mark clearly depict James and John sharing their day when Jesus changes their way of thinking. I want you to follow me and start fishing for men. That meant they were to start pouring their lives into others just like Jesus was doing. These chosen men would now walk the same journey with Jesus and along the way would have plenty of impactful days touching lives and have the power of God with them.

Then we shift to Mary who is just living life normal, she thinks, and then gets blessed with the news from the angel that SHE will become a mother and give birth to Jesus. That is obedience to God to have her heart moved to bring forth a baby, Jesus.

PRAYER: Oh, Lord, we thank You for obedience in the lives of the disciples, Mary and many others in your Word. They provide us great examples to follow. Most of all, may we be obedient to You each and every day. AMEN

DON'T FORGET!

# A PRESIDENT, A POET
# AND A BISHOP

THOUGHT: 'Be united—to become one.'

Message from overview of installation of President Biden, Poet,
Bishop   1/20/2021

PRESIDENT BIDEN

- Press Forward—We are in a winter of peril, jobs lost,
  racial justice no longer
- Much to Build—Virus stalks, businesses close, survival
  climate, domestic terrorism
- Restore the Soul, Action, Unity—Abe Lincoln and the
  Act of Emancipation
- My Soul is in this—Safe schools, leading force for good,
  all created equal
- 1/20/2021—400,000 deaths from the coronavirus and
  growing in number
- History, Faith—Reason to start fresh
- Defend the Truth—Give me a hand, we need each other
  to persevere
- Joy Comes in the Morning—Write the next great chapter
- Thrive—Be a beacon of light

POET

- Light in the never-ending shade, quiet is, nation is
  unfinished, reciting for a president to forge with
  purpose—Have mercy with might and always be the light

BISHOP

- Use our resources—Be a beacon of light
- Discover humanity—Be greater stewards, bring a
  sustainable harvest
- This is our benediction—All human beings' matter, live
  in it, love in it and reconcile in it

- Smile and have a warm embrace—divine factor because I need you and you need me
- Discover common humanity--that binds the wound of the sick and the lonely left out
- Acknowledge sin—reconciliation for the good of a neighbor, elderly, challenged and the poor
- Bring us opportunity—help us to make friends with our enemies

GLORY HALLELUJAH!

PRAYER: Almighty God, witnessed from a prison cell, I hear the message and I share the message. Bless our land, heal our land and bring us all together to be united this day. AMEN

DON'T FORGET!

# SEEK GOD

SCRIPTURES: Psalm 2:8; Psalm 13:5; Psalm 43:5; Isaiah 55:9

WRITERS: Psalm 2—David; Isaiah—Isaiah

Psalm 27:8 'My heart heard you say, 'Come and talk with me.'"

Psalm 13:5 'But I trust in your unfailing love, I will rejoice because you have rescued me.'

Psalm 43:5 'Why am I discouraged? Why is my heart so sad? I will put my hope in God! I will praise Him again—my Savior and my God.'

Isaiah 55:9 'For just as the heavens are higher that the earth, so my ways are higher than your ways and my thoughts higher that your thoughts.'

Boy, when I see the word discouraged in scripture, I can't wait to see what is coming next. Sometimes when things don't go our way, we want to slip off into getting frustrated, flustered and upset. Stop, take deep breaths and seek God. REFUSE to get flustered, it is the devil placing doubt or constructing mind roadblocks that do not need to exist. Tell God what is bothering you and he will show you different ways to understand and trust Him. Yes, it is all about communication with the One that loves you the most. We as humans love being in control and often that is the problem versus trying to be in control. Remember, God is our Savior and we are the followers. Relax and trust in Him while seeking His will for your life.

PRAYER: Dear God, help us today as we seek you and your will for our lives. Yes, we do get frustrated some times and we get off track. Redirect us and bless us in all we do. AMEN

DON'T FORGET!

# FINISHING WELL

SCRIPTURES: II Timothy 4:7; II Corinthians 8:10-11; Romans 1:19

WRITERS: II Timothy—Timothy; II Corinthians—Paul; Romans—Paul

II Timothy 4:7 'I have fought the good fight, I have finished the race, and I have remained faithful.

II Corinthians 8:10-11 'Here is my advice. It would be good for you to finish what you started a year ago. Last year you were the first who wanted to give, and you were the first to begin doing it. Let the eagerness you showed in the beginning be matched now by your giving. Give in proportion to what you have.

Romans 1:17 'This good news tells us how God makes us right in his sight. This is accomplished from start to finish by faith. As the scriptures say, it is through faith that a righteous person has life.'

'From start to finish by faith' That is definitely how I want to finish. I remember Brother Mark Sutton always saying that he wanted to finish well. I will write today's devotion in honor of him. I had the great privilege of working beside him through our deacon board at the church we both served. I was honored to be on the Pastor Search team to bring him to our church and then witnessed as he lost his first wife to cancer. He remained strong and we continued to serve together, which was a blessing to me. For the men I have identified in my life that impact me, Brother Mark Sutton is at the top of the list.

So, what about you the reader? What and how do you want to finish in this life? Will it have a good ending or are there things that you wish to work on to help get you there? Remaining faithful is a key principle as well as finishing what God would call you to as well. Make it a priority today.

PRAYER: Father God, it's hard to think about how we will

finish. Life has all kinds of challenges, bumps in the road, hills and valleys. However, they are there for a reason and that is for us to depend on You and not ourselves. Help us to seek You daily. AMEN

DON'T FORGET!

# ENCOURAGE ONE ANOTHER

SCRIPTURES: I Thessalonians 5:11; Romans 12:8; I Thessalonians 5: 14

WRITERS: I Thessalonians—Paul; Romans—Paul

I Thessalonians 5:11 'So encourage each other and build each other up, just as you are already doing.'

Romans 12:8 'If your gift is to encourage others, be encouraging. If it is giving, give generously. If God has given you leadership ability, take the responsibility seriously. And if you have the gift for showing kindness to others, do it gladly.'

I Thessalonians 5:14 'Brothers and sisters, we urge you to warn those who are lazy. Encourage those who are timid. Take tender care of those who are weak. Be patient with everyone.'

I love encouraging other people in my life and around me. What other way to be positive than to let others see Christ in you through encouragement? I remember growing up having around 10 different coaches, from Boy's Club all the way through college basketball at Centenary College. Coaches are terrific at encouraging you to do what they think you need to do for the end result. That's coaching. But let's think for a minute about what is really important today for people around us. We all need encouragement to push us to completion. To work on family relationships, business continuity, church relations as well as marital relations. We all go through times when we are feeling less that we need to be and that is why our verses today clearly address where we need to land. We are to encourage and build one another up, be with those that are timid and especially those who are weak or sick. The icing on the cake is patience. That's not always easy but God is there to help us. So, what is your gift today? Is it the gift of encouragement? If so, give it all you have to impact those around you.

PRAYER: Father God-God of Mercy, You are the great encourager! You made sure everyone from every walk of life feels important. And You encourage them just as You call us to. Help us today. AMEN

DON'T FORGET!

# VICTORIOUS IN JESUS— 'OVER COMING'

SCRIPTURES: Revelation 21:7; Psalm 62:1; John 16:33

WRITERS: Revelation—John; Psalm 62—David; John—John

Revelation 21:7 'All who are victorious will inherit all these blessings, and I will be their God and they will be my children.'

Psalm 62:1 'I wait quietly before the Lord (God), for my victory comes from him. He alone is my rock and my fortress where I will never be shaken.'

John 16:33 'I have told you all this so that you may have peace in me. Here on earth, you will have trials (many) and sorrows. But take heart, because I have overcome the world.'

When we look at the word victorious, a number of things can immediately come to mind. Winning for your team in a sporting event, perhaps that special recipe from grandma for 'BEET PIE' that wins a blue ribbon. I remember wanting to win the punt, pass and kick competition and have the opportunity to be presented at a real NFL football game wearing my favorite team jersey and being victorious. I won at the local level but did not progress to later rounds but I gave it my best. That's all God asks of us each and every day, to give it our best. That means through the way we lead and live our life, providing forgiveness and grace to those who wrong us as well as those that we wrong. There is victory in living when we are following the will of God and seeking him daily. So, our victory in Jesus may come in a number of ways but it starts with us being obedient to him and following the scriptures to always give our best.

PRAYER: Most Gracious Heavenly Father, we are victorious in You because we have You in us. Today, we are most thankful for Your rich blessings on our life through family, loved ones and friends. Thank You for victory in You. AMEN

DON'T FORGET!

# ENTHUSIASM ABOUT LIFE

SCRIPTURES: Romans 12:11-12; Galatians 6:9

WRITERS: Romans—Paul; Galatians—Paul

DEFINITION: enthusiasm—commit with your whole heart and to be zealous and passionate

Romans: 12:11-12 'Never be lazy, but work hard and serve the Lord enthusiastically, rejoice in our confident hope. Be patient in trouble and keep on praying.'

Galatians 6:9 'So let's not get tired of doing what is good. At just the right time, we will reap a harvest of blessing if we don't give up.'

Wow! When I write the last words of Galatians 6:9 'don't give up' it just reminds me not to give up. I am writing today to you the reader in my 19th day of solitary confinement while awaiting approval from three others to sign off on my COVID retest so I can move to camp where I will be stationed for a while. So far, 454 hours of solitary confinement with short 30 minute to 1 hour shower outing, computer access messages and a few phone calls. God is with me and for me. So, don't give up, no way! I serve a God that I am enthusiastic about and love with my whole heart.

Our verses today speak to that of being a hard worker and serving our Lord with enthusiasm. To rejoice in hope and to be patient in trouble. Think about how enthusiasm or not feeds your life. How about your co-workers, your boss, or closer to home, a spouse, children that are just looking for an encouraging word today? Remember, it's never too late to just give your best to God and to those you love.

PRAYER: Most Important One—Lord, thank You for life, and life abundantly in You. I thank You for peace today that is like a river and make the waters still. Help us to always be enthusiastic about You. We love You. AMEN

## DON'T FORGET!

# MENTORING THAT MATTERS

SCRIPTURES: Acts 18:1-28; III John 1-8

WRITER: Acts—Luke; III John—John

What comes to mind when you think of mentoring? For me, it is someone that is taking me under their tutelage, their instruction and protection. Author Chuck Swindoll mentions mentoring as a relay race. 'One of the most pivotal points in the race is when the person who is running with the baton is in the process of passing it on.' Those who know track and field know that a missed handoff will result in a disqualification.

A good mentor is going to be representative of staying close to you and making sure that you are doing the things that he showed you to allow you to be independent. Kind of the one-on-one approach. Then, as you build your confidence over time, more responsibilities are shared and before long, you are more comfortable.

Challenges can and do arise when you become more independent and that is where trust from the mentor is helpful and can push you to a new lever of belief in yourself.

Enthusiasm from the mentor stimulates others and often has results that are positive.

Is there someone close to you today that you might be able to mentor? Be a wise advisor so that person can grow in the belief in themselves so down the line, they too could become a mentor. Step back and take a look at the person that you are and have become and use that to emulate today for Christ.

PRAYER: Great Redeemer, we are encouraged and blessed by our mentors here on this earth. You are the great mentor with the instructions and examples in Your Word. Help us to strive for excellence in all we do today. AMEN

DON'T FORGET!

# ARE YOU PREPARED?

SCRIPTURES: I Corinthians 2:9; II Timothy 4:2; I Peter 1:13

WRITERS: I Corinthians—Paul; II Timothy—Peter; I Peter—Peter

DEFINITION: prepared—to make or get ready

ARE YOU READY? ARE YOU PREPARED?

I Corinthians 2:9 'That is what the scriptures mean when they say, no eye has seen, no ear has heard, and no mind has imagined what God has prepared for those who love him.'

II Timothy 4:2 'Preach the Word of God. Be prepared whether the time is favorable or not. Patiently correct, rebuke, and encourage your people with good teaching.'

I Peter 1:13 'So prepare your minds for action and exercise self-control. Put all your hope in the gracious salvation that will come to you when Jesus Christ is revealed to the world.'

Have you made your internal list of everything you need to go on your trip out of town this summer? Travel, food, gas, suitcases, medicines, proper summer attire for the pool or beach… Activities planned out that you want to take you and your family to so you can have a great time. We all know this is simply for enjoyment in our life here on earth. Are you ready for what comes after that? Will you be prepared like God calls us to be? We need to be preparing our hearts and minds for what is to come. We need to be making a difference in the lives of people we are in contact with through work, church, civic and just neighborly meetings. Get prepared and don't miss out.

PRAYER: Lord God, please help us to always be prepared. Your word says we need to encourage those around us to be prepared. Help us today Lord. AMEN

DON'T FORGET!

# BEING HUMBLE

SCRIPTURES: James 4:6,10; Ephesians 4:2

WRITERS: James—James; Ephesians—Paul

DEFINITION: humble—not proud or haughty; meek or gentle

James 4:6 'And He gives grace generously. As the scriptures say, God opposes the proud but gives grace to the humble.'

James 4:10 'Humble yourselves before the Lord and He will lift you up in honor."

Ephesians 4:2 'Always be humble and gentle. Be patient with each other, making allowance for others faults because of your love.'

I love James 4:10 for how it advises us to humble ourselves before the Lord and we will be honored. Then we are commanded to be humble and gentle, ultimately, patient with one another. Wow! Then there are 'faults.' Yes, we all have faults and we are called to overlook those faults, in ourselves and most especially in others.

I am so thankful that God has given us grace in abundance. I know I need it every day.

I am taken back by the humble message because it truly is the way God intends for us to be. We see this also in Colossians 3:12, 'Since God chose you to be the holy people He loves, you must clothe yourselves with tenderhearted mercy, kindness, humility, gentleness and patience.

Allow me to encourage you today to always seek the qualities of being humble. God is expects for us to do so.

PRAYER: Heavenly Father, thank You for Your humble nature. A forgiving God that loves us even though we fall short each day. Continue to mold us with Your ever perfect touch. AMEN

DON'T FORGET!

# COMMITTED TO CHRIST

SCRIPTURES: Colossians 4:2-6

WRITER: Paul

Colossians 4:2-6 'Devote yourselves to prayer with an alert mind and a thankful heart. Pray for us too, that God will give us many opportunities to speak about his mysterious plan concerning Christ. That is why I am here in chains. Pray that I will proclaim this message as clearly as I should. Live wisely among those who are not believers, and make the most of every opportunity. Let your conversation be gracious and attractive so that you will have the right response for everyone.

God's word says for us to devote ourselves to prayer and I believe that is one of the major things we can do in being committed to Christ. We do pray for opportunities that will lead us to reaching other people for the Kingdom of Heaven. We are also called to be wise and with our conversation, to be gracious, thankful and wholesome. II Peter 3:1 echoes that same thinking, 'This is my second letter to you dear friends, and in both of them I tried to stimulate your wholesome thinking and refresh your memory.'

Think about your commitment to Christ. It is so easy to have other things that come in and cloud our minds and get us off track of commitment. Are there things that you can identify today that you can work on? Recommit today and devote yourself to Him.

PRAYER: Obedient Father, thank You for devotion and love for us Your children each and every second of the day. Help us as we recommit our walk to You. AMEN

## DON'T FORGET!

# GRACE FILLED—40 DAYS OF FAITH BY PAUL DAVID TRIPP

SCRIPTURES: Hebrews 11:6

WRITER: Unknown

Hebrews 11:6 'And it is impossible to please God without faith. Anyone who wants to come to him must believe that God exists and that he rewards those who sincerely seek him.'

True faith lives on the basis of two unshakable realities—that God really does exist and that he always rewards those who seek him.

Grace has positioned me on two foundation stones that have refined my identity, redirected my purpose, reshaped my desires, rescued my thoughts, and reformed my living.

I have new reason to get up in the morning and face my day with courage, hope, joy, confidence and rest.

Your grace has changed everything, for it has made me sure that you exist and that you reward those who seek you."

In II Corinthians 12:9-10, we see the following verses to confirm grace. 'Each time he said, 'My grace is all you need. My power works best in weakness.' So now I am glad to boast about my weaknesses, so the power of Christ can work through me.

PRAYER: Most Powerful God, we thank You for the outpouring of Your grace. We thank you for Your power when we are weak. Help us to trust in You every waking moment. AMEN

## DON'T FORGET!

# AMBASSADOR—CARRY
# THE MESSAGE

SCRIPTURE: Isaiah 55:4; Psalm 23:2; Deuteronomy 5:32; II Corinthians 5:20

WRITER: Isaiah—Isaiah; Psalm 23—David; II Corinthians--Paul

DEFINITION: ambassador—top ranking, elite

Isaiah 55:4 'Behold, I have made him a witness to the peoples, a leader and commander for the peoples.'

Psalm 23:2 'He lets me rest in green pastures; he leads me beside peaceful streams.'

Deuteronomy 5:32 'Blessed spirit, you must be careful to obey all the commands of the Lord your God, following his instructions in every detail. Stay on the path that the Lord your God has commanded you to follow.'

II Corinthians 5:20 'So we are Christ's ambassadors; God is making his appeal through us. We speak for Christ when we plead, 'Come back to God.'

How would you define the word Ambassador? We perhaps think about top ranking officials that make their way to other countries to represent a particular country. Maybe an Ambassador is a particular individual in a group that has certain responsibilities to carry out to keep that so called worldly status of an Ambassador. That individual is normally one that is carrying the message as to one stance or belief on a certain issue.

For us on the other hand, let's give some thought to one great Ambassador of the world and that being Jesus Christ. He is the one who has led and continues to lead our hearts and our lives based on his living Word. He is the one that is capable of resting us in green pastures when we need it. He is the one who guides us along the right paths and keeps us safe. He also knows the times that we will be in a dark valley wondering how in the world we will get through it. But He is always by our side providing comfort. His kind whisper through the Holy Spirit encourages, uplifts and brings peace for the situation.

PRAYER: Heavenly Father, today we are most thankful to you as our eternal Ambassador, our Lord, our Savior. Thank You for protection and provision. AMEN

## DON'T FORGET!

# BEACON LIGHT

SCRIPTURE: Genesis 1:3; Psalm 27:1; Matthew 5:16

DEFINITION: beacon—a guiding light

Three days into existence of this world, Genesis 1:3 says 'Let there be light, and there was light. And God saw that the light was good.' Then in Psalm 27:1 David shares 'The Lord is my light and my salvation—so why should I be afraid? The Lord is my fortress, protecting me from danger—so why should I tremble? Matthew states 'You are the light of the world—like a city on a hilltop that cannot be hidden. No one lights a lamp and then puts it under a basket. Instead, a lamp is placed on a stand, where it gives light to everyone in the house.' Lastly today, I John 1:5 says 'This is the message we heard from Jesus and now declare to you God is light and there is no darkness in him at all.'

Well, there you have it, a few verses of many in the Bible that clearly declares that He spoke light into existence, He approved of that light, He is the light of the world for all to see and then in Him, believing in Him with your heart, there is no darkness.

I don't know about you but when it is pitch black outside and the storm brings about bad weather and the lights go out in our home, I am looking for a candle, a flashlight, hopefully that has charged batteries or some kind of light. As we are fumbling around, the power comes back on and we have light. Aren't we thankful that Jesus Christ is our beacon of light always beaming the bright light of love, forgiveness, grace and mercy? He is the beacon light that never goes out, constantly glowing for all to see. Look to Him today.

PRAYER: Father God, we thank You for your brightness in our life. We pray for that light to be shared with others. Please direct us today. AMEN

## DON'T FORGET!

# INSPIRATION TO LIVE BY

SCRIPTURE: Isaiah 41:10; Ephesians 6:10-11; II Timothy 3:16

WRITERS: Isaiah—Isaiah; Ephesians—Paul; II Timothy—Paul

DEFINITION: Inspire—to motivate, stimulate as to creating effort, to inhale, to give courage or hope

Isaiah 41:10 'So do not fear, for I am with you; do not be dismayed, for I am your God. I will strengthen you and help you; I will uphold you with my righteous right hand.'

Ephesians 6:10-11 'Be strong in the Lord and in his mighty power. Put on the full armor of God so that you can take your stand against the devil's schemes.'

II Timothy 3:16 'All scripture is inspired by God and is useful to teach us when we are wrong and teaches us what to do right.'

A pretty lofty goal after reading each of these verses. To inspire, to motivate, to encourage others is something I have been blessed with in my life. Probably because I was raised by Christian parents that instilled good traits and wholesome lifestyle characteristics. For that, to my parents, thank you from the bottom of my heart. Also, for a PawPaw and a MeeMee that also instilled the same in my parents, so guess what? It gets passed on through generations. I can see it happening in the lives of my grandkids through my three beautiful daughters. I am so thankful that God tells us and inspires us not to be afraid that He is with us. And no doubt we are thankful that God's word is inspired by Him. Look around, allow the Holy Spirit to have you inspire others today.

PRAYER: Lord Jesus, thank You for the gift of inspiration and encouragement. We receive courage from You today with moving forward to do the same for others that they may know You intimately. AMEN

DON'T FORGET!

# FORGIVENESS—'SYSTEM 77'
## BY STEVEN FURTICK

SCRIPTURE: Matthew 18:21-22

WRITER: Matthew

DEFINITION: forgiveness—giving up, wanting to punish, pardon

Matthew 18:21-22 'Then Peter came to him and asked, Lord, how often should I forgive someone. Who sins against me? Seven times? No, not seven times Jesus replied, but seventy times seven!'

In his book 'The Seven Mile Miracle' Steven Furtick speaks about forgiveness in the idea of system 77. With system 77 Jesus is saying to you and me, there is no limit to how many times I will forgive and, and there is no limit to how many times I can empower you to forgive others. There is no limit to how many times I can heal your broken heart when you hurt. There is no limit to how free you can be.

The Bible tells us, 'Forgive as the Lord forgave you.' So, let me ask you: Are you giving forgiveness the same way you've received forgiveness? That is are you freely, generously—not because the other person deserves it—but because it is the right and reasonable thing to do? Before you answer, think honestly about how you've been acting.

Is there is someone who you haven't forgiven? If there is some bitterness that you're holding in your heart about an event, this is the time at the beginning of your journey to release it to the Father. Search your heart for grudges. Pray for God's help to forgive. Make contact with another person that you need to make things right with today.

PRAYER: Father God, help us to be more like You today in the area of forgiveness. It hurts when things happen against us and others. Encourage us to make things right before the sun goes down as You have commanded. AMEN

DON'T FORGET!

# FOLLOW ME

SCRIPTURES: Mark 1:17; Luke 9:23; Matthew 16:24

Writers: Mark; Luke; John

DEFINITION: follow—come or go after, go along, obey, pay attention to understand, carry out fully

Mark 1:17 'Jesus called out to them, come and follow me and I will show you how to fish for people.'

Luke 9:23 'Then he said to the crowd, if any of you wants to be my follower, you must give up your own way, take up your cross daily and follow me.'

Matthew 16:24 'Then Jesus said to his disciples, if any of you wants to be my follower, you must give up your own way, take up your cross and follow me.

We have the call before us each and every day that we live. 'Come follow me' Chuck Swindoll Study Bible says it this way, 'we must give up our own way, humble ourselves and follow him. Then, we must take up our cross daily which means to die to our own personal agendas and live for Christ. Lastly, we must follow Jesus. That direction is in obedience each and every day.'

Think about when someone you know says follow me, I know the way. You have to trust that person to follow them. Here, we are trusting Jesus to follow Him obediently each day. Will you follow Him today?

PRAYER: Most Gracious Heavenly Father, I thank You for who You are to me personally. Thank You for the call to follow You. May we encourage others to follow and do likewise. AMEN

## DON'T FORGET!

# LIFE IS IMPORTANT

SCRIPTURE: John 14:6

WRITER: John

DEFINITION: life—active existence of plants and animals, living things, a biography; in Webster's New World Dictionary, the words to follow life are lifeboat; lifeform; lifeguard; lifejacket; lifelong; life preserver; life-size; lifestyle; life support and lifetime

Kind of interesting in reviewing the definition of life that I would be shown the above referenced words that all deal with saving and preserving life. Listed last, of course is lifetime, the length of someone's life

John 14:6 'Jesus said to him, I am the way, and the truth, and the life; no one comes to the Father but through me.'

Jesus is our source of life itself. Without him, we would not be able to survive. We not only have life here on earth but also eternal life as a believer in heaven. Definition for heaven; the place where God and his angels are—heavenly.

I would like to challenge you today in this busy world that we live in to think about ALL of the things that you have in your life. Take out a sheet(s) of paper, pray and start writing. You will be amazed that the list is long. God has so richly blessed us with so many things that it is really hard to fathom how and why it has happened this way. I have to say that I have taken for granted many of these things in life and once God halts you and brings you to stand still, you will be awakened and amazed at the results. Breathing fresh air, our senses, touch, taste, thinking ability, eyesight, sky, water, family, love and yes, the list goes on. Take genuine time to thank God for his creation. Praise him, honor him and give him the glory for your life.

PRAYER: Lord God, You are life. You are our life and we praise you. Stuff happens, events take place that are sometimes on the hilltops and some are in deep valleys. You are the way. Help us to be reminded of that each day. AMEN

DON'T FORGET!

# GENEROSITY

SCRIPTURES: I Timothy 6:18; Philemon 1:6; Romans 2:7; Malachi 3:10

WRITERS: I Timothy—Paul; Philemon—Paul

DEFINITION: generosity—giving readily

I Timothy 6:18 'Tell them to use their money to do good. They should be rich in good works and generous to those in need, always being ready to share with others.'

Philemon 1:6 'And I am praying that you will put into action the generosity that comes from your faith as you understand and experience all the good things we have in Christ.'

Romans 2:7 'He will give eternal life to those who keep on doing good....'

Malachi 3:10 'Bring all the tithes into the storehouse so there will be enough food in my temple. If you do, says the Lord of Heaven's armies, I will open the windows of heaven for you.'

How much are you giving in your life to the cause of others? Perhaps you say, well that's none of your business how much money I give. Step back a minute...we are talking about money here. I am simply asking for you to think, what can I do daily to pour into other people's lives in a generous manner. It can be money but it also is about helping people, doing good for our neighbors. When was the last time you went out and met your neighbors personally, spoke with them and truly had a meaningful relationship with them? My PawPaw always taught me to pick up the neighbor's newspaper and deliver it personally to their front door. Yes, even in the rain! That is being generous. What about when someone is sick or they have lost a loved one. You could take a meal or share a meal. You know it truly is the little things that make such an impact in the lives of those around us. Start with your family and work your way out to neighbors and friends.

PRAYER: Heavenly Father, You are most generous in sending your son, Jesus Christ to die for our sins. We thank You and praise You for our salvation. You don't need our money but you teach giving a tenth of our income will impact others. Help us to go beyond the tithe and be generous in other ways. AMEN

DON'T FORGET!

# SIN

SCRIPTURE: Romans 6:23; Ephesians 2:5; Hebrews 12:1; I John 1:9

WRITERS: Romans—Paul; Ephesians—Paul; Hebrews—Unknown; I John—John

DEFINITION: sin—offence against God; good morals, wrong doing, transgression against God's laws

Romans 6:23 'For the wages of sin is death, but the free gift of God is eternal life through Christ Jesus our Lord.'

Ephesians 2:5 'Even though we are dead because of our sins, he gave his life when he raised Christ from the dead.

Hebrews 12:1 'Therefore, since we are surrounded by such a huge crowd of witnesses to the life of faith, let us strip off every weight that slows us down, especially the sin that so easily trips us up. And lets us run with endurance the race God has set before us.'

I John 1:9 'But if we confess our sins to him, he is faithful and just to forgive our sins and to cleanse us from all wickedness.'

God's first sovereign work of grace is summed up in the words from Acts 26:17-18, 'that they may receive forgiveness of sins.' Aren't we thankful that God forgives us our sins? There are plenty of scriptures in the Bible that address sin and what it eventually becomes if we are not a believer in Christ. Romans 6:23 shares that the wages of sin is death, but the free gift of God which is his son, Jesus Christ, is available to us personally if we will simply ask him into our heart. Even after receiving Christ into our hearts, we still sin against God but his scriptures call us to draw from them to help us to rid ourselves of sin.

Once we have received forgiveness of sins, the next mighty work of grace is an inheritance into eternal life. Aren't we thankful for that? Life is not easy and we have many opportunities to sin each and every minute of the day, but if we will fix our eyes on Christ, he will give us the strength we need.

PRAYER: Lord God, thank You for saving us from our sins. You paid the ultimate price for us giving of your Son. Please help us to be mindful to lead upright lives today. AMEN

DON'T FORGET!

# SIN—PART 2

I am continuing part 2 of 'sin' based on a radio broadcast I heard yesterday, Sunday morning. I am going to paraphrase some of my notes that will review the topic of sin.

Sin is not believing in Jesus and that will send you to hell. So, believe in Jesus. Continuing not to believe in Jesus therefore keeps all of your sin mounting up-not trusting and believing is not the way to live.

If you were to die today, what would you do? We are all closer to dying today than yesterday. Do you want to spend eternity separated from Jesus? Believe in Him today.

Jesus is the righteousness of life. Dying to pay the price of our sin. He went to the Father and got God's stamp of approval, The Lamb of God to take away the sin of the world. Jesus defeated Satan on that cross and the Holy Spirit will convict the world of sin. We, the believers, have to share the gospel.

Acts 1:8 'But you will receive power when the Holy Spirit comes upon you. And you will be my witnesses, telling people about me everywhere-in Jerusalem, throughout Judea, in Samaria, and to the ends of the earth.' Here we see the disciples given the power to share.

Our goal is to make day-by-day progress in His Word. The Holy Spirit convicts, directs and confirms Jesus. Inspire others, motivate, stimulate as to a creative effort. Encourage and give hope and courage; be fearless and brave.

Romans 12:8 'If your gift is to encourage others, be encouraging.' It is up to us to reach others for Christ. Join me today in doing that good work.

PRAYER: Heavenly Father, You hate sin. We hate sin that our fleshly side commits. Please help us to turn away from that sin and live more like You. AMEN

## DON'T FORGET!

# WAITING FOR GOD

SCRIPTURES: Romans 8:37; 8:28

WRITER: Paul

DEFINITION: wait—to look forward to expectantly, to stay in place in expectation of

Romans 8:37 'No, despite all these things, overwhelming victory is ours through Christ who loved us.'

Romans 8:28 'And we know that God causes everything to work together for the good of those who love God and are called according to His purpose for them.'

If you hear me tell you to wait, what comes to mind? Don't move? Kind of like the game we played as kids, Simon Says. We are always waiting to hear the next command to move. We see the same thing on our Christian life when we are waiting on God to do certain things, answer certain prayers or not answer. How many times have we moved forward on important decisions that really did not involve God's involvement? I can say it has happened to me plenty of times and all I can say is, I sinned against God not seeking him and praying for this direction rather than my own. Let's look at Romans 8:28 where we see Paul sharing that God causes everything to work together for the good of those who love God. You know, sometimes God is waiting on us and we have to take some action to meet God there where we are to have things take place. God is waiting to pour out his blessings on us if we will simply ask.

PRAYER: Dear God, we pray to You today expectantly, quietly, humbly seeking Your will for our lives as we wait. Help us to wait patiently. AMEN

## DON'T FORGET!

# TOUGH TIMES

SCRIPTURE: Acts 28:17

WRITER: Luke

Acts 28:17 'Three days after Paul's arrival, he called together the local Jewish leaders. He said to them, 'Brothers, I was arrested in Jerusalem and handed over to the Roman government, even though I had done nothing against our people or the customs of our ancestors.

In the scriptures, Paul is under house arrest and is of course seen always going out visiting churches, missionary journeys and such but now is having to ask the other leaders to come to him for a brief time. While Paul was there, he completed the four letters of Ephesians, Philippians, Colossians and Philemon. He was always upbeat and continued to do what he felt he was called to do.

Are you having tough times as you read this today? Do you have so many things on your plate that cannot figure out what to do? Oh, I'm sorry. You said that you are spinning four plates—that would be one on each hand, your shoes off, and on both feet! That's funny because there are a lot of days that perhaps we feel as if we are part of the circus. No worries, because as the plates are tough times, challenges, family, life in general. Are you doing it alone? Are you feeling stale today or are you feeling fresh? We all face tough times at some point in time. I am praying for you the reader today as I am writing you with all my heart from my prison cell at Oakdale.

PRAYER: Dear Holy God, we are blessed beyond measure. Thank You for all You do for us when we get in a rut and want to crawl in a hole. Hold us, encourage us through Your Word, and bless us as we reach out to check on others. AMEN

DON'T FORGET!

# UNFAMILIAR PATHS

SCRIPTURES: Hebrews 13:8; II Corinthians 5:7; Hebrews 4:16

WRITERS: Hebrews—Unknown; II Corinthians—Paul

DEFINITION: unfamiliar—different, not easily recognized, not use to

Hebrews 13:8 'Jesus Christ is the same yesterday, today and forever.'

II Corinthians 5:7 'For we live by believing and not seeing.'

Hebrews 4:16 'So let us come boldly to the throne of our gracious God. There we will receive his mercy, and we will find grace to help us when we need it most.'

Have you ever begun a trip and sometimes, us guys, we know the general area we are traveling but we don't need a map? (this of course is before navigation or smart phones) You know; you travel along and things are not looking familiar but you continue hoping you will reach your destination. What about a new job? Maybe it is totally new field for you. It can make you feel a little uneasy or unsure about yourself. That's when we have to rely on God. He does not waiver. Always the same for us when we call on him. He is steady, a sure thing, our rock that never falters under any circumstance. Something you face today can be different, not easily recognized and you will be able to triumph over the circumstance if you will not go it alone. I am glad that God has laid this on my heart for me to write to you but actually, I am also writing this for myself. I am very much in an unfamiliar place going down an unfamiliar path, waiting to move to camp out of solitary confinement. In confinement the only contact was through a food opening in my door. As I move to camp I will be with other inmates in an open setting. I am trusting God just as I wish to encourage you on whatever new pathway he has you traveling. Don't be afraid, you will do fine. Go boldly to the throne of our gracious Lord.

PRAYER: Holy Precious Father, in the midst of unknowns, You

are known. In the midst of uncertainty, You are certain. In the midst of unsure, You are sure. We come boldly to You now and thank You for controlling our path. May it always be towards You, our LIGHT! AMEN

DON'T FORGET!

# LIKE A TREE PLANTED IN THE GROUND—PLANTING THE RIGHT SEEDS

SCRIPTURES: Hosea 10:12; I Corinthians 3:6; II Corinthians 9:6

WRITERS: Hosea—Hosea; I & II Corinthians—Paul

Hosea 10:12 'I said, plant the good seeds of righteousness, and you will harvest a crop of love. Plow up the hard ground of your hearts, for now is the time to seek the Lord, that he may come and shower righteousness upon you.'

I Corinthians 3:6 'I planted the seed in your hearts and Apollos watered it, but it was God who made it grow.'

II Corinthians 9:6 'Remember this—a farmer who plants only a few seeds will get a small crop. But the one who plants generously will get a generous crop.'

Over the past year, I had the opportunity to visit a plant nursery and select what I thought was a healthy, sturdy tree and transplant it to my client's homes. Then preparation is made to dig the hole sufficient to have a diameter of space around it for roots to openly grow and then proceed to plant the tree root ball. When taking the root ball out of the plastic container, one can only step back and see the miracle of God with all the roots entangled together, pretty amazing. Softening the roots and letting them breathe allows for better distribution in the new soil, of course, new fresh dirt, a bit of balanced fertilizer and then water it in. When we talk about planting the right seeds or to plant a tree in the ground, one must prepare.

Sometimes we face trials that are difficult, tough storms that push and pull at us just like heavy rains and winds blowing at the newly planted tree. Remember, the grace of God, his eternal glory will restore you and make you strong, firm and steadfast. (I Peter 5:10)

PRAYER: Father God, may we always plant seeds of greatness in those around us. Kindness, humbleness, caring and joy to impact someone's life in need of You Father. AMEN

DON'T FORGET!

# YOU CAN BELIEVE

SCRIPTURES: John 3:16; 11:25-26

WRITER: John

DEFINITION: believe—the content of one's conviction on a matter; confidence or reliance upon the truth of a matter; to trust in

John 3:16 'For God so loved the world, that he gave his only Son, that whosoever believes in Him will not perish but have eternal life.'

John 11:25-26 'Jesus told her, I am the resurrection and the life. Anyone who believes in Me will live, even after dying. Everyone who lives and believes in Me will never die.'

Probably the most well known and most recited of all scriptures in the Bible and today, the focus is on believe. My parents were diligent in making sure I went to church, studied my Bible, attended Sunday School to learn more about what I studied and to hear God's Word preached. I still remember nearly some 50 years ago asking my parents questions about what it is to become a Christian and go to heaven when I die. My Dad shared that you have to believe in the Lord Jesus Christ, recognize that I had sin and was sorry for my sin and turn away from that sin. Then, and only then, would I be able to accept Jesus in my heart and begin to live a life in Christ. I thank God today, as I do often, for godly parents who outside of their love for a child, shared about Jesus. There is no doubt it was passed on to me so I could also share that same simple statement with each of my three daughters. I remember the experience of sitting with each of them and going through the plan of salvation. They believed and also asked Christ into their lives. You see, it is God's legacy planning that when we believe in Christ and follow him, the miraculous occurs. A peace, a stillness, a calmness, a joy, a reassurance that has been completed. If you have never come to the place in your life where you have believed and asked Jesus into your heart, perhaps today is the day to believe in Him and start a new life.

PRAYER: Most Gracious Heavenly Father, thank You for a belief in You. A belief that is ever forged in my heart for what You did for me on Calvary's cross. I praise Your name and hope to continue sharing Your great name to those I come in contact with no matter where I go. AMEN

DON'T FORGET!

# SHOW UP

SCRIPTURES: Matthew 24:30; I Peter 5:4; Hebrews 9:24

WRITERS: Hebrews—Paul; I Peter—Peter

DEFINITION: SHOW UP! – my definition is to be present, available and willing; Websters definition – bring into sight, appear, be noticeable, expose, arrive.

Matthew 24:30 'And then at last, the sign that the Son of man is coming, will appear in the heavens, and there will be deep mourning among all the peoples on the earth.'

I Peter 5:4 'And when the Great Shepherd appears, you will receive a crown of never-ending glory and honor.'

Hebrews 9:24 'For Christ did not enter into a holy place made with human hands which was only a copy of the True One in heaven. He entered into heaven itself to appear now before God on our behalf.'

It has come to my attention especially over the last few years the concept of showing up. I say that in the respect of daily work, just show up and good things can happen. Jokingly, I had the great privilege of having to contact a couple of my workers on a daily basis just to make sure we would have a full working crew, most especially the one with the credentials that we needed the most. I then would have conversations with one of my experienced and older gents that agreed with me that showing up was 80% of the battle accomplishing our work.

The Great Shepherd shows up and is present all around us. He desires to be able to meet us but it is us who has to show up and show interest. The Christian life does not occur unless we initiate the desire to be faithful and obedient and seek God. Just like work, showing up and being present, giving our all, then, God will move the relationship to one that is personal and eternally lasting in Christ.

PRAYER: Dear Lord, we thank You for showing up and creating everything. It is in You and only You that we exist and strive to be more like You each day. AMEN

DON'T FORGET!

# COUNTED

SCRIPTURE: Mark 12:29-31

WRITER: Mark

DEFINITION: counted—include or to be included, be important

Mark 12:29-31 'Jesus replied, the most important commandment is this: Listen, O Israel, The Lord Your God is the one and only Lord. And you must love the Lord Your God with all your heart, all your soul, all your mind, and with all your strength. The second is equally important: Love your neighbor as yourself. No other commandment is greater than these.'

When we think about being counted, one might think that they are important. Today our study focuses on being counted in the right way. Our scripture reading speaks of the two most important commandments. First, and foremost, loving God with everything you have. That counts and then loving your neighbor, that counts also. But there is a word equally which links these two together. Equal means same, person that is of equal value, rank. When you really look at what God is saying here, we really find out how important He views how we love our neighbor, care for them, get to know them and take the Godly interest in them that we see here in scripture. Are you and I good neighbors? Do we really care about who just moved in next door or do we have such a busy life that we don't take the time to go and introduce ourselves and love them? Take the time today to follow God's commandment and love your neighbor.

PRAYER: Dear God, thank you for the people, us, our family, our friends and our neighbors that are our brothers and sisters in You. May we take the first step to meet them where they are. AMEN

DON'T FORGET!

# YOU HAVE POTENTIAL—
# OPPORTUNITIES IN LIFE

SCRIPTURES: Matthew 19:26; Mark 10:27

WRITER: Matthew—Matthew; Mark—Mark

DEFINITION: potential—that can be; possible; undeveloped

Matthew 19:26 'Jesus looked at them intently and said, humanly speaking, it is impossible. But with God everything is possible.'

Mark 10:27 'Jesus looked at them intently and said, humanly speaking it is impossible. But not with God. Everything is possible with God.'

There is not a lot of difference in these two different accounts between two different writers except for the word not in Mark 10:27. The writer emphasizes 'but not with God'. This opens up all kinds of discussions to the fact that you and I have plenty of potential right before us in every opportunity that God provides. I love the words possible, potential and opportunity in our everyday life. It means for each of us through Christ, great things can happen if we believe. Check out the other definition of potential and that being, undeveloped. Undeveloped simply means that we still have work to do. Other accomplishments still left at hand to finish. Do you have potential that you have not tapped into yet in your life? Are there things in your relationships with family, friends or loved ones that are undeveloped?

Think about how you can make the most of what God has for us when we truly believe that everything is possible with Him. You have the potential, so make it happen today, your best.

PRAYER: Gracious Heavenly Father, we praise Your name, the name above all other names, the name of Jesus. We thank You that in You, all things are possible with You. Help us to always have Your attitude with us at all times. People need us and we need people. Help us to spread Your word today. AMEN

DON'T FORGET!

# PREVENTIVE FAITH

SCRIPTURE: Matthew 6:24-34

WRITER: Matthew

Matthew 6:24-25'No one can serve two masters, for you will hate one and love the other; you will be devoted to one and despise the other. You cannot serve God and be enslaved to money. That is why I tell you not to worry about everyday life, whether you have enough food and drink, or enough clothes to wear. Isn't life more than food, and your body more than clothing?'

When thinking about being preventive about things in life, it is about stopping something bad from happening. The scriptures above address whom we will serve. We see and know that God provides and truly, life is more than food. Don't be anxious for anything. God meets our needs—all of them. We know that our flesh has worries, yet the bird doesn't' store up food, God provides. Don't worry about tomorrow, don't preoccupy yourself worrying about the things that could happen or when they do happen or how extreme they will be. We as Christian believers have a spiritual right to life. So, don't anticipate a crisis, trust God. Don't assume the worst, God owns the future. Remember, there is no defeat that we cannot turn into victory. God gives victory and God forgives our sin. Today, in your own life, you may be saying, you don't know the family situation going on. I have experienced a loss that I just don't understand. Well, Christ always goes ahead of us and we need to remember life here on earth is exactly that, temporary when we compare that once we give up this life, we will spend the rest of our life with Christ. Therefore, death is not defeat for us, it is victory! We have Christ in us and that is the ultimate as a believer.

PRAYER: Most Gracious Heavenly Father, I write this devotion on a beautiful Sunday morning. You have laid these words on my heart to be able to share about us serving You the best we can each and every day. We as humans are always going to have things that smack us in our face, like death of a loved one or a friend. Help us to remember that this walk, the Christian walk, is about the ultimate goal of eternal life with our Father. When we have You, we experience victory. AMEN

DON'T FORGET!

# BE ALERT AND STAY ALERT

SCRIPTURE: Galatians 1:15-16

WRITER: Paul

DEFINITION: alert—watchful, ready

Galatians 1:15-16 'But even before I was born, God chose me and called me by His marvelous grace. Then it pleased Him to reveal His Son to me so that I would proclaim the good news about Jesus to the Gentiles.'

Are you ready today? Are you prepared? Have you thought out everything in a way that you are prepared to handle it? You say to yourself, what am I waiting on today? Well, it is life and you will choose along with God's help how you will handle things. We have to make room for God and the surprise he brings when we really do expect him to show up, to be a part of an important meeting, a special discussion with a spouse, a breakthrough in an event that is life changing. Be expectant that God will show up when you need Him the most. The best way to do this is to be in constant touch with God and know that he will show himself to you as He decides.

Let me challenge you today to be alert, to be ready for the unknowns that take place. I have come to call them 'grace ticket moments' when God shows up to bless a particular situation when you need him the most.

PRAYER: Heavenly Father, thank You for Your Word and how it shows us Your marvelous grace. We do not deserve grace yet are thankful. Please prepare our hearts to always be alert and ready for what You have in store for us. AMEN

## DON'T FORGET!

# PURENESS OF HEART

SCRIPTURE: Matthew 5:8

WRITER: Matthew

DEFINITION: pure—unmixed; clean; mere; faultless

Matthew 5:8 'God blesses those whose hearts are pure, for they will see God.'

The pureness of heart is no doubt one of the attitudes that we want to be about. No doubt, a character trait of a Christian. How hard is it in our life to strive to be unmixed, clean and faultless? Not easy, but doable as we march forward on our road with Christ. So, we can step back and know that to be pure in heart, we have to watch our actions, our language, our thoughts. I Samuel 16:7 says, for man looketh on the outward appearance, but the Lord looketh on the heart.' Therefore, the promises and blessings of the covenant of grace belong to those who are made pure in heart.

Romans 3:12 says, 'all have turned away; all have become useless no one does good; not a single one.' We find that no one was ever born with a pure heart except Christ. That is why we are blessed to be able to follow the one true pure example and that being Jesus.

Think for a minute the things that we have in our lives that are in the way for us to be pure in heart. I do not have to give you the list because I, the writer, have a list of my own. That is between you and God and He will reveal the things on that list and make a perfect way for each of us to strive for a better way back to the closeness we desire with Him.

PRAYER: Heavenly Father, being pure is hard. It is not easy. We run off the road so many times and we fail You. Forgive us for that. We are excited for the forgiveness given that wipes the slate and gives us another run to be more like You. We love You and thank You for salvation. AMEN

DON'T FORGET!

# A STONG FIVE

SCRIPTURE AND DEFINITION: listed below

I have been listening to some NBA basketball games on my AM/FM radio whereby we can connect to hear the television monitor. I was reminded because Chris Weber, an all-time great with the Michigan Wolverines basketball team during my era at Centenary College during the 1980's. Their team was dubbed the 'Fab 5.' So today you get my version of that in 'A Strong 5.' A look at 5 topics that make up and strengthen the Christian life.

1) FAITH—unquestioning belief; loyalty—I Corinthians 13:13 'Three things will last forever-faith, hope and love and the greatest of these is love.'
2) BELIEF—conviction; faith, trust, opinion—Titus 1:9 'He must have a strong belief in the trustworthy message he was taught; then he will be able to encourage others with wholesome teaching and show those who oppose it where they are wrong.'
3) TRUST—belief in the honesty, reliability of another—Psalm 40:3 'He has given me a new song to sing, a hymn of praise to our God. Many will see what He has done and be amazed. They will put their trust in the Lord.'
4) RIGHTEOUS—virtuous, morally right—Psalm 145:17 'The Lord is righteous in everything He does; He is filled with kindness.'
5) STANDARD—flag, banner, thing set up as a rule or model—Psalm 23:4 'Even when I walk through the darkest valley, I will not be afraid, for you are close beside me. Your rod and your staff protect and comfort me.'

PRAYER: Dear God, we think of 'A Strong 5', these are just a few to highlight how great Thou art. You give us the faith we need, to believe in whom we trust which is you Lord, the most righteous in this world and truly the standard for which we strive. Bless us today. AMEN

DON'T FORGET!

# TAKE THE 'T' OFF OF CAN'T—YOU CAN

SCRIPTURES: Psalm 28:7, Habakkuk 3:9; Philippians 4:13

WRITERS: Psalm—David; Habakkuk—Habakkuk; Philippians—David

DEFINITION: can—verb, ability, likelihood, permission

Psalm 28:7 'The lord is my strength and shield. I trust Him with all my heart. He helps me, and my heart is filled with joy. I burst out in songs of thanksgiving.'

Habakkuk 3:9 'The sovereign Lord is my strength. He makes me as surefooted as a deer; able to tread upon heights.'

Philippians 4:13 'For I can do everything through Christ, who gives me strength.'

You and I have God-given abilities to accomplish nearly everything in this life that we want to. Not too long ago while I was reading, I kept seeing the word can't and it hit me, take the T off and we can! We can choose to look at things in a positive way rather than a negative way. We can view certain circumstances that might look a little rough and overcome our thought process with a 'I can' rather than I can't. It truly is all about our attitude and God's Word says that our attitude should be that of Christ. Are there some things that are before you right now that maybe you are questioning and you do not have a clear-cut answer? Our focus scriptures above give us great comfort to know that we find strength in the Lord and when we trust Him with everything we have, He is faithful. Also, it is good to feel surefooted when we are trying to make right decisions in our life. So, today, choose to say 'I can.' God will give you what you need.

PRAYER: Most High God, thank You for Your word, Your promises and the ability to know that we truly can do all things through You. Help us to always claim Your promises. AMEN

DON'T FORGET!

# GRACE BASED #1

SCRIPTURE: Ephesians 2:8-9

WRITER: Paul

DEFINITION: grace—kind, forgiving, or compassionate treatment, a kindly act

Ephesians 2:8-9 'For by grace you have been saved through faith; and that not of yourselves, it is the gift of God; not as result of works, that no one should boast.'

As we all know, it is easy for us to forget about living a life that is grace based rather than a works related Christian life. We get to thinking that we need to accomplish works to gain our heavenly home or be able to work towards credits based on accomplishments that we are trying to do. Good news…that is simply not the case. Erase that with a BIG eraser on the chalkboard and remember that our Christian walk is one based on God's grace for our life. With this kind of grace upon us, your life will shine with the joy of the Lord. Others will no doubt take notice because your life is different.

Take a look at the definition of grace. Kind, compassionate, and of course forgiving because Jesus was the ultimate example of how grace is poured out and over us.

Romans 12:6 states 'Since we have gifts that differ according to the grace given to us, let each exercise them accordingly.' Let me challenge you to make sure and use your gifts wisely for the Lord and serve Him with a grace-based love.

PRAYER: Most Gracious Heavenly Father, we know that You are not concerned about our works as long as they are Your will. Help us to be reminded that it is all about Your grace in our lives. AMEN

DON'T FORGET!

# UNCONDITIONAL LOVE

SCRIPTURE: John 3:16

WRITER: John

DEFINITION: love—deep affection, a strong enthusiastic liking for something

John 3:16 'For God so loved the world, that He gave His only Son, that whoever believes in Him should not perish but have eternal life.'

When I think about our Bible study group today, someone mentioned how strongly they were moved by John 3:16. So, what are our motives when we think about something that is so unconditional, as love. That means no reservations about a love for us from our Heavenly Father.

God sent his son Jesus to die on the cross for us and He did it with an unconditional love. One that never fades away. The personal touch is always so moving and is one that we should strive to model in our lives.

When we think about unconditional love, our family, our children and grandchildren quickly come to mind because we would go to the mat for each of them. That is what Jesus did for us, paying the price of our sins.

PRAYER: Loving God, Loving Father, I thank You today for Your awesome gift of unconditional love for me in my life and I pray that we will share that same love with those we come in contact with each day. AMEN

DON'T FORGET!

# GRACE BASED #2 – THE WHOLE PACKAGE

Grace truly is the whole package. Grace is defined as the rarest, most theologically significant redeeming activity of God that manifests itself in the redemptive work of Christ by which sinners are forgiven and accepted by God. The word grace is used in the New Testament approximately 150 times. Sometimes referred to as something delightful or beautiful in a person, thing, or an act which brought pleasure to others. Also viewed as the power to unbelievers to believe and the power to build up believers.

My friends, as I am currently inside a federal prison, I am involved in two daily prayer circles with 18-20 men, a bible study on Wednesday evening and a Sunday Bible study-worship. So, when I see those words 'the power to build up believers,' that is exactly what is going on here. Some men have been here and have long sentences where others are less than five years. Grace has permeated the walls of this Oakdale Prison property because someone laid the groundwork before us.

I titled today 'The Whole Package' to encourage you, the reader to strive to your fullest in your Christian walk. To excel in all that you do in your personal relationships as well as being mindful to extend grace to those around you. Grace was meant to be received and lived out to the fullest, not dissected and analyzed by those who would rather argue. Grace is ours today…How will you live it?

PRAYER: Heavenly Father, I thank You for grace. We don't deserve it but You gave it freely and for that we are honored. May Your grace abound in us daily to impact those around us. AMEN

DON'T FORGET!

# RESTORATION IN LIFE

SCRIPTURES: Psalm 30:2; Romans 5:10; I Peter 5:10

WRITERS: Psalm—David; Romans—Paul; I Peter—Peter

DEFINITION: restore—to give back, return, renew

Psalm 30:2; 'O Lord my God, I cried to You for my help, and You restored my health.'

Romans 5:10; 'For since our friendship with God was restored by the death of his Son while we were still His enemies, we will certainly be saved through the life of his Son.'

I Peter 5:10; 'In his kindness God called you to share in his eternal glory by means of Christ Jesus. So, after you have suffered a little while, He will restore, support, and strengthen you, and He will place you on a firm foundation.'

Restoration in anything we do has to start with Christ. We all fall short and mess up in life. I have made plenty of mistakes in my life and no doubt have been seeking restoration with family, friends and loved ones. It has not been easy to know that I made decisions in my business life that crossed over the line and therefore, had to face the fact that I errored in life. I am now paying the price both financially and physically in a federal prison. However, my God restores and he has been doing that since my indictment. His word says that when I cry out for His help, He restores me. Because of Christ's dying on the cross and giving His life, I am restored. God provides the strength, the support and the firm foundation that I need.

My situation may sometimes seem extreme because of where I am, but I am with Christ. That is why the personal relationship through salvation is what gets me through each day and night. I am blessed. I want to encourage you to take a look at things you are facing and perhaps there are things that need restoration and prayer. I am honored that God has allowed me to write to you. James 1:3,4 'For you know when your faith is tested, your endurance has a chance to grow. So, let it grow, for your endurance is fully developed, you will be perfect and complete, needing nothing.'

PRAYER: Father God, we know that we will be tested in this life. When things go wrong because we make wrong decisions, we pray for the restoring of our life. You are our God, the one we put our trust in. Please bless us today. AMEN

DON'T FORGET!

# LOVING OTHERS

SCRIPTURES: Romans 12:9,10; 13:9; Jeremiah 31:3

WRITERS: Romans—Paul; Jeremiah—Jeremiah

DEFINITION: love—unselfish, loyal, and benevolent intention and commitment toward another

Romans 12:9, 'Don't just pretend to love others. Really love them. Hate what is wrong. Hold tightly what is good. Love each other with genuine affection and take delight in honoring each other.'

Romans 13:9, 'These and other such commandments are summed up in this one commandment: 'Love your neighbor as yourself.' Love does no wrong to others, so love fulfills the requirements of God's law.'

Jeremiah 31:3, 'I have loved you, my people, with an everlasting love. With unfailing love, I have drawn Myself to you.'

Love is such a great word with such great meaning. Unselfish, loyal, commitment, just to name a few. What, who, how, comes to your mind when you see or hear the word love? When was the last time you wrote a 'love letter' to the one you love? Perhaps with this being the month of February and Valentine's Day you could think about that. It strikes a nice chord to open up and share with those we love. When we unload, so to speak, the thoughts and feelings that we have on and in our heart.

Now shift that same letter, prayer to the one who loves us the most. God loves us so unconditionally that a lot of times it is really hard to understand. We fall so short, we miss the mark, we don't finish the race, yet, he is still right there, waiting on us to seek him. He gives us the encouragement to love again, to endure again, and to keep fighting the good fight.

Is there someone today that you need to call and tell them you love them? Don't put it off because they might not be there tomorrow. Only God knows that perfect timing, His will.

PRAYER: Dear Lord, thank You for love that You share with us every day. Help us to share with others so they know where it comes from. AMEN

DON'T FORGET!

# DON'T GIVE UP

SCRIPTURE: Galatians 6:9

WRITER: Paul

Galatians 6:9 'So let's not get tired of doing what is good. At just the right time we will reap a harvest of blessing if we don't give up.'

I am a huge basketball fan and student of the game. I played basketball from the time Little Dribblers came on the scene as well as Boys Club, elementary, junior high, high school, and into college. Every coach I had instilled in me to always do my best and to never give up. Of course, the stakes get higher as you move into college because guys are wanting to strive for trying out in the pros of the NBA. I bring up basketball because of Jimmy Valvano, otherwise known as Jimmy V. He coached at North Carolina State and led his team to the National Championships. He later was diagnosed with cancer and lived to promote 'Don't Give Up, Don't Ever, Ever Give Up.'

Paul speaks of this same attitude in Galatians when he says to not get tired of doing good and what is right. But we have to have the faith of not giving up. Sometimes, things are just weighing heavy on our minds and hearts we nearly cannot bear what is going on. How will you handle this challenge? Try to do it yourself, speak and share with a close friend or just try to conquer it by yourself? We like to think sometimes we don't need God and we can go it alone. That is exactly when the wheels fall off, the plates we are spinning all fall off of the twirling sticks and break and we want to turn and run. Don't get sucked into that type of thinking, it is the devil minimizing your abilities with Christ. Be positive, believe, be encouraged and by all means, 'Don't Give Up!'

PRAYER: Most Gracious Lord, we thank You for encouragement and belief. You are the great 'I Am' and we can do all things through You and with You. We believe! AMEN

## DON'T FORGET!

# STAND FIRM

SCRIPTURES: Exodus 14:13; Psalm 84:7; Ephesians 6:14; I Peter 5:9

WRITERS: Exodus—Moses; Psalm—David; Ephesians—Paul; I Peter—Peter

DEFINITION: stand firm—not being moved, strong, unwavering

Exodus 14:13 'But Moses told the people, 'Don't be afraid. Just stand still and watch the Lord rescue you today.'

Psalm 84:7 'They will continue to grow stronger, and each of them will appear before God in Jerusalem.'

Ephesians 6:14 'Stand your ground, putting on the belt of truth and the body armor of God's righteousness.'

I Peter 5:9 'Stand firm against him, and be strong in your faith. Remember that your family of believers all over the world is going through the same kind of suffering you are.'

How hard is it in your life, your daily world, to stand firm and not be moved? We all have influence from outside sources that encourage both positivity and negativity into our lives. I experience that now here where I am and I have a choice each time that comes upon me. I choose to be strong in the Lord and keep his influence number one in my life. We know that peer pressure has always been around and it will not go away totally because we are people and we all sin and are tempted with things that try to knock us off of trying to stand firm. To stand firm, we have to have balance in our life. Think about someone pushing on your shoulder and you are not standing steady. You will get knocked off and pushed over if you are not careful. Let me encourage you to always stand strong and stand firm.

PRAYER: Gracious God, it is not easy to always stand firm in many circumstances we face in life. Would You please guide us and direct us in all we do? AMEN

DON'T FORGET!

# DAILY RELATIONSHIP

SCRIPTURE: Psalm 138:7-8

WRITER: David

DEFINITION: relationship—a connection between two persons

Psalm 138:7-8 'Though I am surrounded by troubles, You will protect me from the anger of my enemies. You reach out Your hand and the power of Your right hand saves me. The Lord will work out His plans for my life-for Your faithful love, O Lord, endures forever. Don't abandon me, for You made me.'

In the worldly sense a relationship is between a group of persons. In the spiritual realm, we are speaking about your relationship with Christ. Today's devotion is directed at each of us not to just have a relationship but to live it 'DAILY.' You know we get so busy, things get rolling, kids have events, a zoom meeting daily during school days or even a business meeting and we forget about God. Draw a big circle on a clean piece of paper and start filling in the 100% pie shapes equal to time and you get the following-sleep, call it 8 hours, work 8 hours, shower, meals, cell phone time, errands, television, computer and then squeeze time in for kid's baths and whew, you are tired and off to bed. What happened to Bible Study, prayer time and quality time with your spouse. It is not easy but guess what? It is about priorities. I would encourage you to start that time early in the morning to kick off your day. It starts off best with Christ in the morning with the sun coming up and kicking off your day on the right foot.

PRAYER: Dear Lord, oh how we want to do the right things daily. Please help us to seek You always knowing that You are there for us. AMEN

## DON'T FORGET!

# FACING AFFLICTION

SCRIPTURE: James 1:27; Hebrews 12:6; II Corinthians 6:4,8

WRITERS: James—James; Hebrews—Unknown; II Corinthians—Paul

DEFINITION: affliction—condition of physical or mental distress, suffering

James 1:27 'Pure and genuine religion in the sight of God the Father means caring for orphans and widows in distress and refusing to let the world corrupt you.'

Hebrews 12:6 'For the Lord disciplines those He loves, and He punishes each one he accepts as his child.'

II Corinthians 6:4,8 'In everything we do, we show that we are true ministers of God. We patiently endure troubles and hardships and calamities of every kind. We serve Gpd whether people honor us or despise us, whether they slander us or praise us. We are honest, but they call us imposters.'

We are all subject to affliction and hardships of life. It just happens and we simply have to prepare ourself for times that we stumble. The real question is how we will act when that happens. Will you fold? Will you quit? Will you have bitterness in your heart or will you allow God to work in you through purity, his understanding, our patience, our kindness and the Holy Spirit within us and our sincere love for Christ to realign with him. We have to be honest here and acknowledge that we have all been through hardships in our life. Death, divorce, financial hardships due to mismanagement, loss of a job or career, a broken or fragmented friendship, a child's poor decision to get involved in drugs or other activities that are not wholesome. These things happen and then it exposes our very being and it is a form of affliction that is painful.

II Corinthians 12:9 "Each time he said, 'My grace is all you need. My power works best in weakness.' So now I am glad to boast of my weakness, so the power of Christ can work through me." So, when things occur, and they will, just know Christ will be there to keep you strong.

PRAYER: Heavenly Father, thank You so much that through our weaknesses, afflictions and hardships, You give us what we need, when we need it and then comfort us and encourage us. AMEN

DON'T FORGET!

# NOTICING YOUR NEIGHBOR

SCRIPTURES: Galatians 5:14; James 2:8,9; Romans 13:8; Luke 10:37

WRITERS: Galatians—Paul; James—James; Romans—Paul; Luke

Galatians 5:14 'For the whole law can be summed up in this one command: Love your neighbor as yourself.'

James 2:8,9 'Yes indeed, it is good when you obey the royal law as found in scriptures: Love your neighbor as yourself. But if you favor some people over others, you are committing a sin. You are guilty of breaking the law.'

Romans 13:8 'Owe nothing to anyone-except for your obligation to love one another. If you love your neighbor, you will fulfill the requirements of God's law.'

Luke 10:37 'The man replied, the one who showed him mercy. Then Jesus said, yes, now go and do the same.'

Do you take notice in your neighbors around you and where you live and where you work? We get so busy and of course, they are busy. We forget about them. Relationships are so important to life and we need to step back and breathe and take notice of our neighbor. Count the neighbors that you can call by name. The ones you know things about, as well as their kid's names, and perhaps, even their pets. I challenge you to change this equation that is too common. Get out and introduce yourself. Yes, I know we are social distancing and that is fine but put on your mask and go out and meet them. Remember, you do not know what is going on in their world. They may be experiencing tough times like missing a mortgage payment or two or three. A loved one may have passed or even be going through tough times of their own. Scriptures clearly depict for us the instructions to love our neighbors and help fulfill God's law. Think back to neighbors that have gone out of their way to meet you and encourage you when perhaps you needed it most. Try it, see how it works and see if you are not blessed in a neat way. Notice your neighbor today.

PRAYER: Most Gracious Lord, we thank You today for neighbors. We ask that You help us and push us to step out of our comfort zone to extend love to our neighbors. We love You and thank You for all you do. AMEN

DON'T FORGET!

# RUNNING WITH PATIENCE

SCRIPTURES: Hebrews 12:1; Psalm 40:1

WRITERS: Hebrews—Unknown; Psalm—David

DEFINITION: patience—the power of capacity to endure without complaint; something difficult or disagreeable

Hebrews 12:1 'Therefore, since we are surrounded by such a huge crowd of witnesses to the life of faith. Let us strip off every weight that slows us down especially sin that so easily trips us up. And let us run with endurance the race God has set before us.'

Psalm 40:1 'I waited patiently for the Lord to help me, and He turned to me and heard my cry.'

I remember training for 5K, 10K and half marathon races. It was something I had to make time for on a scheduled basis to get my body and mind in shape. You don't just go out and start running and think you don't need training to make it happen. Hitting those goals of finishing the race was first, then I could work on lowering my running time as I completed each race.

It is no different in the Christian life that we live. We have to be prepared, grounded and hearts in the right condition to meet our goals. We do have to have patience because it takes time. Patience to build a strong prayer life. Patience to build traits of encouragement, love and grace.

It is hard to be patient a lot of the time. We get frustrated and then we jump into situations and hurt something or offend someone that is not necessary.

Always seek God for direction and allow him to guide you and direct you to where you need to go.

How is your patience barometer today? Is the needle busting out of the glass dial because you are doing things yourself? Try to tune into God for the needed patience to handle each thing that you experience.

PRAYER: Heavenly Father, thank You for Your grace, Your mercy and Your patience with us. We are quick to move, quick to decide and most times get ourselves into trouble. Guide us, Lord. Place Your hand on our lives today. AMEN

DON'T FORGET!

# CLOTHE YOURSELVES

SCRIPTURES: Colossians 3:12,13,14

WRITER: Paul

Colossians 3:12,13,14 'Since God chose you to be holy people he loves, you must clothe yourselves with tenderhearted mercy, kindness, humility, gentleness and patience. Make allowances for each other's faults, and forgive anyone who offends you. Remember, the Lord forgave you, so you must forgive others. Above all, clothe yourselves with love, which binds us all together in perfect harmony."

My friend, God calls us to clothe ourselves with some fruits of the Spirit that are sometimes not easy based on trying circumstances that hit us head on. When we see the words mercy, kindness, humility, gentleness and patience, it makes us stand back and take note very quickly. Verse 14 says 'ABOVE ALL,' which is very direct and definitive for us to act NOW! This is not something Gods say that we can put off to another day. We are called to overlook people's faults and move past that quickly. How can we do that? Well, we can start with our attitudes and by getting our hearts right with God and also being obedient and extending grace to one another.

At the end of the day, we are all in the same business that God is in and that is the people business. He is about saving lives and impacting people for his kingdom. We are also called to forgive others just like God has forgiven us. We are going to have challenges and go through valleys of despair and we simply have to endure and keep fighting to do better. That happens when we show up with the right heart. I encourage you today to look to God for mercy, forgiveness, love, faith, gentleness and patience.

PRAYER: Great Creator, we thank You for forgiveness of our sins. We thank You for patience, love, humility and pureness of heart. Please bless us as we go out in Your name. AMEN

## DON'T FORGET!

# GOOD CHARACTER

SCRIPTURES: James 1:3,4; Philippians 2:13; 4:13

WRITERS: James—James; Philippians—Paul

DEFINITION: character—moral excellence and firmness; main or essential nature

James 1:3,4 'For you know that when your faith is tested, your endurance has a chance to grow. So, let it grow, for when your endurance is fully developed, you will be perfect and complete, needing nothing.'

Philippians 2:13 'For God is working in you, giving you the desire and power to do what pleases Him.'

Philippians 4:13 'For I can do everything through Christ who gives me strength.'

The moral compass in our life is character. It is who we are, every place we go and in everything we do, our business decisions, our personal life decisions, our thoughts, and actions that occur every day. James says that our faith will be tested and because of that, we will have the opportunity to grow. Then, through that growing, we will be totally complete. We see many times in the Bible where Paul said that we would have challenges and that we would face problems and for us to be prepared.

We each have the opportunity to have a strong character and a force that is unstoppable. However, we will not be able to go it alone. May I encourage you today as you peek in to look at what your character looks like to the rest of the world. Unfortunately, they do not see the mirror you look in each day. That is between you and God and no one else. There will be times that your character is questioned by others through judging and you simply have to move on. God is the only one that judges and that is final. Praise God for that because we only need to be worried about ourselves. We have plenty in this life to keep us on our toes. Strive for good character in all you do.

PRAYER: Heavenly Father, thank You for Your perfect character that we can strive to model each and every day. Help us to keep our sights on You always. AMEN

DON'T FORGET!

# HOLD YOUR HEAD UP

SCRIPTURE: Philippians 4:6, 8-9

WRITER: Paul

Philippians 4:6 'Don't worry about anything; instead, pray about everything. Tell God what you need, and thank him for all he has done.'

Philippians 4:8-9 'Fix your thoughts on what is true, and honorable, and right, and pure, and lovely, and admirable. Think about things that are excellent and worthy of praise. Keep putting into practice all you learned and received from me-everything you heard from me and saw me doing. Then the God of all peace will be with you.'

It does not matter the situation that you are living in or have lived in during your past. Remember, the past is behind you and it can only bring you down and have you plunging into negativity that you don't need. Let me encourage you to hold your head up in all you do and look to Christ for all of your needs. The scriptures say not to be worried about anything. God waits on us to hear our prayers but sometimes we don't exercise that privilege until we are in a quagmire of a mess. We get deep into things that clutter our minds and our lives and we don't quite know which way to turn. So here we go, verse 8 says we should fix our thoughts on what is true and that is Christ. Praising Him and thanking Him for giving us true direction that we need. Helping us to model the Christian life and truly practice it every day. Once you put things into practice over and over again, things become easier and then you and I can become more effective in our Christian walk.

PRAYER: Lord God, may we strive to hold our head up in all we do. We pray that our daily focus is always on You and for that we praise You. AMEN

## DON'T FORGET!

# WE ARE SAFE IN CHRIST

SCRIPTURE: Psalm 91:1

WRITER: Paul

DEFINITION: safe—protected, free from harm or risk; secure from harm or loss

Psalm 91:1 'Those who live in the shelter of the Most High will find rest in the shadow of the Almighty.'

The title today clearly states that we ARE safe in Christ. Not that we might be safe, or that it is in the works. We are his and he watches over us in all that we do. God is our refuge, no matter what we are going through, how many struggles we have or uncertain circumstances about us. Sometimes, things might seem long and drawn out but his love for us just gives us the strength we need. He hears your prayers and he is committed to be there for you. Meditate on God's Word day and night trusting in him and always strive to pursue him in all you do.

When we think about safety, we think about protection and we see that in Psalm 91. God being our refuge, our place of safety, our great protector, we have nothing to worry about. He shares with us not to worry, not to be afraid or to dread disease because he is with us. We then are encouraged to make the Lord our refuge, making the Most High our shelter, he protects us in all we do. Have you asked God to rescue you and protect you in your life? No matter what troubles you might be facing, He is there with you if you will simply turn them over to Him. Note, nothing is too big or too challenging for Him because he is God. Stay safe in Christ today because He is always there.

PRAYER: Lord God, thank You for Your promises to always be there for us and keep us safe. We live in a world that sometimes hangs us out to dry, so, protect us in all we experience. AMEN

DON'T FORGET!

# KNOWING HIM

SCRIPTURES: John 14:1,9; Deuteronomy 31:8

WRITERS: John—John; Deuteronomy—Moses

John 14:1, 9.'Don't let your hearts be troubled, trust in God and trust also in me. Jesus replied, 'Have I been with you all this time, Philip, and yet you still don't know who I am? Anyone who has seen Me has seen the Father. So why are you asking me to show Him to you?'

Deuteronomy 31:8 'Do not be afraid or discouraged, for the Lord will personally go ahead of you. He will be with you; he will neither fail you nor abandon you.'

It is exciting to know God and have a personal relationship with Jesus Christ. When you see the confirmation of the scriptures telling us not to have our hearts troubled and to trust in God. That is the reassurance that we are given when we seek God's word and know that He is always with us. The Lord goes before us and is always with our situations and God's care for us is always perfect. Jesus' character, kindness, love and mercy reveal for us God's character and how amazing and awesome He truly is in our lives.

Are you connected in the way you need to be today? Are you following what you feel is God's commands for your life? Intimacy with the Father begins with acknowledging that we need Him and cannot live a single minute without Him weaving his perfect needle into our flesh that punctures our heart. He loves you and me and He hopes that you want to really "know Him." Are you truly sold out for God in your life or are you somewhat on the fence? It happens in life and we sometimes just have to recommit. Will you do it today so you may really know Him?

PRAYER: Lord God, Almighty One, may we know You the way in which You desire to know us. We thank you Lord for your Son, Jesus, who saved us. AMEN

## DON'T FORGET!

# PRAYING FOR OTHERS

SCRIPTURES: Daniel 9:2-3; Colossians 4:2,3

WRITERS: Daniel—Daniel; Colossians—Paul

DEFINITION: prayer-conversation with God-in praise, thanksgiving or intercession

Daniel 9:2-3 'I Daniel, learned from reading the word of the Lord, as revealed to Jeremiah the prophet, that Jerusalem must lie desolate for 70 years. So, I turned to the Lord God and pleaded with Him in prayer and fasting.'

Colossians 4:2,3 'Devote yourselves to prayer with an alert mind and a thankful heart. Pray for us, too, that God will give us many opportunities to speak about this mysterious plan concerning Christ. That is why I am here in chains."

I remember asking one of my married couple classes to close their eyes for a moment, then I asked them to give up their prayer life and their bible study....I am going to ask you the reader for a moment to do exactly the same thing. How does that make you feel down in your gut, your soul, to know that the personal relationship that was afforded to you through Christ is now gone? It is one of the worst, lost feelings you can have. That is, if you are a Christian and that relationship matters to you. I simply ask the question to make each of us think about what should be the norm for us each and every day, seeking God obediently through daily prayer and bible study. I know we all have days that things seem to bombard us, attack us, and truly weigh us down and we miss the things we need to be totally in tune with Christ. Protect against that by keeping an open line straight to the One that loves you and me and patiently awaits us calling on Him. Others need our prayers today such as our family, neighbors, co-workers, church family, homeless, those imprisoned. Remember them today.

PRAYER: Almighty God and Savior, we adore You and praise You for Your greatness and Your mercy. Lord, we thank You for the ability to speak with You and reach You every second of the day. Help us not to miss out on that great blessing. AMEN

DON'T FORGET!

# PERFECT PRACTICE

SCRIPTURES: Philippians 4:9; Colossians 4:5-6

WRITER: Philippians and Colossians—Paul

DEFINITION: practice—to engage in something frequently, to repeat in order to become proficient

Philippians 4:9 'Keep putting into practice all you have learned and received from me-everything you heard from me and saw me doing. Then the God of peace will be with you.'

Colossians 4:5-6 'Live wisely among those who are not believers, and make the most of every opportunity. Let your conversation be gracious and attractive so that you will have the right response for everyone.'

Paul speaks of five things that can be practical and cultivated in our life, reconciliation, joy, gentleness, prayer and focus. These are all things that we are called to live out as followers in Christ. We never practice with our own power. God provides what we need. Are there some things that you need to practice as you seek to imitate Jesus? Also, how can you practice in the power of the Holy Spirit? What is the difference in practice and perfect practice? As we know, it is simply slang to throw in the word perfect. I guess it really just gives us a challenge to strive for the best we can do. Practice sometimes is repetitive and gets boring and sometimes we lose interest in what we are really doing. Stay focused on what you are trying to achieve, such as a strong prayer life, a daily bible study, a phone call to someone that is home bound, a visit to a hospital or nursing home (when it is safe to do so). Always give your best and give your all. God will take care of the rest.

PRAYER: Lord God, You are perfect and we praise You. Please help us to strive for excellence in all we do and practice in our daily walk with You. AMEN

DON'T FORGET!

# WHO IS IN CONTROL?

SCRIPTURE: Hebrews 4:3

WRITER: Unknown

Hebrews 4:3 'For only we who believe can enter His rest. As for the others, God said, in my anger I took an oath: They will never enter my place of rest, even though this rest has been ready since He made the world.'

As we know, no one controls his own life. We do not have control as to when we will die, failing health, accidents or relationships that we will encounter. However, we do control our attitude that we have each day and the things that we pour into our lives. This is why we need to have an intimate relationship with our Creator, the one who does decide what goes on in our life. Sometimes, people resist submitting totally to Christ because they do not want to lose control. Jesus Christ is Lord whether we want to admit it or not. Philippians 2:10 says, every knee shall bow and every tongue shall confess that Jesus is Lord.'

Control issues are always hard to work through, simply because it is the one thing that we think we can do on our own. Then, challenges pop up, situations arise and of course, we want to be in charge and be on top of things. We simply have to step back and recognize that God is in control and He has everything in alignment with His will. We need to trust Him and seek Him in all we do and then and only then will we be able to hand control over to God and be submissive to His direction.

PRAYER: Holy Father, we pray to lean on You for everything we have and need. You meet our desires and we thank You. Please help us not to worry about being in control and totally turning everything over to You. AMEN

DON'T FORGET!

# OBEDIENCE EVERYDAY

SCRIPTURES: Hebrews 5:8; Philippians 2:8

WRITER: Unknown

DEFINITION: obedience—submission, giving into the orders or instructions of authority

Hebrews 5:8 'Even though Jesus was God's son, He learned obedience from the things He suffered.'

Philippians 2:8 'When He appeared in human form, He humbled himself in obedience to God and died a criminal's death on a cross.'

Obedience is something that we are called to in our Christian life. The true test of obedience, however, comes when we, like the Lord Jesus in Gethsemane, face one of God's commands you do not want to obey. You live your life believing that, within limits, you can disobey authority without suffering negative consequences. The price of disobedience is higher than the price of obedience. An omniscient, omnipresent God will call us to account 'in the day when God shall judge the secrets of men by Jesus Christ.' (Romans 2:16) We recognize that no one will go to heaven glad they sinned, but they will be glad they obeyed.

Obedience is total submission to the One that paid the price for us. Jesus Christ gave His life on the cross to provide us eternal life. We have to strive to be the best we can be and that starts with obedience to God.

PRAYER: Most Gracious Heavenly Father, I am so thankful for all You do for us and we seek You in a humble way today. Help us to strive for obedience in everything we do. AMEN

DON'T FORGET!

# WHEN LIFE FEELS EMPTY

SCRIPTURE: Ecclesiastes 1:1-14

WRITER: Solomon

DEFINITION: futile-worthless; useless; no meaning; something that could not succeed; lacking vigor or purpose

What is the most monotonous task you've ever been asked to do? I once saw an example, a warehouse filled with rows and rows of shelving with numbered medical files. I would think filing all day long, five days a week would be my definition of monotonous or boring. I also remember growing up and my siblings and I wanted a hamster so bad. My parents finally got us one. At night, because they are nocturnal, they are awake and exercising and running in the wheel going a hundred miles an hour and go nowhere. Solomon addresses the issue of futility in Ecclesiastes chapter one describing his life in a generation of coming and going, sunrising and sunsetting, wind gusting in and out and streams flowing in and out. Constant movement but no real direction in life. As we know, Solomon was one of the wisest men in the world, he was also one of the wealthiest in the world yet he floundered and wasted time, resources and direction. Apart from God, life is really meaningless. Isaiah 30:15 says, 'This what the Sovereign Lord, the Holy One of Israel says: only in returning to me and resting in me, you will be saved. In quietness and confidence is your strength. But you would have none of it.' Quietness and trust in Christ will help you not to feel empty in placing all you have with him. He knows your circumstances and will give you the power you need.

PRAYER: Father God, we praise You and lift Your name on high for who You are. We thank You for Your grace and mercy over our lives and we pray that You fill our lives with Your Holy Spirit. AMEN

## DON'T FORGET!

# GOD IS IN CONTROL?

SCRIPTURES: II Corinthians 12:9-10; Zechariah 2:13

WRITERS: Corinthians—Paul; Zechariah—Zechariah

II Corinthians 12:9-10 'Each time He said, my grace is all you need. My power works best in weakness. So now I am glad to boast about my weaknesses so that the power of Christ can work through me. That's why I take pleasure in my weaknesses, and in the insults, hardships, persecutions and troubles that I suffer for Christ. For when I am weak, then I am strong.'

Zechariah 2:13 'Be silent before the Lord, all humanity, for He is springing into action from His holy dwelling.'

God is constantly springing into action on our account. I had the great honor to lead our prayer circle last evening and shared these exact verses not knowing how the Holy Spirit would move between 16 men. I greeted everyone, asked for us to join in our time together and read the verses above. As I finished, I noticed a fellow that had been there the last two nights to pray. He said those verses spoke to his heart. The springing into action verses moved him because his family told him of their high school football coach that got the Corona Virus and passed away recently. Fifteen minutes had passed as they pronounced his time of death and then, someone noticed a slight pulse. He came back to life and began to move, to breathe on his own and follow instructions of the nurses. A true miracle that shows us that God is very much in control of everything.

Don't underestimate what God has in store for your life!

PRAYER: Most High God, thank You for miracles like this one mentioned and the miracle of life today. It is so precious and we thank You each day. AMEN

DON'T FORGET!

# GRACE ABOUNDS

SCRIPTURES: I Timothy 1:14; Romans 3:18

WRITERS: I Timothy—Paul; Romans—Paul

DEFINITION: grace—divine love; state of being protected; a temporary immunity or exception

I Timothy 1:14 'Oh, how generous and gracious our Lord was! He filled me with the faith and love that come from Christ Jesus.'

Romans 3:18 'They have no fear of God at all.'

'Beat the odds!' I am strong, resilient, a winner and a fighter. I declare it today. Where I am today is knowing full well that God is in control of my life and I am thankful for his grace that abounds for me. Having a positive mental attitude and outlook on life from prison is something I never planned on, growing up. A departure from day-to-day work, family life and extra-curricular events just never crossed my mind. As I lead my small group Bible study today, my topic is exactly on spot with grace. Grace is kind, compassionate treatment in our disposition toward others. A charitable interest in others and the honor by which favor, was expressed yesterday. Tim, a new inmate was seen in his wheelchair speaking with the case administrator as to which bunk he would be assigned for his 14 month stay here at Oakdale. Not many people were reaching out to him but, I introduced myself to him and told him if he needed anything, not to hesitate and I would be honored to help him. Later, men began to come together to greet and convey their help on this man who had gotten COVID and had a stroke during the illness and now has no movement of his lower body. His wife died before he reported to Oakdale.

I Timothy 1:14 says 'and the grace of our Lord was exceedingly abundant with faith and love which is in Christ Jesus.' Don't ever quit giving and blessing others because God is counting on you.

PRAYER: Lord God, thank You for opportunities with mankind. People are important and we all need Your grace to give attention to others. AMEN

DON'T FORGET!

# CHOOSE TO PRAISE

SCRIPTURES: Hebrews 13:15; Romans 1:2

WRITERS: Hebrews—Unknown; Romans—Paul

DEFINITION: praise—expression of approval; commendation; to exalt or to worship

Hebrews 13:15 'By Him therefore, let us offer the sacrifice of praise to God continually, that is the fruit of our lips giving thanks to His name.'

Romans 1:2 'God promised this Good News long ago through his prophets in the Holy Scriptures.'

Do you know someone that has everything you can possibly think of? What do we offer to God who has no need? God says he owns all and needs nothing from us. However, He desires our offer of thanksgiving and the sacrifice of praise towards Him. When you give the Lord thanks in the midst of your pain you affirm His goodness and His greatness.

Think about the number of ways in which we can praise God and magnify His name. The ways in which we pray, serve and have faith in Christ are important. James 1:2 says, 'Dear Brothers and Sisters when troubles of any kind come your way, consider it an opportunity for great joy. For you know that when your faith is tested, your endurance has a chance to grow.' Examples such as this one definitely point us towards praising the Lord and bringing honor and glory to his name. Faith and endurance are needed when we encounter trials in our lives. My challenge for you today is to choose to praise God in all you do.

PRAYER: Gracious Lord, I thank You for all You do each and every day in my life. I choose to praise You and bring honor and glory to Your names. AMEN

DON'T FORGET!

# TRUTH

SCRIPTURES: Psalm 85:10; John 1:14

WRITERS: Psalm 85—Sons of Korah

Psalm 85:10 'Unfailing love and truth have met together. Righteousness and peace have kissed.'

John 1:14 'So the word became human and made his home among us. He was full of unfailing love and faithfulness. And we have seen His glory, the glory of the Father's one and only Son.'

Christ's death on the cross allowed God to be merciful toward the sinner without doing violence to His truth. Jesus was acknowledged in the book of John as being 'full of grace and truth.' Just as His death made it possible for mercy and truth to meet, so His life was characterized by a blend of grace and truth. Grace and mercy shift and move the blame for your sin from you to Jesus.

Is it not reassuring for us as a Christ follower to know that God is for us and we can always seek the truth in Him?

I think we all know that there have been plenty of times in our life that we have perhaps skirted the truth in the things we have said, exclaimed or gossip we have told others. We have to put the cards on the table to get where we need to be with a right relationship with Christ. Don't take for granted the blessings God gives us through the truth He provides us with His love.

PRAYER: Dear God, thank You for Your truth in our lives. May we strive for excellence in all we do in seeking You. May Your truth be at the forefront of our life. AMEN

DON'T FORGET!

# ANCHOR OF THE SOUL

SCRIPTURES: Hebrews 11:16; Hebrews 6:9

WRITER: Unknown

Hebrews 11:16 'But they were looking for a better place, a heavenly homeland. That is why God is not ashamed to be called their God, for he has prepared a city for them.'

Hebrews 6:9 'Dear Friends, even though we are talking this way, we really don't believe it applies to you. We are confident that you are meant for better things that come with salvation.'

When we think about being on a boat, getting ready to drop anchor so the boat can remain steady and in place, not to move about. An anchor is made of iron and is cast to give a lot of weight to spear itself into the bottom of a body of water. It is important to know this anchor will hold and be dependable. God created you and me with the desire of immortality. Those who know their Creator understand that He has given them this life to prepare for eternity. The promises of God truly are the Anchor of the Soul. Remember that Heaven is not a reward, but a gift. The reward of faith is for God to say to you, 'I am not ashamed to be called Your God.'

Try to think about the anchor being the example for you that reminds you to be steadfast in our beliefs, our actions, our faith and the works we do to move things toward God's kingdom. Jesus Christ is that anchor for you and I and he will never allow us to waiver if we are obedient and living in the right step with him. Hang on to the Anchor today.

PRAYER: One True God, we thank You for being that strength that we need and desire to hang on to each day. Thank You for the direction You give through our trials. AMEN

## DON'T FORGET!

# FAITH AND BELIEVING

SCRIPTURES: II Timothy 1:12; II Corinthians 1:24; Hebrews 6:12

WRITERS: Timothy—Apostle Paul; II Corinthians—Paul; Hebrews—unknown

DEFINTION: faith—reliance, loyalty or complete trust in God; a system of religious beliefs

II Timothy 1:12 'That is why I am suffering here in prison. But I am not ashamed of it, for I know the One in whom I trust, and I am sure that He is able to guard what I have entrusted to Him until the day of His return.'

II Corinthians 1:24 'But that does not mean we want to dominate you by telling you how to put your faith into practice. We want to work together with you so you will be full of joy, for it is by your own faith that you stand firm.

Hebrews 6:12 'Then you will not become spiritually dull and indifferent. Instead, you will follow the example of those who are going to inherit God's promises because of their faith and endurance.'

Walking by faith is what God wants us to do in our life each and every day. A lot of times we find ourselves not walking by faith because of events and the stuff of the world around us taking us in other directions. As Paul wrote, he was too, following the ministry path of Jesus. Being persecuted for his stance and following God. It is no different for us today. We must keep our faith strong even when things in our life try to waiver our beliefs. We have placed our faith in Christ when we asked Jesus in our heart and that is where it all started. If we are walking with God and seeking Him in all we do. Do you know of someone in your circle that may be struggling with their faith and their walk? Encourage them today for God.

PRAYER: Faithful Father, we come to You today to say thank You for our faith. We pray for strength, guidance and joy in our walk. May we give thanks to You constantly. AMEN

DON'T FORGET!

# CHANGE HOW YOU THINK

SCRIPTURE: Romans 12:2

WRITER: Paul

DEFINITION: think-to reflect, ponder or remember

Romans 12:2 'Don't copy the behavior and customs of this world, but let God transform you into a new person by changing the way you think. Then you will learn to know God's will for you, which is good and pleasing and perfect.'

Our mind is a wonderful thing that God has created. Our brain which is comprised of the cerebrum which controls and integrates motor, sensory and higher mental functions, such as thought, reason, emotion and memory. The cerebellum on the other hand is responsible for regulation and coordination of complex voluntary muscular movement as well as the maintenance of posture and balance. Pretty smart stuff that God put together for each of us here in the world. We can look at things in a very technical sense but Paul sticks to the basics of simply saying that we should not conform to this world and surely not be conformed into that as well. He says that we need to think differently and act differently as in God's will. How do you think each day? Is it with Godly things in mind? Is your thinking about others or are you simply concerned about yourself and how your life is going? You and I both know the right answer and we must always strive to keep our mind in check for exactly what God set out for us in the beginning, for us to impact those around us in a positive way.

PRAYER: Holy God, thank You for our mind, body, and spirit. May we think clearly about You and how You long for us to be transformed in our life seeking You. AMEN

DON'T FORGET!

# THE NAIL

SCRIPTURES: Matthew 27:35; Colossians 2:14

WRITERS: Matthew—Matthew; Colossians—Paul

DEFINITION: nailed-to fasten with or as if with a nail; to keep fixed on motionless; a slim, pointed piece of metal hammered into material

Matthew 27:35 'After they had nailed him to the cross, the soldiers gambled for his clothes by throwing dice.'

Colossians 2:14 'He canceled the record of changes against us and took it away by nailing it to the cross.'

I received an email from a friend today with the story of a good carpenter using a bent nail. It occurred to me that Jesus, the Master Carpenter, does that with us. We are all bent nails at one time, but he straightened us and makes us useful for his work. You have to get pretty rough with some of these bent nails in order to get them out of their useless state. Christ has to get pretty rough with us sometimes to get us 'unstuck' from the messes we get ourselves into. But He can straighten us out and use us in some of His marvelous works. After all, He is the Master Carpenter!

Jesus paid the ultimate price for you and I by being nailed to the cross with painful metal nails. Thankfully, He canceled our debt and transgressions when that occurred on our behalf. Live for Christ today.

PRAYER: Most Gracious Lord, I thank You for the unbelievable sacrifice you made for my life. You are the Great Carpenter and thank You for Your special touch each and every day in my life. AMEN

DON'T FORGET!

# CONTENTMENT

SCRIPTURE: I Timothy 6:6-8

WRITER: Paul

DEFINITION: contentment—a source of satisfaction

I Timothy 6:6-8 'Yet true godliness with contentment is itself great wealth. After all, we brought nothing with us when we came into the world, and we can't take anything with us when we leave it. So, if we have enough food and clothing, let us be content.

How is your life going today in the midst of the pandemic, a new Presidential Cabinet, social distancing and masks? Are you content with life as you live it today? Do you have enough stuff? Is money and retirement a concern at your current age? These are things to think about as we navigate through each day and truly look at the things that are really important and meaningful in our life. These things lead us into our topic of being content. We live in a world that has us surrounded by the most up to date phone devices, pads and computers. We are able to navigate through online apps to pinpoint a direction or a location. Yet sometimes it is just not enough for us to be content.

Paul in I Timothy shares that there is contentment in godliness. But, remember, stuff and worldly things will not make a difference in the end because we will not be taking it with us. So, get your priorities on Godly things like faith, prayer, thanksgiving, grace, humility and love of your neighbor. Don't let things control or run your life. Just be content in Christ today and your life will be blessed.

PRAYER: Heavenly Father, may we be content in our life for You and how You bless us each day with Your presence in our life. Help our source of satisfaction always align with You. AMEN

DON'T FORGET!

# REPENTANCE

SCRIPTURES: Matthew 11:20; Acts 2:38; Matthew 3:2

WRITERS: Matthew—Matthew; Acts—Luke

DEFINITION: repent-to turn from sin and change one's heart and behavior; to feel regret and contrition

Matthew 11:20 'Then Jesus began to denounce the towns where he had done so many of his miracles, because they hadn't repented of their sins and turned to God.'

Acts 2:38 'Peter replied, each of you must repent of your sins and turn to God, and be baptized in the name of Jesus Christ for the forgiveness of your sins. Then you will receive the gift of the Holy Spirit.'

Matthew 3:2 'Repent of your sins and turn to God for the Kingdom of Heaven is near.

When we speak of repenting, what comes to mind? We have done something wrong, crossed the line, we went against God and what he wants us to have in our life. Thankfully through salvation and our ability to repent, we can be made whole again. We are commanded to repent of our sins daily and turn to God and ask for forgiveness. We do not need to allow sin to build up in our lives and then get overwhelmed because we have that sin binding us and keeping us from a right relationship with God. The verses shared today clearly mark the path for us when we sin. Let me challenge you to do an ongoing evaluation of where you are with your daily walk with God and then work towards obedience in Him. Repentance brings about obedience and our desire to seek Christ and continue to grow.

PRAYER: Almighty God, help us to repent of our sins and wrong doings so we may grow closer to You each and every day. AMEN

## DON'T FORGET!

# SEPARATION

SCRIPTURE: Romans 8:38-39

WRITER: Paul

Romans 8:38-39 'And I am convinced that nothing can ever separate us from God's love. Neither death nor life, neither angels nor demons, neither our fears for today nor our worries about tomorrow – not even the powers of hell can separate us from God's love. No power in the sky above or in the earth below-indeed, nothing in all creation will ever be able to separate us from the love of God that is revealed in Christ Jesus our Lord.'

Nothing can separate us from God's love. We are still going to experience trouble and calamity. Persecution, hunger and trips down into the valley will take us on a ride that makes us feel as if we are going it alone. Take heart that God does not want separation from us. Can we think of some examples that take us through the separation process? Sin, of course does that most notably. How about troubles from within a family, a business or even issues with a possible neighbor? Our verses today clearly claim just how strong God's love is for us each and every day. Neither death nor life, neither angels nor demons, neither our fears for today or worries for tomorrow, not even the powers of hell can separate us from God's love. That pretty much encompasses everything we need in our daily life. God has already made promises for us to have exactly what we need to be connected to him. Praise God for that promise!

PRAYER: Heavenly Father, we don't ever want separation from You in our lives. Please keep us on the pathway that we need to follow each day. Help us to have a strong confidence that You are there for us no matter what we face. AMEN

DON'T FORGET!

# WITH MY HEAD HELD HIGH

MY STORY

I have accomplished two months of my sentence and would love to update and share how God has blessed me and allowed me to hold my head high the entire way. God has blessed me with an appearance of 3 crosses, a Jesus stamp, a Christian orderly, 4 unsaved correctional officers, mail, Christian books, motivational books, 696 hours of solitary confinement behind bars in a 10' X 7' cell, a landscape job given to me on the first interview, Godly co-workers, a Godly boss and men in a prayer group that have made me feel welcome and who have poured into me each and every day.

I began my time walking the prison yard on a 10' wide concrete walkway that was separated by rows of jail cells with small windows. Words, phrases and pounding on windows taking place but my grace ticket reminded me to hold my head high, looking to Christ and being constantly reminded that this is now my story. This is adversity at its greatest and I intend to conquer with the promises I have from my Lord and Savior, Jesus Christ.

God has blessed me in so many ways but most of all, impacting men that have all done wrong, been forgiven and are now rebuilding their lives through forgiveness for themselves and being obedient to God moving forward.

For me, I am thankful for Jesus and His love for me that I may press forward every day, with my head held high praising His name.

PRAYER: Lord God, You are the great I Am. There is no other like You and I thank You for all you do for me each and every day in a very different atmosphere, yet it is where my story continues. AMEN

## DON'T FORGET!

# PURSUIT

SCRIPTURE: I Timothy 6:11-12

WRITER: Paul

DEFINITION: pursuit-to follow in order to overtake; capture or to seek

I Timothy 6:11-12 'But you, Timothy, are a man of God; so, run from all those evil things, pursue righteousness and a godly life, along with faith, love, perseverance and gentleness. Fight the good fight for the true faith. Hold tightly to the eternal life to which God has called you, which you have declared so well before many witnesses.'

When I think about the things that I now want to pursue in life, it is building my relationship with Jesus Christ, the one who died for me. When you spend 29 days with 16-18 hours of that being quiet time, you can really focus on the connection one needs to be right at God's feet. Timothy tells us to stay away and run from evil in this life and more towards seeking righteousness, a godly life which is filled with good things. Those are faith, perseverance and gentleness. Lastly, to fight the good fight of true faith which clearly means following Christ. To pursue means to seek and to follow the One who seeks us as well. The question is whether we will do the right thing and follow Christ as we are called. Pursuit is not always easy because we get side tracked and derailed by sin. We can't do that and don't need to be that if we want an effective witness. Pursue the godly things in life today.

PRAYER: Heavenly Father, thank You for pursuing us each and every day. Help us always to seek You and know that we will find You. AMEN

DON'T FORGET!

# THE STORY I WILL TELL

I have a close friend that shared with me something that had been placed on her heart months ago and sent to me here in prison in a letter. It talks about how we each have our own story to tell and I am very excited about the story that God is writing in my life being where I am and doing what I am doing each day. Twenty five percent of our prison camp where I am housed attends our Prayer Circle and Bible Study weekly. We meet at 4:15pm and 10:15pm each day; 6:00pm on Wednesday and 9:00am on Sunday morning. This has become my story simply in a different location; Oakdale, Louisiana. Hence, Devotions from Oakdale. Here is the song....

The hour is dark and it's hard to see what you are doing here in the ruins and where this will lead. Oh, but I know that down through the years I'll look on this moment and see your hand on it and know you were here.

I'll testify of the battles you've won, how you were my portion when there wasn't enough and I'll testify of the seas we've crossed, the waters you parted, the waves that I've walked. Singing Oh my God did not fail Oh the story I'll tell.

Believing gets hard when options are few. When I can't see what you're doing I know that you are proving you're the God that comes through. Oh, but I know that over the years I'll look back on this moment and see your hand on this and know that you were here. I'll testify of the battles you've won, how you were my portion when there wasn't enough. I'll testify of the seas we've crossed, yes, I will, the waters you parted, the waves I've walked. And all that is left is highest praises so sing hallelujah to the Rock of Ages, come on sing, sing it, all that's left is the highest praises.

Singing, Oh my God did not fail, never ever failed me, Oh, the story I'll tell. It's my testimony. Oh, I know it is well—That's the story I'll tell!

This is why I say, through all of this....I have a 'story to tell.'

PRAYER: Dear Lord, thank You for the story that You are writing through my life in a very unfamiliar place. I pray for Your guidance and direction, Your ways and not my ways. AMEN

DON'T FORGET!

# HIS VOICE

It is Sunday morning and I am preparing to attend 9:00am Bible Study here at Oakdale. I will quote the email I received verbatim so the effect of the words shared will impact you like they impacted me. 'I came across something in my daily reading a few days ago that reminded me so much of you (Greg). Did you know your writing voice is a reflection of what is in your heart? I never thought about our writing being a 'voice.' We become familiar with God's voice in the same way. By reading what He has written, we learn who He is and how He expresses Himself. God went to extremes to make sure we recognize His voice. He gave us His word and He gave us the word made flesh-Jesus!'

Through the writings of the Oakdale Devotionals, I have been able to strengthen my relationship with Christ and to continue building on every word that I write. My goal is to encourage you the reader but I have to say selfishly, my transcriber is a very special person who is editing all of my writings and I owe a debt of love and gratitude to her and that is my beautiful wife, Cheri. Thank you, my love, for allowing my voice to be heard through God's voice through the ink that hits the paper each time God moves my heart to write. His voice is all we need to listen for daily.

PRAYER: Most Gracious Lord, thank You for Your small still voice. May it impact many for the cause of Christ. I love You. AMEN

DON'T FORGET!

# GREATER AWARENESS

SCRIPTURE: II Corinthians 7:5-6

WRITER: Paul

II Corinthians 7:5-6 'When we arrived in Macedonia, there was no rest for us. We faced conflict from every direction, with battles on the outside and fear on the inside. But God, who encourages those who are discouraged, encouraged us by the arrival of Titus.'

One of our purposes in life is to bring a greater awareness of our dependence upon Christ. God is constantly trying to teach us how dependent we really are on Him, that we are held completely by His hand and we must totally rely on His care alone.

We must stand not with our self-made strength but always leaning on Him and trusting Him for guidance. Also, our stand must exhibit a trust that would never dare to take even one step alone. This will teach us to trust him more.

Take it from Paul, there was no way to learn faith except through trials. They are God's school of faith and it is much better for us to learn to trust Him than to live a life of enjoyment.

You and I are challenged every day on how we will handle challenges, conflict and adversity in our life. When we try to do things on our own is when the wheels fall off. We can't do it and deep down, we know that our trust simply needs to be in Christ.

PRAYER: Most Gracious Lord, thank You for awareness in You and all the great things You have lined out for us if we simply place our trust in You. AMEN

DON'T FORGET!

# THE FIRE TEST

SCRIPTURES: Job 23:10; Hebrews 6:12

WRITERS: Job—Unknown; Hebrews—Unknown

Job 23:10 'But He knows where I am going. And when He tests me, I will come out as pure as gold.'

Hebrews 6:12 'Then you will not become spiritually dull and indifferent. Instead, you will follow the example of those who are going to inherit God's promises because of their faith and endurance.'

I don't know about you, but I definitely do not want to become spiritually dull and indifferent. Today, I want to take you down into the village. We are at the blacksmith shop. The old village blacksmith once said, 'there is only one thing that I fear: being thrown onto the scrap heap. You see, in order to strengthen a piece of steel, I must first temper it. I heat it, hammer it, and quickly plunge it into a bucket of cold water. Very soon, I know whether it will accept the tempering process or simply fall to pieces. If, after one or two tests, I see it will not allow itself to be tempered, I throw it onto the scrap heap, only to later sell it to the junkman for a few cents per pound.

I realize the Lord tests me the same way: through fire, water and heavy blows of his hammer. If I am unwilling to withstand the test, or prove to be unfit for his tempering process, I am afraid he may throw me onto the scrap heap. 'When the fire in your life is the hottest, stand still, for later on...it produces a harvest.' (Hebrews 12:11) of blessings. Then we will be able to say with Job, 'when he has tested me, I will come forth as gold. (Job 23:19)

Will you accept the tempering process today or simply fall to pieces? Are you producing a harvest today? I want to encourage you to be the best you can be for the Lord.

PRAYER: Lord God, thank You for strengthening us each and every day. We pray for refinement and tempering. We want to produce a harvest for You today. AMEN

DON'T FORGET!

# GOD'S TIMING

SCRIPTURES: Malachi 3:3; Romans 8:28

WRITERS: Malachi—Malachi; Romans—Paul

Malachi 3:3 'He will sit like a refiner of silver, burning away the dross. He will purify the Levites, refining then like gold and silver, so they may once again offer acceptable sacrifices to the Lord.'

Romans 8:28 'And we know that God causes everything to work together for the good of those who love God and are called according to His purposes for them.'

God prepares us as His instruments and matures our strength at the appointed time and He is able to meet the tasks we encounter. God is not in a hurry. He spends years preparing his plans for us and His planning is never too long for us.

The most difficult ingredient of suffering is often time. When things are monotonous in our life, sometimes our heart loses strength. In Malachi, the true goldsmith which is God, stops the fire the moment he sees the image in the glowing metal.

There is a reason behind every lesson, and when God sees that we are ready, our deliverance will definitely come. He is in the process of educating us for future service and greater blessings.

Learn to await his timing—the second, minute and hour hands must all point to the precise moment for action. You and I both know that God's timing is so perfect, so rely on Him today.

> He never shows up late; He knows just what is best;
> Fret not yourself in vain; until He comes just rest.
> Selected Poem

PRAYER: Most Gracious Heavenly Father, Your timing is always perfect and we thank You for that. May You work through our situations to keep us on track with You. AMEN

## DON'T FORGET!

# HIS STRENGTH

SCRIPTURES: Philippians 3:10; Romans 8:28; I Timothy 1:12

WRITERS: Philippians—Paul; Romans—Paul; I Timothy—Timothy

DEFINITION: strength—the quality of being strong; power to resist attack; an attribute or quality of particular worth

Philippians 3:10 'I want to know Christ and experience the mighty power that raised Him from the dead. I want to suffer with Him, sharing in His death.'

Romans 8:28 'And we know that God causes everything to work together for the good of those who love God and are called according to His purpose for them.'

I Timothy 1:12 'I thank Christ Jesus our Lord, who has given me strength to do his work. He considered me trustworthy and appointed me to serve Him.'

Have you ever worked out at a gym day after day working your upper body one day and your legs the next? You get into a rotation getting your body into shape. You also work on eating properly so you can attain your goal of losing weight or tuning up your body so you feel better and have more energy each day. The Christian life is a lot like working out and getting into shape. However, you are working out your mind spiritually, your heart along with the way in which you live your life. Constant workouts in the gym becomes hard at first until you start getting into shape. Same with conditioning yourself in Bible study, daily prayer time and quiet time along with application of what we read and study. You need 'His strength' to be successful in a daily walk that is obedient to our Lord and Savior. I want to challenge you to step back and evaluate your workout and conditioning of your Christian walk.

PRAYER: Dear God, may we have Your strength in all of our

daily workouts of reading and studying Your Word as well as living it out each and every day. I love You Father and praise Your name today. AMEN

DON'T FORGET!

DEVOTIONS FROM OAKDALE

# GOD'S GIFTS

SCRIPTURE: I Peter 4:10-11

WRITER: I Peter—Peter

I Peter 4:10-11 'God has given each of you a gift from his great variety of spiritual gifts. Use them well to serve one another. Do you have the gift of speaking? Then speak as though God himself were speaking through you. Do you have the gift of helping others? Do it with all the strength and energy that God supplies. Then everything you do will bring glory to God through Jesus Christ. All glory and power to Him forever and ever! AMEN

What comes to mind when you hear about gifts? Perhaps Christmas time, a birthday or a special occasion honoring someone or a special event. We all love to receive gifts and give gifts to show our appreciation or love for others. God showers us with His gifts in our own lives and the big question is whether or not we are able to recognize those gifts. Peter writes that we all have at least one gift given to us in our life. They are spiritual gifts ranging from speaking, teaching and encouraging others. We are called to use them well. Not half-heartedly, not recognizing that a special blessing of a gift in the form of a talent needs to be maximized to bless the One who has given it to us. I definitely love the verse about the gift of helping others. I have my good friend Dave who is the epitome of serving others regardless of the situation. Picking up limbs, blowing off a roof, helping someone clean out a storage room or just bringing someone a gallon of milk and eggs in a winter ice storm. Always give your best because God has provided his special gifts to us.

PRAYER: Dear Lord, we thank You for Your blessings on our lives through spiritual gifts. May we use them to bless You and others each and every day. AMEN

DON'T FORGET!

# WHOLESOME THINKING

SCRIPTURES: I Timothy 1:13-14; Philippians 2:3-4

WRITER: Timothy—Paul; Philippians—Paul

DEFINITION: thinking—to reflect; ponder or remember; to subject to processes of logical thought; to have as an opinion; to conceive or reason

I Timothy 1:13-14 'Even though I used to blaspheme the name of Jesus. In silence, I persecuted his people. But God had mercy on me because I did it in ignorance and unbelief. Oh, how generous and gracious our Lord was! He filled me with the faith and love that come from Christ Jesus.

Philippians 2:3 'Don't be selfish; don't try to impress others. Be humble, thinking of others as better than yourselves. Don't look out only for your own interests, but take an interest in others, too.

My PawPaw, Aubrey Boswell and my Father, Don Smith have had the most impact on my life over the years as it pertains to wholesome thinking. I have never heard a harsh word or slang expression because God is in their heart and therefore, they expressed it daily by what came from their mouths. My PawPaw passed away some 30 years ago and I miss him dearly. He made a great impact on my life. Wow, how he loved his grandkids and that has instilled in me how to love my family and to be thankful for the relationships that I have been blessed with in my life. Now, when it comes to my Dad, oh what an example he has been. He always went to work every day, worked hard and then came home and spent time with his kids in the yard playing ball and showing us what it meant to live and share a wholesome life.

PRAYER: God Almighty, thank You for my grandparents and my parents. They have shown me what wholesome living is all about. I love You and thank You for Your blessings upon my life. AMEN

DON'T FORGET!

159

# SHIELD OF FAITH

SCRIPTURES: Ephesians 6:16; Matthew 9:29

WRITERS: Ephesians—Paul; Matthew—Matthew

DEFINITION: faith—reliance, loyalty or complete trust in God; a system of religious beliefs

Ephesians 6:16 'In addition to all of these, hold up the shield of faith to stop the fiery arrows of the devil.'

Matthew 9:29 'Then he touched their eyes and said 'Because of your faith, it will happen.'

Praying though it might be looked upon as praying your way into full faith; being assured while still praying that your prayer has been heard and accepted in advance of the event, and during confident anticipation becoming aware of your prayer being answered, are among the exciting mysteries that grow our faith. We live in an ever-changing world and we are called to be steadfast. As His Word says, we have to be loyal and give Him complete trust each day. We all know that we are traveling some ups and downs in our life. A lost job, a mortgage payment delayed, a sickness, a loss of a loved one, a cancer diagnosis…things just keep coming and sometimes, we would like to just hold up our hands and say I can't take any more. You see, it is when we are at our weakest and in a corner that God just looks in and wonders, are you going to acknowledge Me and call upon my name? He is our shield of faith and we can depend on Him.

PRAYER: Most Gracious Lord, thank You for being the shield we need each and every day. We depend on You and love You. AMEN

## DON'T FORGET!

# STAND FIRM

SCRIPTURES: I Corinthians 16:13; Hebrews 3:14; I Corinthians 9:24

WRITERS: I Corinthians—Paul; Hebrews—Unknown

I Corinthians 16:13 'Be on guard, stand firm in the faith. Be courageous, be strong and do everything with love.'

I Corinthians 9:24 'Don't you realize that in a race everyone runs but only one person gets the prize? So, run to win!'

Hebrews 3:14 'For if we are faithful to the end, trusting God just as firmly as when we first believed, we will share in all that belongs to Christ.'

The finish line is right in front of you. You can see it since you are at the last of your race. The archway with bold letters FINISH LINE awaits you. You are tired, your body heaving and sometimes people are passing you to get in front of you in this race of life. Don't be dismayed by things that go on around you. Your life and your relationship are with Christ and no one else. Stand firm and expect blessings to come your way because of your faithfulness. Sometimes, we see what we think is a short straight road but becomes a winding road with lots of curves and plenty of danger. Satan loves to tempt us and puts up road block signs that really have no meaning to us if we just keep our eyes and focus on Christ. He is our true roadmap when we are navigating through life. So, will you finish the race with confidence? Let's run the race to win and stand firm for Christ.

PRAYER: Dear Heavenly Father, thank You for all that You do for us when we can't see over the hills and down in the deep valleys. We do not have to travel alone when we have You. AMEN

DON'T FORGET!

# REPENTING

SCRIPTURES: Matthew 3:2; Acts 2:38; Acts 20:21

WRITERS: Matthew—Matthew; Acts—Luke

DEFINITION: repent—to ask for forgiveness of sin against God and man; a radical change of heart resulting in a radical change in the direction of one's life; it is only possible if there is the power to change; to turn from sin and change one's heart and behavior

Matthew 3:2 'Repent of your sins and turn to God, for the Kingdom of Heaven is near.'

Acts 2:38 'Peter replied, each of you must repent of your sins and turn to God, and be baptized in the name of Jesus Christ for the forgiveness of your sins. Then, you will receive the gift of the Holy Spirit.'

Acts 20:21 'I have had one message for the Jews and Gentiles alike-the necessity of repenting from sin and turning to God, and having faith in our Lord Jesus.

When we are seeking repentance, we truly have to be sorry for our sins and we have to live a Godly life. A genuine decision must be made to live the life we are called to live. We can't pick and choose which sins we want to identify. We have to have a new knowledge, a new beginning regretting the life behind us. Think about your friendships that you are a part of on a daily, weekly and monthly basis. Do any of those relationships cause you to compromise your relationship with Christ and even more importantly, cause you to sin where you then evaluate your sin and then pick and choose which ones to bring to God for forgiveness? We can do that if we are truly going to walk with God in obedience. Give great thought to this topic of repenting because it is the very foundation of the Christian life. We sin, we seek God and we repent to have newness of life.

PRAYER: Most Gracious Father, thank You for sending Your son, Jesus to die on the cross for our sins so that we might have eternal life in You. AMEN

DON'T FORGET!

# KINGDOM AGENDA

SCRIPTURES: Matthew 13:11

WRITER: Matthew

The Kingdom Agenda is intended to control our hearts and transform our lives. Christ is our Redeemer and HE is our only hope. He has conquered sin on our behalf! He willingly offers us His heart-transforming life altering grace! Colossians 2:8 'See to it that no one takes you captive through hollow and deceptive philosophy, which depends on human tradition and the basic principles of this world and not on Christ.'

God uses ordinary people to do extraordinary thing in the lives of others.

Matthew 13:11 'He replied, you are permitted to understand the secrets of the Kingdom of Heaven, but others are not.'

Ephesians 5:5 'You can be sure that no immoral, impure or greedy person will inherit the Kingdom of Christ and of God. For a greedy person is an idolater, worshipping the things of the world.'

God's Word is very clear about how we are to live to inherit His Kingdom. Paul talks about living in the light. Ephesians 5:1-2, 'Imitate God, therefore, in everything you do, because you are His dear children. Live a life filled with love, following the example of Christ. He loved us and offered himself as a sacrifice for us, a pleasing aroma of God.'

We have our work cut out for us when we are striving to be Godly and live the life Christ has for us. A step lock walk, side by side with Him is what He desires. Keep the Kingdom Agenda where it needs to be today.

PRAYER: Lord God Almighty, we thank You for Your Heavenly Kingdom and we praise You today. May You help us as we strive to be extraordinary in You today. AMEN

DON'T FORGET!

# THANKFULNESS

SCRIPTURE: Thessalonians 5:16-18

WRITER: Paul

DEFINITION: thankfulness—a prayer expressing gratitude; a public acknowledgement or celebration of God's goodness

I Thessalonians 5:16-18 'Always be joyful. Never stop praying. Be thankful in all circumstances, for this is God's will for you who belong to Christ Jesus.'

When we think about 'thankfulness,' we are able to 'pray without ceasing' by consistently referring life's input to God; your thinking process becomes prayer. Your thoughts, victories, discouragements and defeats are all committed to God in prayer with a spirit of gratitude. I have been reading a book by Jim Stovall titled 'Today's The Day.' The introduction to his book begins as follows…'As a blind person, I live in a different world than those of you reading the words on this page; however, that doesn't mean that I don't 'see.' Here is an individual that has a vision impairment that has made the most of where he is and has continued with his life making a difference and has sold over 3 million copies of his first book 'The Ultimate Gift.' We are so blessed each and every day to have our senses. To smell, taste, touch, hear and to see, are so powerful and we do not need to forget and take them for granted. Paul speaks about always being joyful in everything we do and to never stop praying. Be thankful in all circumstances because, we belong to Christ.

PRAYER: Dear God, today I am especially thankful for life and all that You do for me each day. I thank You for favor and Your blessings on me. I thank You for family, friends and life. AMEN

DON'T FORGET!

# WAITING FOR GOD

SCRIPTURES: Deuteronomy 2:31; Romans 9:37-38

WRITERS: Deuteronomy—Moses; Romans—Paul

Deuteronomy 2:31 'Then the Lord said to me, look, I have begun to hand King Sihon and his land over to you. Begin now to conquer and occupy his land.'

Romans 9:37-38 'And I am convinced that nothing can ever separate us from God's love. Neither death nor life, neither angels nor demons, neither our fears for today nor our worries about tomorrow; not even the powers of hell can separate us from God's love.'

The Bible has a lot to say about waiting for God and the teaching cannot be too strongly emphasized. We so easily become impatient with God's delays. Another situation that exists is that God often waits for us. Many of God's promises are conditional, requiring some initial action on our part. Once we begin to obey, He will begin to bless us.

God is waiting to pour out His richest blessings on you and me. We are called to 'go forward' with a strong confidence and take what is ours.

Is it hard for you when things are going on in your life with family, friends or business associates for you to patiently wait on God? It can sometimes be hard if you lose connection with the ONE who truly make the difference. We will never be separated from God as long as we are obedient and walk with Him each day.

PRAYER: Most Gracious Heavenly Father, thank You for always being there for us when we are lost and looking for our way. Life can be challenging a lot of the time and we simply have to be connected to You. May we seek You today. AMEN

DON'T FORGET!

# DEPEND ON ME

SCRIPTURES: I Kings 12:24; Philippians 4:19; II Thessalonians 2:16

WRITERS: I Kings—unknown; Philippians—Paul; II Thessalonians—Paul

DEFINITION: depend—to rely, especially for support or maintenance; to place trust or confidence

I Kings 12:24 'This is what the Lord says: Do not fight against your relatives, the Israelites. Go back home, for what has happened is my doing! So, they obeyed the message of the Lord and went home, as the Lord had commanded.'

Philippians 4:19 'And this same God who takes care of me will supply all your needs from his glorious riches, which have been given to us in Christ Jesus.'

II Thessalonians 2:16 'Now may our Lord Jesus Christ himself and God our Father, who loved us and by His grace gave us eternal comfort and a wonderful hope, comfort you and strengthen you in every good thing you do and say.'

'This is my doing.' God says that your weaknesses need my strength, and your safety lies in letting me fight for you. Are you in a difficult situation right now? Are you surrounded by people that you don't need to be around because of their questionable views or character? God says, I am the God of all circumstances and you did not come to this place by accident. You are exactly where I meant for you to be. God's word addresses that He will take care of all of our needs but we have to depend on Him and trust Him. Think about the times in which events in your life have occurred and they could have gone either way, good or bad. The situation tips your way and hopefully you recognized that God was there waiting for you to depend on Him.

PRAYER: Almighty God, thank You for dependence on You and the strength that You provide through Your grace and comfort. AMEN

DON'T FORGET!

# POSSIBILITIES

SCRIPTURES: Matthew 17:20; I Peter 5:7

WRITERS: Matthew—Matthew; I Peter—Peter

Matthew 17:20 'You don't have enough faith, Jesus told them. I tell you the truth, if you had faith even as small as a mustard seed, you could say to the mountain, move from here to there, and it would move. Nothing would be impossible.'

I Peter 5:7 'Give all your worries and cares to God, for He cares about you.'

All things are possible with Christ. God calls us to daily cast all our anxiety upon Him. It is possible to see God's will in all of our circumstances. It is possible to stay strong in our daily life even when things are sometimes upside down. We can become stronger when things have not gone our way and we are wondering, what in the world is going on. We all face challenges with the decisions we make and sometimes, they are poor decisions at that.

Again, all things are possible with Christ. Are you depending on Him each day or only when things explode and you have no other option but to turn to Him? I want to challenge you to be proactive about your daily walk and seek Him through the possibilities. Don't miss the opportunities that are waiting for you today.

PRAYER: Father God, we thank You for all of the great possibilities that are before us today just waiting for us to take advantage. We thank You and praise You and ask for You to guide us. AMEN

DON'T FORGET!

# WHO YOU ARE

SCRIPTURE: Psalm 37:7

WRITER: David

Psalm 37:7 'Be still before the Lord and wait patiently for him; do not fret when people succeed in their ways, when they carry out their wicked schemes.'

If I introduce myself to you and share my name with you, most likely, you will do the same by giving me your name and acknowledging one another. As one grows up, your name continues to have things added to it like doctor, nurse, pro athlete and so on. I received a neat quote from a friend who knew I was writing daily devotionals. Here is how it goes-

> 'Who you are is not who society says you are,
> Not who the courts say you are,
> Not who your enemies say you are,
> Not even who your friends say you are.
> Who you are is who you are in Christ.'

I like that because it really directs us as to who we really are with Christ, who matters the most. Things in our lives may sometimes seem to be going all wrong, but God knows our circumstances better than we do. He will work at the perfect moment, if we completely trust Him to work in His own way and in His own time. Living a life of faith often requires us to leave things alone. The scripture that I am reminded of is Psalm 37:7 'Be still before the Lord and wait patiently for Him; do not fret when people succeed in their ways when they carry out their wicked schemes.' Ask yourself the question today, is 'who you are' who you need to be?

PRAYER: Heavenly Father, we all make mistakes in our lives and because of that we get separated from Your will. Please continue to help us to know who we are in our walk with You. AMEN

DON'T FORGET!

# TRUST IN HIM

SCRIPTURES: Mark 9:23; Psalm 37:5

WRITERS: Mark—Mark; Psalm—David

DEFINITION: trust—to place confidence, depend (on God); to be confident; to hope; to commit or place in one's care or keeping.

Mark 9:23 'What do you mean, IF I can? Jesus asked. Anything is possible if a person believes.'

Psalm 37:5 'Commit everything you do to the Lord. Trust Him and He will help you.'

When you have trust, you have everything you need in this life. Think about the people you trust. How long did it take for that trust to be built? Sometimes, years is what it takes for that communication line to be open to get strong. Marriage is built on trust from the day you meet your fiancé until the day the marriage begins. This is all on you and cannot be given to anyone else no matter what the situation holds. The language of faith is, commit everything you do to the Lord. Trust Him and He will help you.' That verse does not stand for anything other than the core value of faith and trust. We cannot make it in life without first trusting God and then seeking Him as to who He would have us trust as we enter into relationships for a lifetime as well as friendships we enter.

I love the word 'anything,' as in anything is possible if we believe in God. Do you believe that today in your life? If not, try trusting in Christ today. Place your confidence in Him and then commit.

PRAYER: Lord God, I continue to place my trust in You for everything I have going on in my life. My Bible study, my quiet time, my marriage, my family and my friendships. AMEN

DON'T FORGET!

# ARE YOU HUNGRY?

SCRIPTURE: Matthew 5:6

WRITER: Matthew

Matthew 5:6 'Blessed are those who hunger and thirst after righteousness for they shall be filled.'

I came across the quote from Dr. Benjamin Mays and wanted to share to impact your thinking...

'It must be borne in mind that tragedy of life doesn't lie in not reaching your goal. The tragedy lies in having no goal to reach. It isn't a calamity to die with dreams unfulfilled, but it is a calamity not to dream. It is not a disaster to be unable to capture your ideal, but it is a disaster to have no ideal to capture. It is not a disgrace not to reach for the stars, but it is a disgrace to have no stars to reach for. Not failure, but low aim is sin.'

Do you ever find yourself being hungry in life? What is satisfying in your life? If you died today, what dreams, what ideals, what gifts, what inventions, what innovation, what voice, what story would die with you?

Is it time for each of us to move forward with the things that God has placed on our hearts? To move forward and to complete while we are alive?

Perhaps you have special talents and abilities that you are not fully tapped into. My encouragement today is to remain hungry and seek out God's will for your life.

PRAYER: Most Gracious Father, thank You for a hunger in our heart. May that hunger always be for You and towards growing a better us. May we strive to always to live for You. AMEN

DON'T FORGET!

# CONFIDENCE

SCRIPTURE: Psalm 27:1

WRITER: David

Psalm 27:1 'The Lord is my light and my salvation—whom should I fear? The Lord is the stronghold of my life—whom shall I be afraid?'

I am very blessed to have received a morning devotion from a very special person today. In addition, I received a letter from a kind lady from my favorite barbeque restaurant in Shreveport. Here is how the coincidence occurred and how it blessed my heart today. Both the email and the letter were based on the same scripture, Psalm 27:1!

I received an email stating the following, 'I stand strong in the face of enemy threats. I remain confident even when an enemy rises against me. I declare that if God is for me, who can stand against me. Far more significant is He who is in me than he who is in the world. I am God's beloved. He is my mighty fortress. My strong tower. A shelter against my foes. He is my deliverer, my defender, a fierce warrior, and a wonderful Father. I am his beloved. He will guard and guide me, shelter and provide for me, bless and establish me. Learn to live in the stronghold of God. Gain confidence in His character. He never changes; is always faithful and refuses to let me go. I live secure because I am his beloved.' Anonymous

God provides exactly the confidence we need on a daily basis for us to make it in this life. His light shines so bright that we don't have to look far to see it. He is always seeking us and hoping that we will seek Him. Don't miss out—Jesus truly never changes, we do, so let's change for the good and have confidence in our relationship with Jesus Christ.

PRAYER: Heavenly Father, we are moved today for like-minded individuals, my wife and a friend both being compelled to share Psalm 27:1 with me today to bless me. Thank You for Your Holy Spirit moving in them to in turn move me. AMEN

DON'T FORGET!

# A CLOCK WITH NO HANDS

SCRIPTURE: Psalm 91

WRITER: David

Psalm 91:1 'Whoever dwells in the shelter of the Most High will rest in the shadow of the Almighty.'

I am working on the property at Oakdale through landscaping, hedge trimming and beautification of a 200 acres government reservation property not far from Kisatchie Forest. I happened upon something a bit unusual today. Then, it hit me, I need to write about this clock I found. So, imagine, 2 clock hands, fastened by a brass brad stuck in the middle of a round clock face with handwritten numbers to tell time, one hand longer than the other. Apparently, a child had made this clock, perhaps learning how to tell time and studying with a parent and maybe blew from a vehicle. My blessing today because the hands were dangling and then it hit me….a clock with no hands. That's really what we have with Christ, a clock that is God's clock. His perfect timing, a vapor of time to Him is our life. What are we doing with our lives daily with our families, our businesses, our friends? More importantly, what are we doing with our time spent developing our relationship with Jesus Christ? The relationship that trumps every relationship in this world. We need to pay attention to what time it really is and know that we can easily rest in the shelter of the Most High One, Jesus.

PRAYER: Most Gracious Heavenly Father, thank You for Your timing in relationships, friendships and You moving in our hearts. May we be mindful of what You are doing for us each day. AMEN

DON'T FORGET!

# DIFFICULT PEOPLE

SCRIPTURES: Proverbs 15:1; Joshua 1:7-8

WRITER: Proverbs—Solomon; Joshua—Joshua

Proverbs 15:1 'A gentle answer turns away wrath, but a harsh word stirs up anger.'

Joshua 1:7-8 'Be strong and very courageous. Be careful to obey all the instructions Moses gave you. Do not deviate from them turning either to the right or to the left.'

The tongue, when it is used to encourage, brings healing, like a medication used on a wound. If it is necessary to address a wrong, just know it is good Biblical wisdom for you to confront situations that are difficult with a positive word. We are instructed in Joshua 1:9 'This is my command—be strong and courageous! Do not be afraid or discouraged. For the Lord your God is with you wherever you go.' God told Joshua to keep the Book of Law always on your lips. Meditate on it all the time.

Have you ever met difficult people or difficult situations that you may have wondered how you would handle? We are on a walk of life with people and we are always going to encounter situations that are sometimes very difficult and we really don't know how to respond. Follow the lead from Proverbs 'a gentle answer turns away wrath.' Also, to be strong and courageous when things are not so easy and do not deviate in our position. Sometimes, that is way easier to say than to do, but in Christ all things will work for the good of the Lord. We have to sometimes step back and recognize that it is us that is being difficult and need to watch our attitude towards others.

PRAYER: Heavenly Father, help me to not be difficult around people that I work with or associate with. Even closer to home, my family and loved ones need my gentleness. Help me to answer with Your gentle spirit. AMEN

DON'T FORGET!

# HOPE FOR TODAY

SCRIPTURES: Ephesians 2:10; Romans 15:13

WRITERS: Ephesians—Paul; Romans—Paul

DEFINITION: hope—confident trust with the expectation of fulfillment

Ephesians 2:10 'We are God's handiwork, created in Christ Jesus to devote ourselves to the good deeds for which God has designed us.'

Romans 15:13 'I pray that God, the source of hope, will fill you completely with joy and peace because you trust Him. Then you will overflow with confident hope through the power of the Holy Spirit.'

'Hope is being convinced that you are surrounded and pursued by the goodness of God. That He works all things for good in the end so, if it is not good it is not the end, and that there is no story of tragedy or grief where He won't have the last word.' Anonymous

What do we think about when we hear the word hope? I think of a new baby, a new relationship, a new opportunity, a remedy for cancer, a chance to reestablish a friendship, hope to reconnect with family and hope to love again. You will have your own list, these are simply a few that come to my mind. We have all heard hundreds of cancer stories where something that appears very dismal turns out good because of a miracle. It is hope that believing in God and having His guardian angels all around a situation that makes it in alignment with God's will. I am so very thankful to be able to hope for the day I exit prison and return to a more normal life with family, loved ones and trusted friends. You don't know what you are missing until you don't have it. Don't miss out on having hope every day. Trust God and He will bless you and fulfill you.

PRAYER: Father of Hope, we praise You Lord. Thank You for hope each day. We thank You and ask that You continue to bless us in our lives as we hope for living the way to which You have called us. AMEN

DON'T FORGET!

# CALL OUT FOR HIM
# AND BELIEVE

SCRIPTURES: Titus 1:9; Romans 10:9

WRITER: Paul

DEFINITION: believe—to trust in; to hold a firm conviction about; to accept as true, genuine, or real

Titus 1:9 'He must have a strong belief in the trustworthy message he was taught; he will be able to encourage others with wholesome teaching and show those who oppose it where they are wrong.'

Romans 10:9 'If you openly declare that Jesus is Lord and believe in your heart that God raised him from the dead, you will be saved.'

'God is not counting your curse words (we know we don't do that), your cigarettes (this either), your fits of anger (oops) or your relapses. In fact, He is not counting any of your weaknesses or mess ups. He is not a petty God. The only thing He is counting is how many times you cry out for help, how many times you say, God I'm sorry and I need You. The only thing He is counting on is that you do your best and let Him pick you up and help you.' Anonymous

Isn't it nice to know that God is simply waiting on us and listening for us if we will just call out for him and also believe that he is there for us? He does not care what we have gone through or the challenges we have faced this past week. He gently says, I know the things you are up against and I want to help you. We can go through the toughest times and think that we will not make it navigating on our own because that is what we sometimes do. Try to trust in God and allow Him to keep you strong.

PRAYER: Most Gracious Father, thank You that You are always there for us in the valleys and the mountain tops. Help us to accept exactly where we are and call on You. AMEN

DON'T FORGET!

# CIRCUMSTANCES

SCRIPTURE: John 17:20-23

WRITER: John

John 17:20-23 'My prayer is not for them alone. I pray also for those who will believe in me through their message, that ALL of them may be one, Father just as You are in me and I am You. I have given them the glory You gave me, so they may be one as we are one. I am in them and You are in me. May they experience such perfect unity that the world will know that You sent me and that You love them as much as You love me.'

In John 17, we find our Savior praying for His disciples. He doesn't just pray for those who are in earshot, but He prays for all of us who would come to faith through the centuries... He knows His time is short, so He wants his disciples to hear these important words. He wants us to have the same oneness. Through the Spirit, we are enabled to love others in Christ in the midst of divisions, God calls us to serve and love each other in His power. This scripture is great to recognize when one has strange circumstances and are bringing God's glory to a place that they had not planned on being. I am there personally.

Never, ever would I have thought I would be where I am today, but I am for a reason that only God knows. I am safe, secure and protected right where I am in Oakdale, Louisiana. We all have circumstances that come about in our life and God will always help us through them if we will recognize 'why' to glorify God because we are not smart enough to know His timing.

PRAYER: Most Gracious Lord, thank You for circumstances that we encounter so we can trust You more and more. Help us to take the easy way out and turn away from You when You are trying to do a great work in us. AMEN

DON'T FORGET

# FORGIVENESS WHEN NEEDED

SCRIPTURES: Genesis 50:16-17; Matthew 6:14-15; Matthew 7:1-2

WRITERS: Genesis—Moses; Matthew—Matthew

DEFINITION: forgiveness—to pardon or acquit of sins

Genesis 50:16-17 'So they sent this message to Joseph: Before your father died, he instructed us to say to you, 'please forgive your brothers for the great wrong they did to you-for their sin in treating you so cruelly.' So, we the servants of the God of your father, beg you to forgive our sin.'

Matthew 6:14-15 'If you forgive those who sin against you, your heavenly Father will forgive you. But if you refuse to forgive others, your Father will not forgive your sins.'

Matthew 7:1-2 'Do not judge others, and you will not be judged. For you will be treated as you treat others. The standard you use in judging is the standard by which you will be judged.'

I am sharing today about forgiveness two-fold. First, it is Saturday and I have a small group Bible Study studying forgiveness. Second, I need the topic smack dab in my heart since it is a cornerstone to the Christian life that we live. We don't have to go very far into the Bible to see the early sin committed and the stories that merited the request for forgiveness. We as Christians must first forgive ourselves and then we will be able to forgive others to allow God to flow into them. Ask yourself this question, why did this situation occur in a way that got so wrong and so out of control. Things will always cross our paths and create havoc. When that happens, give it to the Lord. We need to say, in the future, I am going to wait on you Lord. We are called to be equally yoked together in our relationships, business dealings and in our followings of Christ. Are you about to enter into a business relationship? A marriage? A joint venture with someone you think you can trust? Seek God's revelation. Be a good follower and seek Godly co-workers. We know that we will have sin in our life and forgiveness is the key to a Godly life. If you have sinned against someone and not asked for forgiveness, do it today. Seek them out, ask for forgiveness with a genuine heart and make it right. God calls us to do it, so trust in Him today.

PRAYER: Most Gracious Father, I thank You for forgiveness in my life for my sins, my wrong doings and the times that I have crossed the line. I also pray today that You will show me any areas of my life that I need to ask for forgiveness or to extend forgiveness. AMEN

DON'T FORGET!

# MY HELP

SCRIPTURE: Psalm 121:1-3

WRITER: David

Psalm 121:1-3 'I look up to the mountains – does my help come from there? My help comes from the Lord, who made heaven and earth! He will not let you stumble; the One who watches over you will not slumber.'

How many times have you called out for help in your life? Think about instances when you bit off way more than you could chew and you needed some help to get you out of a jam. You thought you could make your own way and do it yourself, but you figured out quickly that you needed help. God's word is very clear that our help comes from the Lord. He truly watches over us in every situation and has us protected from harm's way.

You can have confidence in your daily walk knowing that whatever you are facing in life, God will be there for you. Are you facing some challenges or tough decisions today centered around work, business decisions, relationships or even family initiatives? God knows and desires to help you only if you will lean on Him and turn things over to Him. You need His help and He wants to give it to you so look to Him for the right guidance. I know what you are thinking. You've got this, correct? That's where things often run right off the road into a caution area, a hazard zone…. You don't have to do that if you just ask God to help.

PRAYER: Almighty God, helper of all things, may we seek You instantly in all things that we do in our life to keep us on track with You. AMEN

DON'T FORGET!

# LOSE SOMETHING

SCRIPTURES: Jonah 3:9; I Samuel 10:6

WRITERS: Jonah—unknown; I Samuel—Samuel

DEFINITION: change—to make different or transform; to shift, exchange or transfer

Jonah 3:9 'Who can tell? Perhaps even yet God will change his mind and hold back his fierce anger from destroying us.'

I Samuel 10:6 'At that time the Spirit of the Lord will come powerfully upon you, and you will prophesy with them. You will be changed into a different person.'

Have you ever wanted to change something in your life? Maybe your appearance, your hair color, your body, some habits, your attitude. I heard an advertisement yesterday on the radio stating to lose weight…do it now…and on…and on. So I thought, what are some things that we want to lose? Mine would be gray hair but I don't have a lot of hair so I am okay. I wish to lose negativity around me, some friendships that were not really friendships, some opportunities that perhaps did not need to take place and then certain opportunities that were not all good. I think we are all faced with things that we want to change in life and it does have to start with us. We do need the Spirit of the Lord powerfully upon us so we can lose the things that we don't need and also for the good that we need surrounding our lives.

So today, let's rid ourselves of the negative and replace with the positive. Dump the bad stuff out and load up on the good stuff. Change the small things that make big differences and then last but not least, lose the things that we don't need and add back in the things that really build our lives toward Christ. That's right, gaining Christ is the ultimate goal for all.

PRAYER: Most Gracious Father, thank You Lord for shedding us of all the things that we don't need. Add back to us the things that build us-character, attitude, hope, love and joy. AMEN

DON'T FORGET!

# ATTENTION

SCRIPTURES: I Timothy 4:15-16; Proverbs 5:1

WRITERS: I Timothy—Paul; Proverbs—Solomon

DEFINITION: attention—the act or state of applying the mind to an object or thought

I Timothy 4:15-16 'Give your complete attention to these matters. Throw yourself into your tasks so that everyone will see your progress. Keep a close watch on how you live your life and on your teaching. Stay true to what is right for the sake of your own salvation and the salvation of those who hear you.'

Proverbs 5:1 'My son, pay attention to my wisdom; listen carefully to my wise counsel.'

I heard the words from my father many times on certain topics. Topics to live by and to grow by. 'Pay attention; I am speaking to you. This is important and I don't want you to miss out on what I am about to say.' I would then listen and try to apply what he shared with me to keep on the 'straight and narrow' to honor my father. You have been there before and probably had the same discussion but hopefully in a loving way and caring way where it did not make you want to turn and run the other way.

God's Word in our scripture references today clearly address how we are to give complete attention to certain matters. Keeping a close watch on how we live and how we teach. Those things are important to how we live and react to things imparted into our daily walk. Wise counsel also directs us to pay careful attention and to listen well. That is great advice to us when God wants our complete attention, our heart, mind and soul.

PRAYER: Lord God, help us to be focused solely on You in all we do. We pray that our attention is where it needs to be to be able to share with others around us. May we glorify Your name in all we do. AMEN

DON'T FORGET!

# APPRECIATION FOR LIFE

SCRIPTURES: I Thessalonians 5:18; Psalm 107:1-2

WRITERS: I Thessalonians—Paul; Psalm—David

DEFINITION: appreciation—expressive of thanks, kindly or grateful thoughts; gratitude

I Thessalonians 5:18 'Be thankful in all circumstances, for this is God's will for you who belong to Christ Jesus.

Psalm 107:1-2 'Give thanks to the Lord, for He is good! His faithful love endures forever. Has the Lord redeemed you? Then speak out! Tell others He has redeemed you from your enemies.'

Today, I am very thankful for you, the reader. I pray honor and blessings for you and your life, your families and your friends. We all have so much to be thankful for in our life and sometimes we do get a little busy and forget to appreciate that part of life. Please take out a clean piece of paper and a pen and take as long as you need to write down all of the things that you are thankful for in your life. I will list a few just to get you going on your list. Mine would be Jesus, wife, children, family, friends, food, shelter, clothing, Bible Study, prayer time, grace tickets, don't forget Jesus coins, books, newspapers, Christian writers, motivational books, favor, devotions and so on... So now, take time to complete your list and put it on your breakfast table for reflection each day. You can add to the list as you get new things that you are thankful for that comes to mind.

Now, here is the challenge for today concerning appreciation and thankfulness. I want to ask the question, what would you do if you had to do without the things that you placed on your list that you are thankful for? We would all say that we would not approve. We don't want those important things that make up my life to evaporate. Be thankful and appreciative for life today, because you never know the day all that changes could occur.

PRAYER: Dear God, we thank You for our list today of so many great things and want You to help us not to take them for granted. Sometimes we get too busy and things get cluttered in our heart. Help us to keep our focus on You. AMEN

DON'T FORGET!

# START YOUR DAY RIGHT

SCRIPTURE: Exodus 34:2-3

WRITER: Moses

Exodus 34:2-3 'Be ready in the morning to climb up Mount Sinai and present yourself to me on the top of the mountain. No one else may come with you. In fact, no one is to appear anywhere on the mountain. Do not even let the flocks or herds graze near the mountain.'

As I walk to my landscape job each day, I walk on the sidewalk overlooking a whole host of pine trees, oak trees, magnolias and beautiful Bradford pear trees with the sun rising. It jumpstarts my day since the morning is an excellent time to acknowledge God's creation and to face our creator with a 'Good Morning Lord.' We cannot do anything by our own strength and we need to yield to God for his influence over us. No need to meet with family, a business associate or neighbor until you have met the creator at sun up.

I know for myself, when I can get up early and start to prepare for my day, it always goes smoother with a special reading time with God. Then prayer time throughout the day just to acknowledge that Christ has influence over my character, my being, my attitude and the things that will come out of my heart throughout the day.

Think for a moment what your schedule looks like for a typical morning. How is your time filled with the things that really matter? So today, start your day right with God. Take each first step with Him and let him go before you blessing the things that you do and having influence over your walk.

PRAYER: Most Gracious Heavenly Father, thank You for the early mornings with You. May You direct them for us so we are in step and in tune with You. Thank You for Your insight into our lives when we are fresh at the start of the day. AMEN

DON'T FORGET!

# STAY STRONG

SCRIPTURES: Hebrews 3:14; I Corinthians 16:13; Galatians 6:9

WRITERS: Hebrews—unknown; I Corinthians—Paul

Hebrews 3:14 'For if we are faithful to the end, trusting God just as firmly as when we first believed, we will share in all that belongs to Christ.'

I Corinthians 16:13 'Be on guard. Stand firm in the faith. Be courageous. Be strong. And do everything with love.'

Galatians 6:9 'Let us not become weary in doing good, for at the proper time we will reap the harvest if we do not give up.'

'The greatest challenge for us in receiving great things from God is holding on for the last half hour.' Anonymous

I am around a bunch of men who are constantly working out, lifting weights, doing reps, jumping rope, pounding pushups to make sure their body is in good shape and their process is basically breaking down to build up. This happens to us as we are doing life and encountering certain challenges, obstacles and situations that break up right before our eyes. It breaks down the continuity of life and what we are doing and then we recognize that we of course need spiritual direction and we turn to God and trust in Him for the courage that we need. We are called to be on guard and to stand firm. On top of that, we are encouraged to never give up.

How hard is it for you to stay strong in the world in which we live? Do you find that certain times are harder than others? You are not alone because we all encounter those challenges. Remember, when good times come upon you because you stayed strong, pass it on to others.

PRAYER: Most Awesome God, thank You for Your strength that You provide exactly when we need it. During difficult situations and decision times, we ask that You intervene on our behalf. AMEN

DON'T FORGET!

# GREATER AWARENESS

SCRIPTURE: II Corinthians 7:5-6

WRITER: Paul

II Corinthians 7:5-6 'When we arrived in Macedonia, there was no rest for us. We faced conflict from every direction, with battles on the outside and fear on the inside. But God, who encourages those who are discouraged, encouraged us by the arrival of Titus.'

Why do we always have a constant pressure on us? Probably to show us that we need God's sufficient strength and grace upon our lives. Another purpose is to bring us greater awareness of our dependence upon Him. There is no way to learn of faith except through experiencing trials. I consistently see a retired judge walking the grounds outside our landscaping building walking with two ski poles for balance. The day it hit me about awareness it was pouring down rain and he had a raincoat on, holding an umbrella being consistent to get his walk in regardless of the elements.

We as Christians have to continue our daily walk in Christ even around the elements. The elements are the battles, the discouragements, the short comings, the tragedies and just everyday life. Strive to have a greater awareness that you are not alone and that God is there to give you what you need. Think about the things you or a close family member might be facing and point them in the direction of God and His promises.

PRAYER: Gracious Lord and Savior, thank You for awareness in You! It truly is all we need to make it in our life each and every day. I truly desire to love You more and more each day. AMEN

DON'T FORGET!

# TURN THE KNOB -
# CLAIMING GOD'S WORD

SCRIPTURES: I Chronicles 17:23-24; Romans 4:21; II Peter 1:4

WRITERS: I Chronicles—Ezra; Romans—Paul; II Peter—Peter

I Chronicles 17:23-24 'And now, O Lord, I am your servant; do as You have promised concerning me and my family. May it be a promise that will last forever. And may Your name be established and honored forever so that everyone will say, 'The Lord of Heaven's Armies, the God of Israel, is Israel's God!' And may the house of Your servant David continue before You forever.'

Romans 4:21 'He was fully convinced that God is able to do whatever He promises.'

II Peter 1:4 'And because of his glory and excellence, He has given us great and precious promises. These are the promises that enable you to share His divine nature and escape the world's corruption caused by human desires.'

How well are we claiming God's word? We have to surround ourselves with Bible Study, adequate prayer time and asking in accordance with God's will. It is not something that costs us money, no anguish, struggle or wrestling with a situation. We simply have to depend on God's truth. As we know in the world we live in, broken promises are human and often times worthless. Take note of the scriptures above and know that God is there for us and is capable of doing whatever he wants to impact our lives. Also, we have great and precious promises that can carry us through tough times.

Turn the knob that opens the door to a personal relationship with Christ. Do you find yourself at the threshold of the door and just can't walk through the door? Jesus is waiting on you if you will trust Him and place your heart in His nail pierced hands. Jesus paid the ultimate price for sin on the cross and is wanting to share His unconditional love with you today. Turn the knob and walk through the door and experience the greatest decision you will ever make in your life.

PRAYER: Most Trusted Heavenly Father, thank You for salvation and a life full of abundance in You. Thank You for Your word and the direction it gives us each day. May we be obedient to follow Your Word. AMEN

DON'T FORGET!

# OVERCOMER

SCRIPTURES: Hebrews 10:38; Romans 12:21

WRITERS: Hebrews—unknown; Romans—Paul

DEFINITION: overcomer—to get the better of; to overwhelm; to gain; to acquiring force of arms

Hebrews 10:38 'And my righteous ones will live by faith. But I will take no pleasure in anyone who turns away.'

Romans 12:21 'Don't let evil conquer you, but conquer evil by doing good.'

Sometimes our emotions get mistaken for faith. Trials, conflicts, battles and testing lie along our path and are to be counted as part of our discipline personally. Keep your eyes firmly fixed on Christ's greatness and his finished work and righteousness. Don't allow your life to be tossed around like a football all over the field. Put 100% of your trust in God and know that he will help you to overcome anything that you are going through. Psalm 42:5 says, 'Put your hope in God.' Have you completely put your hope in God?

I think about all the athletic events I have been involved with along with business contests that I have participated in to try to finish at the top. It always made me feel like I was an overcomer. One who saw the challenge and met the goal. It was never easy because it pushed me out of my comfort zone and made me dig deep for the extra 10%. How about your life? Are you giving the extra percentage to be an overcomer and do for your family what you are striving for today? Perhaps your faith seems weak to you and you just don't think you can get there. Give an extra push and make it happen today. God is there with you. You are never alone, I promise.

PRAYER: Mighty God, we praise You for who You are and thank You for giving us an extra push to be where we need to be. Please help us each day to meet your mark. AMEN

DON'T FORGET!

# PRESS ON

SCRIPTURES: Hebrews 12:2; Galatians 5:22

WRITERS: Hebrews—unknown; Galatians—Paul

Hebrews 12:2 'We do this by keeping our eyes on Jesus, the champion who imitates and perfects our faith. Because of the joy awaiting Him, He endured the cross, disregarding its shame. Now He is seated in the place of honor beside God's throne.'

Galatians 5:22 'But the Holy Spirit produces this kind of fruit in our lives, love, joy, peace, patience, kindness, goodness, faithfulness, gentleness and self-control.'

Some time ago, you experienced sorrow and your life seems empty and all alone. One crisis after another and one misfortune here and a deep valley there. When is it going to end so you can go back to a 'normal' life? As we know, normal gets knocked around because we get out of sync with our Christian walk and we just make bad choices.

God's Word says that if we keep our eyes on Jesus, He will perfect our faith. The reason is because He paid the price for us and He truly does go before us. Then we see in Galatians all of the great things that the Holy Spirit produces for us to help in our goal of pressing on. They are love, joy, peace, patience, kindness, goodness, faithfulness, gentleness and self-control. No doubt, we can get excited about those things being in our life and us literally putting those things to great use each and every day. Let's just pour love and joy into our neighbors and see the great things that take place and the blessings that we reap because of that. Press on today to be the best you can be.

PRAYER: Great Almighty God, You are the champion and initiator of all good. Thank You for our faith that keeps us strong and allows us to believe in what Your Word says and does. It allows us to truly make a difference in everything we do. AMEN

DON'T FORGET!

# HANDLING SETBACKS

SCRIPTURE: I John 4:9-11

WRITER: John

I John 4:9-11 'God showed how much He loved us by sending his one and only Son into the world so that we might have eternal life through him. This real love—not that we loved God, but that he loved us and sent his Son as a sacrifice to take away our sins. Dear friends, since God loved us that much, we surely ought to love each other.'

'God loves us. We are not our weaknesses. We are not our sins. We are not even our own strengths. God loves us, enjoys and redeems us. In Christ Jesus, we are brand new, through and through. We don't have to look back in regret or look down in shame. We can look up and honor the name of Jesus, who lived, died and rose again so we can live powerfully, abundantly and eternally. Refuse to let setbacks and mess-ups define who you are. They don't, they can't, they won't. Walk intimately with God. Revere His name. Do what He says. Trust Him to be the miracle working God that He is. Be bold, be brave, and be happy in Jesus. He is thrilled to claim us as His own.'    Anonymous

If you have experienced a setback in your life, turn to God and trust Him. A cancer, the loss of a loved one, a parent, a lost job, maybe even a business deal gone south, can be an opportunity to trust. Trust in Him to help you work through what is going on in your life.

PRAYER: Most Gracious Heavenly Father, please help us to handle setbacks that we face with our daily walk. We need You and depend upon You to give us direction. AMEN

DON'T FORGET!

# CHOOSE FORGIVENESS

SCRIPTURES: Galatians 6:1; Ephesians 4:31-32

WRITER: Paul

Galatians 6:1 'Brothers and sisters, if someone is caught in a sin, you who live by the Spirit should restore that person gently.'

Ephesians 4:31-32 'Get rid of all bitterness, rage and anger, brawling and slander, along with every form of malice. Be kind and compassionate to one another, forgiving each other, just as in Christ God forgave you.

So, we know that God expects you and I to forgive others when we are wronged. Is it healthy and what does forgiveness look like from the perspective of the Bible?

- 1. We have to notice that no one is perfect. 'Not a single person on earth is always good and never sins.' (Ecclesiastes 7:20) We're all imperfect.
- 2. Put it out of your mind to get back even with someone. 'Never avenge yourselves. Leave that to God, for He has said that He will repay those who deserve it.' (Romans 12:19) Leave the repayment to God.
- 3. Do good when someone does evil to you. 'Love keeps no record of wrongs.'     (I Corinthians 13:5)

Live the life God has called you to live today. Choose forgiveness!

PRAYER: Most Gracious Heavenly Father, we pray for forgiveness today in our lives. We do wrong often and we want to realign to choose forgiveness today. AMEN

DON'T FORGET!

# MERCY

SCRIPTURES: Romans 9:18; Hebrews 4:16

WRITERS: Romans—Paul; Hebrews—unknown

DEFINITION: mercy—a blessing that is an act of divine favor or compassion; withholding of punishment or judgement our sins deserve

Romans 9:18 'So you see, God chooses to show mercy to some and He chooses to harden the hearts of others so they will refuse to listen.'

Hebrews 4:16 'So let us come boldly to the throne of our gracious God. There we will receive His mercy, and we will find grace to help us when we need it most.'

I will not forget this day. It has significance for me as to where I am. I had an accident yesterday while pruning some hedges. I accidently cut about 4 inches above my knee. It is a nice cut! I was placed on medical leave which I do not care for at all. I felt a loneliness, a solitude feeling because I felt as if I was headed back into solitary confinement again. I am in need and God is showing me that He is super strong and He cares deeply for me and my feelings. Jesus was tested in every way on His walk to the cross and yet He did it without sinning. I am thankful that I can come boldly to the throne that is full of grace and there be given mercy to help me grow my own strength in God. Today, I am thankful that God is always with me whatever I am experiencing.

PRAYER: Dear Merciful God, thank You Lord for Your grace and mercy over my life. May we accept it and apply it to our hearts today. AMEN

DON'T FORGET!

# SPIRITUAL GROWTH

SCRIPTURES: Hebrews 5:11, 14; II Peter 3:18

WRITERS: Hebrews—unknown; II Peter—Peter

Hebrews 5:11, 14 'There is much more we would like to say about this, but it is difficult to explain, especially since you are spiritually dull, and don't seem to listen. Solid food is for those who are mature, who through training have the skill to recognize the difference between right and wrong.'

II Peter 3:18 'Rather, you must grow in the grace and acknowledge of our Lord and Savior, Jesus Christ.'

When you think about growth in a literal sense, you have to think about babies growing into children growing into school years and then to college and then to grown men and women. As we know, this entire process takes time, nourishment, exercise, study and making mistakes and growing from them. There are many cases when we as God's children get older during different stages of our Christian life but we remain idle or at a standstill with our actions. How can that happen when we serve an awesome God? We can look in from the outside and notice that perhaps we have no wind in our sail. Liken it to little or no Bible study life, little to no prayer life and couple that with a weak faith and you get a big bowl of 'little things soup.' You are not growing and we are called to grow and to acknowledge our Savior because He has us covered. We need one-on-one time, a quietness about us with Him and a concerted effort to show up.

PRAYER: Dear God, we thank You today for all that You do for us and we praise You for that. We ask You to grow us through Your Word and through our time with You. AMEN

DON'T FORGET!

# COURAGEOUS

SCRIPTURES: Deuteronomy 31:6; Psalm 31:24

WRITERS: Deuteronomy—Moses; Psalm—David

DEFINITION: courageous—having courage or being brave; mental or moral strength

Deuteronomy 31:6 'So be strong and courageous! Do not be afraid and do not panic before them. For the Lord your God will personally go ahead of you. He will neither fail you nor abandon you.'

Psalm 31:24 'So be strong and courageous, all you who put your hope in the Lord!'

Exclamation points abound in each of our focal verses today which emphasizes a strong feeling. What are you going through today that you need to be courageous about? Perhaps you are up against a really tough situation and like most of us, we feel as if we can handle it on our own. This may be a decision that affects the life of someone you love, a close friend or maybe even yourself. So, what are you going to do?

First, you take courage in knowing that no situation is too tough for God. He was courageous throughout His life even His walk to the cross dealing with people spitting on Him, hurling nasty phrases at Him along with people challenging Him on why He could not save Himself on the cross. Jesus denied getting Himself off of the cross because He was obedient to his Father. He paid the cost for all of our sins that we might have eternal life. Have courage today in whatever you are going through.

PRAYER: Mighty One, Heavenly Father, I pray for needed courage today for myself as well as the reader. We earnestly need You every second of every day. We love You and praise You. AMEN

DON'T FORGET!

# ADVOCATE

SCRIPTURES John 14:16; John 15:26

WRITER: John

DEFINITION: advocate—one that pleads the cause of another; one that defends for someone

John 14:16 'And I will ask the Father, and he will give you another advocate who will never leave you.'

John 15:26 'But I will send you the Advocate – the Spirit of Truth. He will come to you from the Father and will testify all about me.'

Someone that you feel strongly about stands beside you and vouches for you and your character when things are sometimes on the line. Things happen sometimes when your character gets challenged and you might want to hide under a rock. We all know that we cannot do that because that is not our way to do things. We need to claim God's Word and know that we have the greatest Advocate in the Holy Spirit. The Holy Spirit works in our hearts and keeps us in check in our daily lives and we simply need to come to the Father and speak with Him, live in Him and love in Him. As fast paced as our life is with all kinds of activities going on and situations that we are faced with, we need an advocate to stand in the gap. Call on the Holy Spirit to be there for you and trust in God's Word that He will never leave you.

PRAYER: Most Gracious Father, we thank You today for the Advocate, Your Holy Spirit. We are mindful that You are exactly what Your word says about being here and not leaving us. Thank You. AMEN

DON'T FORGET!

# GOD IS ALL AROUND

SCRIPTURE: Psalm 139:1-12

WRITER: David

Psalm 139:1-12 'O Lord, You have examined my heart and know everything about me. You know when I sit down or stand up. You know my thoughts even when I'm far away. You see me when I travel and when I rest at home. You know everything I do.'

It really doesn't matter what you do in life or where you might be in life, God is there with you. The Holy Spirit often reminds us that He is there with us and we are never alone. He really is our best friend. Depend on God to be there for you all of the time. God is able to be everywhere at all times and we gain a lot of comfort from the promise. Sometimes we may think that God doesn't see certain things or know things about us, but He does. God knows everything. He is there when we sit down, when we walk, when we sleep. He walks with us on life's highway, hemming us in, step lock walking, in v.5 'You go before me and follow me. You place Your hand of blessing on my head.' There is no place we can go where God's Spirit is not there. God is everywhere, and His presence with us through all of life's circumstances should bring us comfort each day.

PRAYER: Great Redeemer, God, we thank You that You are in everything and You are everywhere. We ask that You continue to bless us in all we do. AMEN

DON'T FORGET!

# WILLINGNESS TO
# ADMIT WRONG

SCRIPTURE: Numbers 21:3

WRITER: Moses

Numbers 21:3 'The Lord heard the Israelites' request and gave them victory over the Canaanites. The Israelites completely destroyed them and their towns, and the place has been called Hormah ever since.'

We know that in life, it is easy to say, 'If I hadn't been abused as a child' or 'If I had gotten to go to school to finish my education' or 'If this had not happened to me, I would be in a different situation.' IF is a word that can be used to defer blame. We see Adam and Eve being confronted by God in the Garden doing wrong. Adam blamed Eve, that is where the blame game began. When we do wrong, we have to admit it, ask for God's forgiveness and start a new day. Sometimes, we don't want to wait on God and we rush to do things on our own and then, we fall short. That is why it is important to stick to the Bible and study it over and over again.

We need to remember not to be judgmental of other people or even blaming others. A lot of times, we may pass people and nothing is said to one another. Remember, we don't know what people are going through in their lives.

In our focal passage, we see that God and Moses were blamed by the Israelites. They stayed in the wilderness because they would not face the truth and they were not obedient.

We need to face the truth and look into ourselves. We cannot be truthful to others if we are not truthful with God and ourselves. In Psalm 51, we see David is requesting a cleansing of his life. He is conscious of his mistakes and he brings his requests that are sincere and earnest to God. He states that he takes responsibility even knowing he was wrong. Take note that he was asking for mercy. Verse 10 says, 'Create in me a clean heart, O God. Renew a loyal spirit within me.' He is asking for forgiveness and that is the same for us. We have to admit our sins one to another and confess our sins to the Lord. That is the key in life for you and me.

PRAYER: Dear God, today we acknowledge that we have done wrong. We have sinned against You and we are sincerely sorry and ask that You would forgive us. AMEN

DON'T FORGET!

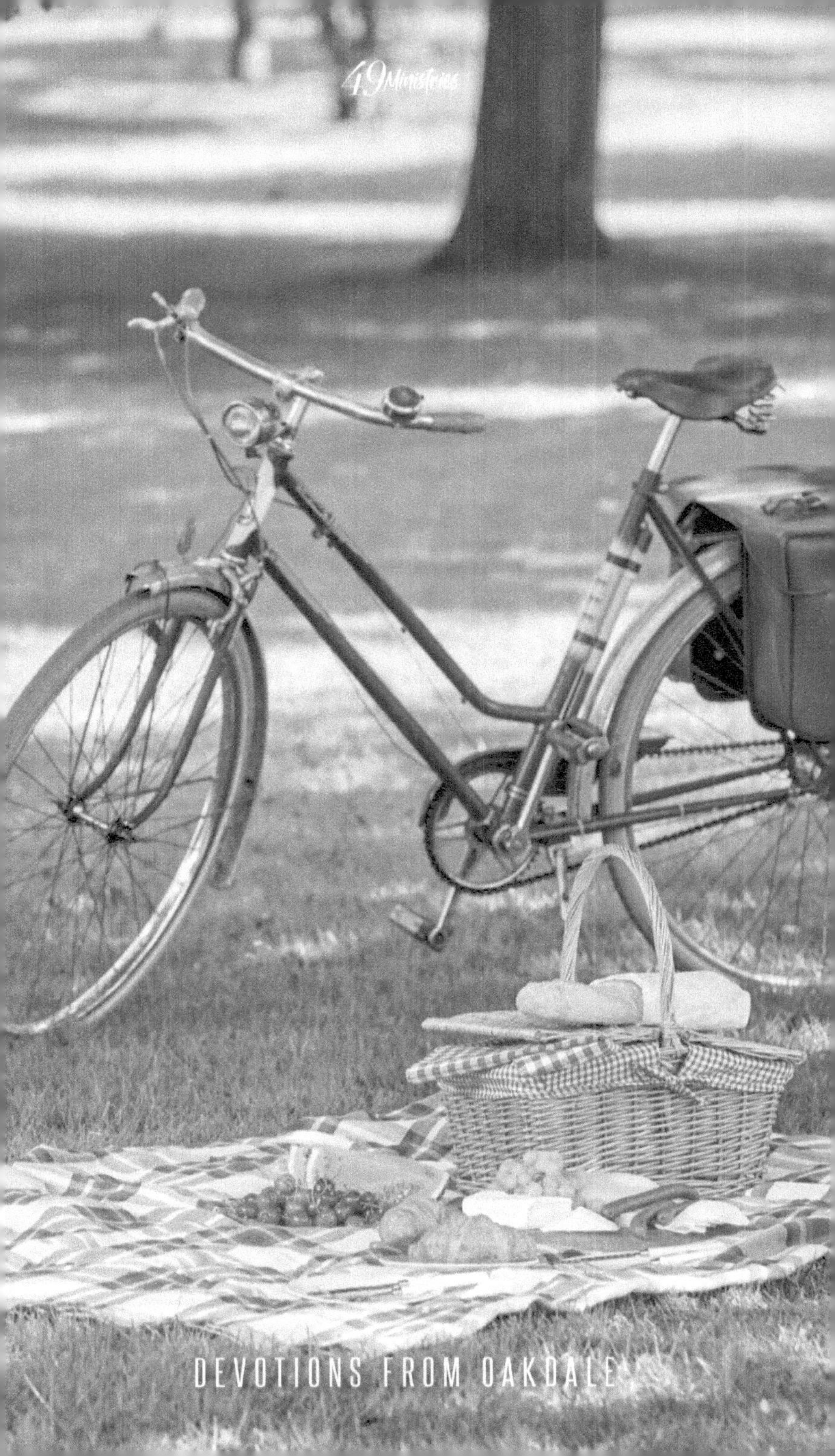
49 Ministries
DEVOTIONS FROM OAKDALE

# YOU MAKE THE CALL

SCRIPTURE: Psalm 37:23-24

WRITER: David

Psalm 37:23-24 'The Lord directs the steps of the godly. He delights in every detail of their lives. Though they stumble, they will never fall, for the Lord holds them by the hand.'

Right now, you have all kinds of things going on in your life. And, sometimes you are going to have an unexpected circumstance take place in your life. Life really is one crisis after another. Don't let anyone tell you any different. You have either finished a crisis or you are currently in one now. Lastly, you are about to be in another one. So, get prepared.

The main question and what matters most is how you will choose to deal with it when it happens?

'The ultimate measure of a man is not where he stands in the moments of comfort, but where he stands at times of challenge and controversy.' Rev. Dr. Martin Luther King, Jr

Where are you today when you experience challenges that seem way out of hand and appear to be way over your head? Will you call on God, or try to handle it yourself? You make the call.

PRAYER: Most Gracious Father, thank You for all You do for us each day. We love You and thank You that You are always with us. AMEN

DON'T FORGET!

# IF YOU HAD 24 HOURS

SCRIPTURE: Proverbs 21:21

WRITER: Solomon

Proverbs 21:21 'Whoever goes hunting for what is right and kind finds life itself.'

The challenge for us today is to think differently for a few minutes and get in the zone of living life to the fullest for 24 hours. We are not talking about dying, just what we will do with the next 24 hours. Will you just move through life as normal or will there be specific purposes that will impact others? You know, fulfillment doesn't come from exceeding others, it comes from elevating others. Are you looking into the future to use your talents and abilities to help the less fortunate? It truly is about spiritual transformation. We can all set a different course in the next 24 hours and notice that it will be a more rewarding life.

Look for the next act of kindness that you can share with someone. Do it until it becomes who you are. Invest in the lives of others because you have more power and influence than you think. This comes from the Lord. You can change your home, workplace, school and community. Kindness offers hope, heals wounds, combats loneliness and restores what is broken.

Give to others and expect nothing in return. NOTHING! A model of living that Jesus prescribed thousands of years ago. Be mindful that kindness is your ticket to health and happiness.

PRAYER: Most Gracious Lord, I thank You for time and how precious it is to me. Lord, I am in awe of the great things that You do around me even in a new place of life. Help me to share kindness to those around me. AMEN

DON'T FORGET!

# MERCY MATTERS

SCRIPTURES: Psalm 37:23-24; Hebrews 4:16

WRITERS: Psalm—David; Hebrews—unknown

Psalm 37:23-24 'The Lord directs the steps of the godly. He delights in every detail of their lives. Though they stumble, they will never fall, for the Lord holds them by the hand.'

Hebrews 4:16 'So let us come boldly to the throne of our gracious God. There we will receive mercy, and we will find grace to help us when we need it most.'

What is mercy and when does it matter the most to you? Mercy is a blessing that is an act of divine favor or compassion. To withhold punishment or judgement. Forgiveness, clemency and in the Latin, a payment. Our payment, thankfully is Jesus. We need mercy in our lives each day since we sin and fall short. Why do we get mercy? So people can see Christ in us, is one reason. Along with mercy comes longsuffering and we see a great example of that in I Timothy 1:16, 'But God had mercy on me so that Jesus Christ could use me as a prime example of His great patience with even the worst sinner. Then others will realize that they too can believe in Him and receive eternal life.'

Remember that God's love has the power to do anything and that is why we need to remember to be patient and allow God to work. God gives us time in being longsuffering so we will come to Him. The door is open and He has great patience towards us. Therefore, strive to have mercy in our life and show mercy as an example as an image of Christ, a likeness of His character.

PRAYER: Heavenly Father, thank You for Your mercy in and upon our lives. Please help us to be more like You, extending mercy to others that have wronged us. AMEN

DON'T FORGET!

# UNANSWERED PRAYERS

SCRIPTURES: Colossians 4:2; Psalm 4:1

WRITERS: Colossians—Paul; Psalm—David

DEFINITION: prayers—conversation with God

Colossians 4:2 'Devote yourselves to prayer with an alert mind and a thankful heart.'

Psalm 4:1 'Answer me when I call to you, God who declares me innocent. Free me from my troubles. Have mercy on me and hear my prayer.'

When our prayers go unanswered, remember God is kind. Everything begins and ends with His character. We all have difficult seasons and many of us live with many unanswered prayers. What helps you get through a time of unanswered prayers? We have to understand that our God is a God of Good Heart. He knows exactly what we need so lean into the goodness of God. Trust that He will do what is right. Kick the negative out the door and believe that at the right time and in the right way, God will answer our prayers. We can always trust in God.

Are you facing a time in your life where you question God's timing and why your prayers seem to get voiced by you but nothing happens? Don't give up on prayer and be consistent with your requests and thanksgiving. God is steadfast and timely with answering prayers, so trust in Him today.

PRAYER: Heavenly Father, thank You for the opportunity to offer up our prayers and to know that You hear us. Help us to stay strong in our daily walk and be obedient in praising You. AMEN

DON'T FORGET!

# HOPE FOR THE DAY

SCRIPTURE: Lamentations 3:21-23

WRITER: unknown

Lamentations 3:21-23 'Yet I still dare to hope when I remember this: The faithful love of the Lord never ends! His mercies never cease. Great is His faithfulness; His mercies begin afresh each morning.'

Think about the hope that you start off with each morning. Hopefully, a personal walk and relationship with Jesus Christ is at the forefront of your heart. Scripture shares with us that our Lord is faithful and that His love never ends. Along with that, His mercies never end either. His faithfulness and mercies start over for us every morning. So, why would we not want everything that situation can offer us? It truly is everything that we need if we simply show up at the table where He awaits us each day. Don't get pulled into excuses of my schedule is too full or my commitments for the week are overwhelming. Take your ink pen, not a pencil, and commit to a fresh start each day. It is the spiritual nutrition that we all need to handle the day-to-day stuff.

PRAYER: Most Gracious Lord, thank You for morning prayer time to start the day right with You. I pray for hope and confidence that You will work through me in a new place. AMEN

DON'T FORGET!

# A BEND IN THE ROAD

SCRIPTURE: Psalm 118:6

WRITER: David

Psalm 118:6 'The Lord is on my side; I will not fear. What can man do to me?'

We all experience turning points and defining moments throughout our life. Most contain fear and that is truly a terrible thing about the bend in the road. An overriding theme of letters that are sent into syndicated columnists have an overwhelming common denominator....fear.

Fear is simply a part of the fabric of living. God has equipped us so when we encounter things in life that are unexpected, we are able to go to Him and overcome.

Fear can build its power over us and it completely ties our hands and keeps us from doing the routine things of life such as working, playing, living and serving God.

Fear also can discourage as well as devastate during the process. Fear causes us to drain away the vitality of the people that we love.

How does God view fear in the big scheme of things? Fear is disobedience, plain and simple. How can it be anything but disobedience?

How are you confronting fear in your life? Deuteronomy 31:6 says, 'Be strong and of good courage, do not fear nor be afraid of them, for the Lord your God, He is the One who goes with you. He will not leave you nor forsake you.' And we also see in Psalm 27:1, 'The Lord is my light and my salvation; whom shall I fear? The Lord is the strength of my life; of whom shall I be afraid?'

Today, let's maintain a strong relationship and be near to God. That will help us to keep our road straight.

PRAYER: Most Gracious Father, thank You for helping us to

conquer our fears. Sometimes we have things we experience that are just too overwhelming and it creates fear. Help us when that happens. AMEN

DON'T FORGET!

# DON'T STAND ALONE

SCRIPTURES: I John 1:7; Ecclesiastes 4:9-12

WRITERS: I John—John; Ecclesiastes—Solomon

I John 1:7 'But if we are living in the light, as God is in the light, then we have fellowship with each other, and the blood of Jesus, his Son, cleanses us from all sin.'

Ecclesiastes 4:9-12 'Two people are better off than one, for they can help each other succeed. If one person falls, the other can reach out and help. But someone who falls alone is in real trouble. Likewise, two people lying close together can keep each other warm. But how can one be warm alone? A person standing alone can be attacked and defeated, but two can stand back-to-back and conquer. Three are even better, for a triple-braided cord is not easily broken.

Have you ever felt alone? Standing by yourself because you are shy, timid or maybe even because your self-esteem may be a bit low. God's Word shows us some great direction on not being by oneself. Psalm 27:10 says, 'When my father and mother forsake me, then the Lord will take care of me.' I John 1:7 says, 'If we walk in the light as He is in the light, we have fellowship with one another.'

Loneliness is a choice, so get connected in church, in small groups, with friends and use the spiritual gifts that God has blessed you with. I love the verses in Ecclesiastes 4:9-12 that say, "Two are better than one, because they have a good reward for their labor. For if they fall, one will lift up his companion. But woe to him who is alone when he falls, for he has no one to help him up.'

God wants us to be alive and dynamic. So, be bold and be greater than yourself. Take the initiative today to step out.

PRAYER: Most Gracious Lord, thank You for helping me to overcome the fear of being alone and really afraid to be out in public. I was so shy and timid and my self-esteem was non-existent.

Look at what you did with my life. I love being in front of people, groups and doing one-on-one meetings with individuals. I love You with all my heart and I praise You for Your love. AMEN

DON'T FORGET!

# DON'T HIT THE WALL –
# KEEP YOUR FOCUS

SCRIPTURES: Philippians 4:8; Joshua 1:8-9

WRITERS: Philippians—Paul; Joshua—Joshua

Philippians 4:8 'And now, dear brothers and sisters, one final thing. Fix your thoughts on what is true and honorable, and right, and pure, and lovely, and admirable. Think about things that are excellent and worthy of praise.'

Joshua 1:8-9 'Study this book of instruction continually. Meditate on it day and night so you will be sure to obey everything written in it. This is my command—be strong and courageous. Don't be afraid or discouraged. For the Lord your God is with you wherever you go.'

I read a story about NASCAR rookies and the training process they go through and the main concern all drivers share with them. Guess what it is? 'THE WALL' No one wants to hit the wall and especially not at the high speeds these guys drive for sometimes 250-500 laps. And, they do it with other drivers jockeying for position and they get bumped and pushed and even forced into accidents. So, the wall is a constant problem for all drivers but is the primary fear for all new drivers.

Let's think for a minute about the correlation in our Christian walk of something very similar. As new Christians, the fear is maybe how to interact, how to pray, how to study the Bible and just how to deal with the pressures of a new life. Sometimes there is a fear of hitting the wall. Getting pushed around with situations that sometimes are very hard to navigate through. Then out of the blue, fear sets in and we move from the area of comfort, the pit stop zone, and we accelerate through life and we once again get pushed into the wall. Today's verses can help us have the focus we need to obey God's commands and to be strong.

PRAYER: Most Gracious Heavenly Father, we know that we are making laps around the track of life and we need Your help keeping us off the wall. We do pray for Your guidance and direction today. AMEN

DON'T FORGET!

# IMAGINATION

SCRIPTURES: James 1:6,8; Matthew 6:25

WRITERS: James—James; Matthew—Matthew

DEFINITION: imagination—the power of forming a mental image of something not present; creative ability

James 1:6,8 'But when you ask him, be sure that your faith is in God alone. Do not waiver, for a person with divided loyalty is as unsettled as a wave of the sea that is blown and tossed by the wind. Their loyalty is divided between God and the world, and they are unstable in everything they do.'

Matthew 6:25 'That is why I tell you not to worry about everyday life. Whether you have enough food and drink, or enough clothes to wear. Isn't life more than food, and your body more than clothing?

Today we see James writing about the indecision that man has in life. James knew that it was impossible for a man to achieve what he wants until he first knows what he wants. He speaks of the unstable man driven by the winds of what might be happening in their lives at any given moment.

Whether you like it or not, you are going to have to live in the future to some degree. So, start planning, be a dreamer and a planner and imagine where you want to go in life. Jesus was not telling people to stop planning their lives or to just drift along in life without purpose. He was telling people to stop worrying and fretting over those things that God was providing for them on the journey.

Where are you today? Are you waiting for things to happen to you and for you or are you planning for your future? God wants us to push forward with purpose and not to sweat the small stuff.

PRAYER: Father God, thank You for the imagination that You give us through the complex brain and nervous system. May we use it to the fullest to glorify You. AMEN

DON'T FORGET!

# RELATIONSHIPS—BEING ABOUT OTHERS

SCRIPTURES: Romans 12:9-10; Corinthians 12:7

WRITER: Paul

Romans 12:9-10 'Don't just pretend to love others. Really love them. Hate what is wrong. Hold tightly to what is good. Love each other with genuine affection, and take delight in honoring each other. Never be lazy, but work hard and serve the Lord enthusiastically.

Corinthians 12:7 'A spiritual gift if given to each of us so we can help each other.'

Our need to create relationships and to nurture friendships is so important on all levels. Both men and women who would be great must have relationships on different levels. Some are personal and lifelong, others are casual, professional or some just temporary. However, all relationships are important on the journey to excellence. We as Christians are called to excellence in all we do, so always give your best. Our focal scriptures teach us that God gives a person one or two specific strengths so that person can share his strengths with others. God gives another person one or two different strengths so the first person will be encouraged to nurture a strong relationship with Him in order to utilize the strengths he has.

Remember, we are never good alone. God created us for one another and we need to remember to love our neighbor as ourself and to keep reaching out.

PRAYER: Most Gracious Heavenly Father, we thank You first for our personal relationship with You. Without it, we are nothing. With it, we are everything and we thank You. Without people around us, we would be lonely. Help us to reach out today with a smile, a handshake or fist bump to show we care. AMEN

DON'T FORGET!

# KINDNESS

SCRIPTURES: Proverbs 18:21; Galatians 5:22-23

WRITERS: Proverbs—Solomon; Galatians—Paul

DEFINITION: kindness—a kind deed; affection; the quality or state of being kind

Proverbs 18:21 'The tongue can bring death or life; those who love to talk will reap the consequences.'

Galatians 5:22-23 'But the Holy Spirit produces this kind of fruit in our lives: love, joy, peace, patience, kindness, goodness, faithfulness, gentleness and self-control. There is no law against these things.'

'For beautiful eyes, look for the good in others; for beautiful lips, speak only words of kindness; and for poise, walk with the knowledge that you are never alone.' Audrey Hepburn

Have you ever written a handwritten note to someone? No doubt, you gave hope and joy to the recipient because that is what happens when you share kindness with others. I personally love to be able to write a personal note to someone thanking them or encouraging them in something that they are involved with in their journey.

As we have read in Proverbs, we choose to either give people bouquets or bayonets, so choose your words and your tone carefully. Our world needs positive signs that can be shared with others. Then, people can be uplifted and hopeful. We need more of that in the world today. The song goes, 'What the world needs now, is love sweet love…..'

Just remember to share a little kindness and then step back and check out what happens to others around you. You may be amazed at the outcome that you are not expecting.

PRAYER: Dear Lord, thank You from the bottom of my heart for Your kindness towards me as a sinner and as Your child. Your ways teach me each day how to be more like You. AMEN

DON'T FORGET!

# SELF CONFIDENCE

SCRIPTURES: Romans 12:3; Hebrews 11:1,2

WRITERS: Romans—Paul; Hebrews—unknown

DEFINITION: self-confidence—confidence in oneself and one's powers and abilities

Romans 12:3 'Because of the privilege and authority God has given me, I give each of you this warning: Don't think you are better that you really are. Be honest in your evaluation of yourselves, measuring yourselves by the faith God has given us.'

Hebrews 11:1,2 'Faith shows the reality of what we hope for; it is the evidence of things we cannot see. Through their faith, the people in days of old earned a good reputation.'

When I look back over my life, I can pick out the men who had the most influence over my life and the things they imparted to make me the man I am today. Of course, my parents, my grandparents, my coaches and the business owners I worked for, taught me business principles and ethics along the way. However, the one thing that had to grow with me over the years was self-confidence. You are not born with it and it has to be developed as we go through life experiences, pitfalls, peaks and valleys. We work through things, we overcome, we persevere and we conquer fear. We step out of our comfort zone eventually and we see that things are building for us. To be great and to be successful in achieving your dreams, you must believe in yourself. Self-confidence is not prideful and I believe that it is godly. Remember, in heaven, God sees us as perfect. He already sees us as successful. In Romans 12:3, Paul never tells us that we needed to think of ourselves as lowly. He said to think highly of yourself and be seen the way God sees them. Just as it is a choice to be negative – or a choice to be positive, be confident in oneself and one's abilities to succeed.

PRAYER: Almighty God, I thank You for self confidence that I have in my life that You have blessed me with. I know that it comes from You and I ask that You humble me to serve You the best way I can. AMEN

DON'T FORGET!

# PERSISTENCE PAYS OFF

SCRIPTURES: II Timothy 4:7l I Corinthians 16: 13,14; Proverbs 24:16

WRITERS: II Timothy—Paul; I Corinthians—Paul; Proverbs—Solomon

DEFINITION: persistence—to take a stand, to go on resolutely or stubbornly in spite of opposition

II Timothy 4:7 'I have fought the good fight, I have finished the race, and I have remained faithful.'

I Corinthians 16:13,14 'Be on guard. Stand firm in the faith. Be courageous. Be strong. And do everything with love.

Proverbs 24:16 'The godly may trip seven times, but they will get up again. But one disaster is enough to overthrow the wicked.'

I love being able to accomplish a task that is before me, yet, it has a great deal of challenges associated with it. Keeping with a persistent outlook keeps you on your game. Persistence, therefore, is one of the key traits that separate those who just get by from those who are truly remarkable. Some choose to quit when tough times hit them. Quitting is a permanent solution for a temporary problem, because a man who is down can always get back up, but a man who quits will never take another step forward. The key to long-term success is to keep getting back on your feet and keep trudging forward. If you can just do that, you will be amazed how far you can go in life.

So, don't quit! Don't ever give up! And never give in! You never know when something great is just around the corner. Dr. Norman Vincent Peale, one of the pioneers of positive thinking, said, 'It's always too early to quit.'

Let me challenge you today to always believe in yourself, encourage others when they are down and have a joyful attitude while serving Christ.

PRAYER: Most Gracious Lord, thank You today for persistence.

Thank You for continually tugging at my heart through Your Holy Spirit. The ability to know right from wrong and then to do it. Thank You always for the gentle nudge to keep pushing forward. AMEN

DON'T FORGET!

# LIVING TO GIVE

SCRIPTURES: I Timothy 6:10; Exodus 20:3; Ecclesiastes 10:19, II Corinthians 9:8

WRITERS: I Timothy—Paul; Exodus—Moses; Ecclesiastes—Solomon; II Corinthians—Paul

I Timothy 6:10 'For the love of money is the root of all kinds of evil. And some people, craving money have wandered from the true faith and pierced themselves with many sorrows.'

Exodus 20:3 'You must have no other god but me.'

Ecclesiastes 10:19 'A party gives laughter, wine gives happiness, and money gives everything!'

II Corinthians 9:8 'And God will generously provide all you need. Then you will always have everything you need and plenty left over to share with others.'

People love to give. That can be time, material resources and of course, the almighty dollar, cash, moolah. Money is said to make the world go around and each of us knows that we have to have it to live economically. Money gives you choices in life. It gives you the ability to live what your heart has always imagined. To live your life as you pictured it to be.

According to the Bible, money is a good thing. Money is never referred to as 'evil' in God's word. It is the love of money that is the root of all evil. God designed money to be the fuel that drives all aspects of economic life. You need it to eat, pay your rent, feed your family, provide yourself medical care and support your aging parents.

Remember, no person can give to 'every good work' out of an empty pocket. We need abundance in order to be able to give. In the Bible, giving is encouraged and commanded. This is a tough subject, but, peer into your checkbook ledger and you will notice the priorities in your life. Pray for God's will and what he would have you do in the area of giving. So, live to give today and bless others.

PRAYER: Most Gracious Lord, we are blessed each day to receive what we have. Help us to flip the coin over and remember that it is all about the giving and we pray You will direct our paths today. AMEN

DON'T FORGET!

# REMOVE THE HANDCUFFS

SCRIPTURES: Mark 11:25; Luke 17:4

WRITERS: Mark—Mark; Luke—Luke

DEFINITION: forgive—to grant relief from a payment, to pardon or acquit of sins

Mark 11:25 'But when you are praying, first forgive anyone you are holding a grudge against, so that your Father in heaven will forgive your sin, too.'

Like 17:4 'Even if that person wrongs you seven times a day and each time turns again and asks forgiveness, you must forgive.'

We all need to remove the handcuffs from individuals that we have wronged or has wronged us. There are many instances in our lives that we see a head on accident that removes a family member from his or her family. Alcohol may have been involved or even drugs and now, someone is gone. Pent up feelings and judgement overwhelm the remaining family to the point that life is tough. Bishop T.D. Jakes says, 'I think the first step is to understand that forgiveness does not exonerate the perpetrator. Forgiveness liberates the victim. It's a gift you give yourself.'

Unforgiveness has been found to also cause health problems. It increases blood pressure, affects cholesterol levels, and decreased blood flow through the coronary arteries. I choose to forgive and so can you. We all find peace and perspective and so can you.

Perhaps you need to send a letter of apology to someone you may have hurt. Or, release a small debt that someone owes you. Maybe even encourage a family member to say, 'I'm sorry' even for the little things. It is the Godly thing to do today. Don't keep putting it off and not having total release. Remove the handcuffs today.

PRAYER: Most Gracious Lord, thank You for choosing to forgive us. We don't deserve it. We thank You for all You do. Your grace, Your mercy and Your perfect love is a blessing for us. AMEN

DON'T FORGET!

# HAVING HOPE

SCRIPTURES: Lamentations 3:21-23; Romans 15:4

WRITERS: Lamentations—Jeremiah; Romans—Paul

DEFINITION: hope—confident trust with the expectation of fulfilment

Lamentations 3:21-23 'Yet I still dare to hope when I remember this: The faithful love of the Lord never ends! His mercies never cease. Great is his faithfulness, his mercies begin afresh each morning.'

Romans 15:4 'Such things were written in the scriptures long ago to teach us. And the scriptures give us hope and encouragement as we wait patiently for God's promises to be fulfilled.'

Having hope in Christ is something we as Christians can count on every day. I am living a personal experience serving a prison term for decisions I made in business that were not right. I have apologized to the victims in my case and I also asked for forgiveness and pleaded for mercy in my sentence. The judge in my case administered me a 6-year sentence for wrong doing and today, I am making it daily having hope in Christ and that is sufficient for me. I serve an awesome God that sent his son for me and died on the cross for me and my sins. I thank God for forgiveness, grace and mercy on my life. Think about hope today in your life. Your situations in your life may not be as extreme as serving a prison sentence but life is life. We still live each day with hope and the desire to follow Christ so we may impact others around us. I love the words 'never end' and 'never cease' while waiting for the new mercies each day. So, have hope today!

PRAYER: Thank You for hope today in You. Lord, we are blessed to have salvation in and through You. Help me to impact those around me today. AMEN

## DON'T FORGET!

# DOING THINGS YOUR WAY
# STUBBORNESS AND REBELLION

SCRIPTURES: Joshua 1:8; Psalm 78:7-8

WRITERS: Joshua—Joshua; Psalm—David

Joshua 1:8 'Study this book of instruction continually. Meditate on it day and night so you will be sure to obey everything written in it. Only then will you prosper and succeed in all you do.

Psalm 78:7-8 'So each generation should set its hope on God, not forgetting his glorious miracles and obeying his commands. Then they will not be like their ancestors, rebellious and unfaithful, refusing to give their hearts to God.'

We have all at one time or another heard the song by Frank Sinatra, 'I Did It My Way.' There are many times in our lives that we thought doing things our way was for sure exactly where we needed to be. Then we find out that we made the wrong decision. We did it on our own without following God's instruction and prayer over the situation and how things seem to be upside down.

The Israelites over and over committed sin, then they would come back over and over again. That is insanity if the same thing continues and you expect different results. It will not happen that way in life.

We need to walk in wisdom each day. Consider your family roots, your experiences in the past and you will notice that the traits sometimes carry on to your life as well. Obeying is important when God gives you a command. Do it and be obedient. God is in control. Choose to do things God's way and life will flow much easier for us all.

PRAYER: Most Gracious Heavenly Father, I pray today for wisdom in my life and for the ability to recognize stubbornness and rebellion. Please help me to stay away from these areas and be obedient each day. AMEN

DON'T FORGET!

# FORGIVENESS FOUR WAYS

SCRIPTURES: Ephesians 4:31-32; Romans 12:19

WRITERS: Ephesians—Paul; Romans—Paul

Ephesians 4:31-32 'Get rid of all bitterness, rage, anger, harsh words, and slander, as well as all types of evil behavior. Instead, be kind to each other, tenderhearted, forgiving one another just as God through Christ has forgiven you.'

Romans 12:19 'Dear Friends, never take revenge. Leave that to the righteous anger of God. For the scriptures say, 'I will take revenge; I will pay them back' says the Lord.

We know that sometimes in life, things happen and misconceptions occur and we hurt those we love and maybe find it difficult to forgive. We need to understand forgiveness and know that as Christians, we are clearly called to forgive others. Here are some ways to think about how to forgive others in a healthy way.

- Recognize no one is perfect

- Choose not to get even. This is the heart of forgiveness

- Respond to evil with good (Romans 12:21 says, 'Don't let evil conquer you but conquer evil in doing good.'

- Refocus on what God has for your life-Don't let another person control you. You must release the person that wronged you or you will become like them.

Instead, refocus on what God has in store for you and know that His purpose is greater than any problem you are facing.

Forgiveness is not easy when something bad has occurred and someone has pointedly wronged you. We are called to step forward and make it right by extending forgiveness. Review the four ways to forgiveness and be free today.

PRAYER: Dear Lord, thank You for Your forgiveness in our life. We don't deserve it but we thank You for your loving kindness that overwhelms us. We love You and praise You today. AMEN

DON'T FORGET!

# HIS FAITHFULNESS IN
# TIMES OF SUFFERING

SCRIPTURES Psalm 119:71; Psalm 34:19

WRITER: David

DEFINITION: affliction—any difficult or painful circumstances

Psalm 119:71 'My suffering was good for me, for it taught me to pay attention to your decrees.'

Psalm 34:19 'The righteous person faces many troubles, but the Lord comes to the rescue each time.'

Have you ever experienced suffering in your life or the life of someone close to you? It is difficult and it is a painful circumstance to have to go through. Sometimes when we experience a failure, it brings about an attitude that now becomes teachable. What we need to realize is that God is intimately involved in every aspect of our troubles. Nothing happens—no matter how bad it may seem—by accident.

Trials are about God. What a good thought that is. Your troubles are not about you. Your troubles are about God. They are sent to teach you things about God you couldn't learn any other way.

Most of us would have a hard time saying, 'It was good for me to be afflicted.' Affliction is painful to endure. How could we ever view it as good? One of the purposes of affliction is to teach us things we would not otherwise know. Until hard times come, our knowledge of God and his word tends to be just hanging out there in the theoretical realm. When God is involved, things are much different. Trust God today to be there for you in every aspect of your life.

PRAYER: Most Gracious Lord, we don't like affliction and we sure don't like to experience suffering. Please be with us and guide us through our life and strive to be more like You. AMEN

DON'T FORGET!

# GOD'S EQUATION

SCRIPTURES: Psalm 27:14; Galatians 5:22-23

WRITERS: Psalm—David; Galatians—Paul

Psalm 27:14 'Wait patiently for the Lord. Be brave and courageous. Yes, wait patiently for the Lord.'

Galatians 5:22-23 'But the Holy Spirit produces this kind of fruit in our lives, love, joy, peace, patience, kindness, goodness, faithfulness, gentleness and self-control. There is no law against these things.'

Do you like math? Did you like it as a child when you were in school? Mathematical equations, multiplication, division, trigonometry, simple addition and subtraction. These are some of the things involved with solving equations to come up with 'THE ANSWER.' Sometimes, the number of steps in the more complex equations would lead us to scratching our heads. I think that is why I don't have much hair these days!

Seriously, God's equation for our lives is pretty simple. Wait patiently for the Lord, be brave and be courageous. We have a very nice list throughout the Bible that gives us encouragement we need to follow the right steps to solve life's equation.

When we factor God into any equation, things do look very different for us. Often when we want things to change in our life, God's word to us is to 'wait,' 'endure,' 'be patient,' and 'persevere.' This is why long suffering is a fruit of the spirit. God is always faithful and he will see us through our struggles.

PRAYER: Almighty Redeemer, thank You for a beautiful day today where we can praise Your name and bring honor and glory to You. Thank You for always being the equation we need when we are trying to figure things out in life. Help us to always trust You. AMEN

DON'T FORGET!

# WHAT DO I KNOW TO BE TRUE ABOUT GOD?

- God's grace is all we need – II Corinthians 12:9-10 'My power works best in weakness.'
- 'If you openly declare that Jesus is Lord and believe in your heart that God raised him from the dead, you will be saved.' Romans 10:9
- 'And we know that God causes everything to work together for the good of those who love God and are called according to his purpose for them. Romans 8:28
- Regardless of what we are going through, God is with us.
- 'God saved you by His grace when you believed. And you can't take credit for this; it is a gift from God.' Ephesians 2:8
- We know that we can do all things through Christ who gives us strength. (Philippians 4:13)
- God canceled the record of charges against us and took it away by nailing it to the cross. (Colossians 2:14)
- He calls us to always be joyful and to never stop praying. Also, to be thankful in all circumstances. (I Thessalonians 5:16-18)
- 'For God so loved the world, that He gave us His only begotten son, Jesus, that whosoever believes upon Him will not perish but have everlasting life.' (John 3:16)

These are just a few things listed that we know about God and are true. There are so many more to not and recognize but that is today's challenge for you. Write today's title and put it on your breakfast table and think and prayerfully consider all of the true things about God that you know and we are thankful for today.

PRAYER: Gracious Heavenly Father, thank You for who You are in my life. I pray today for the reader. I pray Your blessings over their life and their situation. Please take the words You have placed on my heart and impart them into someone's life to make a difference. AMEN

DON'T FORGET!

# A DIFFERENT DESCRIPTION

SCRIPTURES: Philippians 1:6; Romans 8:28

WRITER: Paul

Philippians 1:6 'And I am certain that God, who began the good work within you, will continue his work until it is finally finished on the day when Christ Jesus returns.'

Romans 8:28 'And we know that God causes everything to work together for the good of those who love God and are called according to His purpose for them.'

I am thinking that if I asked a close friend of mine that I have known for over 40 years to write down a description of me then and to also do the same today, what would that conclusion look like. He would say, 'These are two distinctly different people.' I was in college then and knew each other through the Fellowship of Christian Athletes. Since that time, we have both grown families, both gone through financial service careers and then changed business fields and I ended up working for his company as a contractor through my landscape and tree company since my indictment. Our relationship has been nothing short of a miracle. God has reconnected us through the years. God has grown me to a different person.

A lot of times our problem is that we look for outward, spectacular results when God's work, like the tiny mustard seed, begins in a hidden place inside the human heart.

Think about going through the same exercise in your life and see where it takes you. God will continue His work in your life and will continue doing great things as you change over the years.

PRAYER: Almighty God, thank You for changing us and making us a different person as life goes on. May we continue to place our trust in You and always remain obedient. AMEN

DON'T FORGET!

# BETTER DAYS ARE COMING

SCRIPTURES: Jude 1:24; Hebrews 13:20-21

WRITERS: Jude—Jude; Hebrews—unknown

Jude 1:24 'Now all glory to God, who is able to keep you from falling away and will bring you with great joy into his glorious presence without a single fault.'

Hebrews 13:20-21 'Now may the God of peace-who brought up from the dead our Lord Jesus, the great shepherd of the sheep, and ratified an eternal covenant with His blood, equip you with all you need for doing His will.'

I recently read about a sanctification example that caught my eye. A change that was going on inside of a person that was described as faint hammering and sawing. Having been in the tree removal business and using saws, it reminds me of removing the old and replacing with the new. That is what actually takes place in the life of an unbeliever who turns toward God and starts a new life. That new life echoes a hammering and sawing that continues in the life of a believer as we watch the Holy Spirit work. Here are some facts that we know about sanctification:

- It is the work of God
- It is an ongoing process
- It is never complete in this life
- God won't stop until the job is done
- God uses everything that happens to us – the good and the bad – to make us more like Jesus

These examples are the reason that we can know that better days are coming inside and out as we seek Christ.

PRAYER: Most Gracious Lord, we always want to desire better days with You, in Your timing and by Your love for us. We pray that you will equip us to always be our best. AMEN

DON'T FORGET!

# I DON'T KNOW WHO YOU ARE

SCRIPTURES: Joshua 1:9; Psalm 31:5

WRITERS: Joshua—Joshua; Psalm—David

Joshua 1:9 'Have I not commanded you? Be strong and courageous. Do not be terrified, do not be discouraged, for the Lord your God will be with you wherever you go.'

Psalm 31:5 'Into your hands I commit my spirit; redeem me, O Lord, the God of Truth.'

My time this morning at Oakdale began with walking in the dark from my living area towards to computer room for me to do my writings and study. I passed a gentleman by the name of John who is on a walker and has some eye issues. I have put drops in his eyes each morning for the last 2 months, only because we both are up early. This morning, things were different. Today, I hear the question, 'I don't know who you are.' I identified myself to John so he would know who I am and then he was comforted that I was there. I cannot imagine being in that state of blurredness, not seeing color and just having that unsure feeling.

I liken our lives before Christ to somewhat of the same situation. We have blurred vision of rights and wrongs. Situations that are wrong and cloud our vision and make it difficult to see the road ahead. John 1:9 states, 'for us to be strong and courageous and to not be frightened or dismayed because God is with us.' That is great encouragement to know that God is right beside us the entire way even if we sometimes have a blurred vision. God brings things back into focus just as soon as we align with him. Psalm 31:5 states, 'I've put my life in your hands and you won't drop me, and you will never let me down.' That is the God we serve and yes, HE KNOWS WHO WE ARE!!

PRAYER: Dear God, thank You for sight, taste, touch, smell and the senses You created in our miracle bodies. Help us not to take these for granted. We love and praise You! AMEN

DON'T FORGET!

# PRIDE

SCRIPTURES: Proverbs 6:3; Mark 7:21-22; I John 2:16

WRITERS: Proverbs—Solomon; Mark—Mark; I John—John

DEFINITION: pride—inordinate self-esteem or conceit; disdainful behavior or treatment of others

Proverbs 6:1-3 'My child, if you have put up security for a friend's debt or agreed to guarantee the debt of a stranger, if you have trapped yourself by your agreement and are caught by what you said, follow my advice and save yourself, for you have placed yourself at your friend's mercy.'

Mark 7:21-22 'For from within, out of a person's heart, come evil thoughts, sexual immorality, theft, murder, adultery, greed, wickedness, deceit, lustful desires, envy, slander, pride, and foolishness. All these vile things come from within, they are what defile you.'

I John 2:16 'For the world offers only a craving for physical pleasure, a craving for everything we see, and pride in our achievements and possessions. These are not from the Father, but are from this world.'

The one thing I do not want to happen in this world is being kept from God. What are you chasing in this world that makes you think you need 'stuff' so you can be fulfilled? The harsh truth is that I have experienced this to a degree in my life and because of my situation, that has me in prison. I made mistakes in the 'stuff' category. You the reader, deserve transparency and I intend to give it. This is the trust that is needed when I am sharing to grow people and to pour into their lives. So, my story in a nutshell is that I ran after the stuff in life and then would get more and then discover that it was never enough. After I was indicted, all material possessions were stripped away so that God could once again begin to shape and mold His child. The last three years have been totally amazing. I recognize that I love a simple life and am striving to leave pride exactly where it belongs, on the street at the dumpster. Let me encourage you to step back and evaluate the list of things in scripture that can corrupt your personality if you are not careful.

PRAYER: Most Gracious Father, thank You for Your love for us. Help us not to awaken sinful cravings and desire things that we don't need. We don't need success, status, or identity to be who You call us to be. AMEN

DON'T FORGET!

# HANDS, OVERCOMING DISCOURAGEMENT

SCRIPTURES: II Corinthians 4:1; Ephesians 3:13; Luke 18:1

WRITERS: II Corinthians—Paul; Ephesians—Paul; Luke—Luke

II Corinthians 4:1 'Therefore, since God in His mercy has given us this new way, we never give up.'

Ephesians 3:13 'So please don't lose heart because of my trials here. I am suffering for you, so you should feel honored.'

Luke 18:1 'One day Jesus told his disciples a story to show that they should always pray and never give up.'

I recently read a story about a lady that had many talents and gifts based on the works of her hands. Her name was Sally and she was so gifted at playing piano, typing eighty-five words per minute, needlework, cooking, and just about anything one could think of, she could do.

A few years later, a stroke occurred and things changed for Sally. First, a miracle that she lived through the stroke to begin with and then, she had to relearn everything from reading, to writing and to speaking again. She stated, 'God didn't want me to give up' and so with the help of her husband, their love and a lot of determination, she once again plays the piano, and types on the keyboard.

Think about your hands today, your ability to cook, to be a master gardener, to wash clothes, to paint beautiful pictures and to show affection to those you love with a gentle touch of your hand and of course, a smile. Don't miss out on appreciating what you have before giving thanks to God for safety, good health and His provisions for your life.

Our scriptures today share with us to never give up and to never lose heart. So, let's be the best we can be today.

PRAYER: Most Gracious Lord, we are thankful for the day

today. For our senses, our hands, and our mind that You have blessed us with. Lord, help us to not take for granted all You do for us. AMEN

DON'T FORGET!

# BUILDING BLOCKS

SCRIPTURES: II Thessalonians 3:13; Psalm 46:1-3

WRITERS: II Thessalonians—Paul; Psalm 46—David

II Thessalonians 3:13 'As for the rest of you, dear brothers and sisters, never get tired of doing good.'

Psalm 46:1-3 'God is our refuge and strength, always ready to help in time of trouble. So, we will not fear when earthquakes come and the mountains crumble into the sea. Let the oceans roar and foam. Let the mountains tremble as the waters surge!'

When we recognize discouragement in our life, fatigue sets in and turns us all into cowards. When energy runs short, so does courage. Haven't you found this to be true? You work long hours each day. You finish month end reports and now, you have to come home to a zoom meeting for your second time to go to school in your life because kids are studying virtual school at home.

Each of us has to deal with the crunch of time, pressure, exertion. Things get tense, you get irritable and sometimes even gloomy. That is exactly the time to use building blocks of faith to get you through things. Stay away from negative talk and turn it into positive. Stay away from discouragement and add back encouraging words that build up. In these times, run, don't walk to the word of God. When your heart is hurt, get a transfusion of hope and power. Galations 6:9 says, 'And let us not grow weary while doing good.' For in due season, we shall reap if we do not lose hope (heart) that is, become discouraged.'

Go fill the needs of others. You will reap what you sow, and the love you share will come back to you many times over.

PRAYER: Dear God, thank You for Your building blocks that You give us each day. Hope, love, joy are things we can share daily. Help us to be proactive and help encourage others around us. AMEN

## DON'T FORGET!

# KEEPING YOUR MIND STRONG

SCRIPTURES: John 8:31-32, I Corinthians 10:13

WRITERS: John—John; I Corinthians—Paul

John 8:31-32 'If you abide in My Word (hold fast to my teachings and live in accordance with them), you are truly my disciples. And you will know the Truth, and the Truth will set you free.'

I Corinthians 10:13 'The temptations in your life are no different from what others experience. And God is faithful. He will not allow the temptation to be more than you can stand. When you are tempted, He will show you a way out so you can endure.'

Whether we want to believe it or not, our warfare is not with other humans, but with the devil and his demons. Satan is our greatest enemy and he attempts to destroy us with anything he can throw our way. Are you prepared for each day against him? How will you handle your day to day knowing that you need to keep your mind, heart and soul strong? Remember, Satan is clever and can creep into your thoughts, cause you to have poor ideas, cause fear and your reasonings turn to doubts. Satan eases in at a time, a weak time, and he will work on your mind. The devil is also patient and always has a plan when we least expect it.

The good thing for us is that we have our own weapons, our Bible, our Bible studies, Christian books, music and movies. Praise, prayer and fellowship in Christ are also other tools we use daily to fight back. Learn to use God's Word to defeat the devil and live a life God calls us to live.

There is no reason for us to have to go it alone. Jesus stands waiting on us to call on Him and live in Him each day. Keep your mind strong today and impact those around you.

Remember God's word states that He will not give us more than we can handle.

PRAYER: Most Faithful Lord, thank You for the strength that

You give us as Your children each day. The devil lurks around and tries to destroy us. Keep us strong in You each day. We love You. AMEN

DON'T FORGET!

# A DO OVER

SCRIPTURE: Galatians 1:11-24

WRITER: Paul

Galatians 1:12 'I received my message from no human source, and no one taught me. Instead, I received it by direct revelation from Jesus Christ.'

What in the world is a 'do-over?' Well, if you are a golfer, it is called a mulligan. It is a chance for you to re-hit a bad shot. You know, the one you hooked out of bounds and went over the ditch that is 40 feet deep and into a par 3 with people on the putting green. Wow, you might want to try again to improve your shot from the fairway you are playing on. The mulligan is normally allowed on the first hole and first ball of the game since you are not warmed up.

Guess what? You get a 'do-over' in life which is exactly what happened to Paul before his life with Christ. Paul was trying to destroy the church. He was doing all the wrong things and definitely needed an opportunity to change. We see in Galatians that Paul was a people pleaser. After God called Him, everything changed. God reveals Himself through His Word directly from Jesus. A new quality comes through once a person has a 'do-over' in life. For us, that is about having the zeal in life that runs off the chart and simply showing we want to follow Christ and be changed for life. Sometimes, just as Paul went away to Arabia to have focus and listen to God, we have to find our quiet place so God can work in us. A 'do-over' in golf is extended to a player as an act of courtesy. God extends His love to us to allow us the opportunity to have a 'do-over' to change our life for eternity. Make that shot today.

PRAYER: Heavenly Father, You are magnificent, joyful and triumphant in our lives. We thank You for second chances to be able to follow You. Lord, help us to be passionate about You even when we are faced with the fears of life. AMEN

DON'T FORGET!

# BE HUMBLE

SCRIPTURE: James 4:6-7

DEFINITION: humble—not proud or haughty; can imply lower social or economic status; meek or gentle

James 4:6-7 'And He gives grace generously. As the scripture says, 'God opposes the proud but gives grace to the humble.' So, humble yourselves before God. Resist the devil, and he will flee from you.'

We are called not to give into the world and to pursue a worldly attitude. We are to have a humble heart and to always seek grace, and therefore we will get it. It is grace that makes us humble, and grace that finds in this humanity an opportunity for the pouring in of more grace.

We have plenty of opportunities in our daily life when meetings and get togethers are taking place. There is no need to think that we have to run over people and not step back and have a humble attitude. We all know that our normal tendency is to always move forward and be in charge.

It is okay for us to go down that we may rise. It is okay for us to be poor in spirit that God may make us rich in Him.

So, today, take a lower place. Be smaller in your own esteem, that God may have the opportunity to make much of you.

PRAYER: Almighty God, thank You for all You do for our lives. We pray to stay humble in our actions and deeds. May everything glorify You. AMEN

DON'T FORGET!

# THE 3 R'S

SCRIPTURE: Psalm 103:2-5

WRITER: David

Psalm 103:2-5 'Let all that I am praise the Lord; may I never forget the goods things He does for me. He forgives all my sins and heals all my diseases. He redeems me from death and crowns me with love and tender mercies. He fills my life with good things. My youth is renewed like the eagle's!'

Are there specific things in your life that are intentional for you? Do you have them on the top of your head at all times? Here are three to consider on a daily basis to help you in life.

The 3 Rs are rest, release, and remember. We had an example in our prayer circle the other evening and the leader asked us to clench our right fist. Place in that fist all of the things that take up your time and control your life. Material wealth, cars, homes, paintings, country club memberships, second homes....'stuff.'

Now, RELEASE your hand and the stuff so God can bless you in what you are experiencing.

REST, because in Christ, we know that He is in control of everything and we need not worry.

REMEMBER, we are loved by a God that is the creator of the universe and He controls everything. So, open your hand and your heart to things like forgiveness, job, longsuffering, patience, mercy and love.

The 3 Rs are important in life because we all need rest from the things of live, we need release from the busyness of life and its struggles and lastly, we need to remember that in Christ we have it all.

PRAYER: Dear Majestic Father, we praise You today for who You are and how wonderful this world is. Things move so fast and we do not want to miss Your blessings. Father, help us to rest in You today. AMEN

DON'T FORGET!

# LIVE LIFE LIKE YOU ARE ALIVE

SCRIPTURE: Psalm 31:5

WRITER: David

Psalm 31:5 'I've put my life in your hands. You won't drop me, you'll never let me down.'

What is your reason for getting up in the morning? What motivates you to make it through the day? Christ came to restore you and me with the exact purpose that you were made for: to live every aspect of your life worshipful, and be obedient to Christ. So, are you living life just to do life each day or are you really alive in Christ? We have to figure this out so we can really be who God calls us to be.

I have spoken with many readers in years gone by that describe to me their life and the things that satisfy them and it comes to me that most are not really alive. They have so much debt hanging over them, living paycheck to paycheck and hoping that nothing goes wrong to push them over the edge. Now, our country is faced with pandemic conditions and stimulus checks are so needed just to place a band-aid on the situation.

God intends for us to live life like we are alive. God cares about you and me and He places people in our path that we are to help. God never gives a wrong address and He intends for us to help those around us. God uses ordinary people to do extraordinary things in the lives of others. Make everything you do today count for being alive and just not living to live.

PRAYER: Most Gracious Lord, help me to help others to be alive today, speak through me to impart the words that You would have me to share. AMEN

## DON'T FORGET!

# ABLE

SCRIPTURES: Ephesians 3:20; Ephesians 6:13; II Timothy 1:12

WRITERS: Ephesians—Paul; II Timothy—Paul

DEFINITION: able—marked by power, intelligence, competence, skill, giftedness

Ephesians 3:20 'Now all glory to God, who is able, through His mighty power at work within us, to accomplish infinitely more than we might ask or think.'

Ephesians 6:13 'Therefore, put on every piece of God's armor so that you will be able to resist the enemy in the time of evil. Then, after the battle, you will still be standing firm.'

II Timothy 1:12 'That is why I am suffering here in prison. But I am not ashamed of it, for I know the one in whom I trust, and I am sure that He is able to guard what I have entrusted to Him until the day of his return.'

Isn't it great to be able to do things each day? For me, it was getting up, getting ready in the morning, having breakfast, quiet time, going to work, doing work, fellowshipping during lunch and then coming home to dinner and being able to relax after the day. We are able. How about you, are you able to do the things you need to day each day? You know that we all have choices as to how we spend our time and in that, God does a number of things for us that sometimes get overshadowed.

First, our God is able to accomplish way more than we ever ask or expect. Second, God helps us to resist the enemy along with the things that can harm us. Third, God guards us against Satan and the outside things that we need protection from day to day.

So, today, go about your day looking to the One who is able and He also makes us able to do our best to glorify Him.

PRAYER: Heavenly Father, thank You for the word 'able.' Without it, we would be in a fix. We need Your special touch to be able to meet others, able to speak to others, and able to share with others. AMEN

DON'T FORGET!

# AWESOME ATTITUDE

SCRIPTURES: Philippians 2:5; I Peter 3:8; 4:1

WRITERS: Philippians—Paul; I Peter—Peter

DEFINITION: attitude—a mental position with regard to a fact or state; a feeling or emotion toward a fact or state

Philippians 2:5 'You must have the same attitude that Jesus did.'

I Peter 3:8 'Finally, all of you should be of one mind. Sympathize with each other. Love each other as brothers and sisters. Be tenderhearted, and keep a humble attitude.

I Peter 4:1 'So then, since Christ suffered physical pain, you must arm yourselves with the same attitude He had, and be ready to suffer too. For if you have suffered physically for Christ, you have finished with sin.'

We all have choices each day as to whether we will choose to have a positive attitude or if we will choose to be negative. Attitude is everything and is so very important. We have all worked at jobs where the atmosphere is not really what we would like for it to be. How about God using us to change that atmosphere through our actions.'

We are called to have an attitude of Christ. How hard is that for us each day? Checks and balances throughout the day are simply ways to live a life in tune with Him, prayerful and seeking Him in all things.

Attitude starts with us each morning. When we get up, we make a choice to either be positive toward others or taint the day for everyone. God calls us to have a humble attitude, one that exudes a smile, joy and to be uplifting. Try to have an impactful attitude today so we affect those around us in a positive way.

PRAYER: Dear God, we pray for an awesome outlook on the day that You have blessed us with each day. Help us to have Your smile on our face daily. AMEN

DON'T FORGET!

# EXPERIENCING TRIALS

SCRIPTURES: Luke 22:28; I Peter 1:7

WRITERS: Luke—Luke; I Peter—Peter

DEFINITION: trials—a legal proceeding based in court; a test of faith, patience, or staying through subjection to suffering or temptation

Luke 22:28 'You have stayed with me in my time of trial.'

I Peter 1:7 'These trials will show that your faith is genuine. It is being tested as fire tests and purifies gold-though your faith is far more precious than mere gold. So, when your faith remains strong through many trials, it will bring you much praise and honor and glory on the day when Jesus Christ is revealed to the whole world.'

We are encouraged to rejoice and be happy in the midst of trials. God's word shares that we are protected even during the trials and we are to be encouraged when we experience tough situations. Situations like divorce, prison time, loss of a loved one, a cancer diagnosis, a job loss or just a major setback in life.

God is able to put us right back where we were before our trial situation and make us stronger than before if we will trust Him.

Even when we experience trials in our life, we need to remember to be faithful and to also offer forgiveness to those we have wronged and sinned against. During my time in prison, I have had time to reflect and to ask God to show me areas in my life that I need to work on and one of those have been forgiveness or the state of unforgiveness which is a sin.

PRAYER: Heavenly Father, all praise, honor and blessings be upon Your name today as we strive to work through trials and setbacks that we experience. Please give us strength to endure and to be able to overcome. AMEN

## DON'T FORGET!

# STRONG DETERMINATION

SCRIPTURE: Mark 2:3-4

WRITER: Mark

DEFINITION: determination—to decide, to resolve

Mark 2:3-4 'Four men arrived carrying a paralyzed man on a mat. They couldn't bring him to Jesus because of the crowd, so they dug a hole through the roof above his head. Then they lowered the man on his mat, right down in front of Jesus.'

I love the story of the paralyzed man on the mat. First of all, Jesus is busy sharing with the crowds and He appears to be in a tight home teaching having standing room only inside and outside the door. This situation does not keep the man from having faith and determination to just get inside to see Him. Well, if you can't go in the normal way, come in through the top. I love that! Where there is a will, there is a way. The will here involves faith but also a few other basics that I believe get overlooked in this story. They needed ropes to let this man down through the roof. They needed tools to dig out the roof. They had to carry the man up the ladder and then also decide which part of house they were going to cut through to lower him down. So many things to think about, but these guys along with the paralyzed man had a strong determination and faith.

What about you, the reader? Have you ever experienced an event that you know was something that you needed to do and you had the determination and faith to accomplish the task? It is a good feeling when everything works together and comes to completion.

Maybe you have serious doubts and lack the faith to move forward with something you have been praying about. Believe in God and trust Him today.

PRAYER: Dear Lord, thank You for this miracle we have read about You today. May we also have the same faith to accomplish great things in our life. AMEN

DON'T FORGET!

# INTEGRITY

SCRIPTURES: Psalm 119:1-2; Proverbs 10:9

WRITERS: Psalm—David; Proverbs—Solomon

DEFINITION: integrity—honesty; without compromise or corruption

Psalm 119:1-2 'Joyful are people of integrity, who follow the instruction of the Lord.' Joyful are those who obey his laws and search from him with all their hearts.'

Proverbs 10:9 'People with integrity walk safely, but those who follow crooked paths will be exposed.'

Honesty, with compromise or corruption are all good topics to discuss when someone wants to depict integrity. To live with integrity is to live your life with the best of intentions and with honesty.

I remember my PawPaw early in my life taking me to a local drugstore. While in the store, he noticed that someone had dropped a $5 dollar bill on the floor. My PawPaw, not making a big deal of it put it in his pocket then went to find the manager and turned in the money as lost. By the way, he made a huge impression on his grandson and that has been 50 years ago. Amazing how something so small could have such a large impact on me and how I live my life today.

I can't say I have not made mistakes in my life in the area of integrity because I have. But that is why I am thankful that Jesus died on the cross for my sins and sees them no more.

I also experienced finding money in a store while with one of my daughters. So, I went through the same process of returning it to the store manager. Always strive to do the right thing. That continues to build integrity just as Christ would want.

PRAYER: Lord God, You call us to a high standard of integrity. Help us not to miss the mark and to bring honor and glory to Your name. AMEN

DON'T FORGET!

# WHO DO YOU SAY GOD IS?

SCRIPTURES: Proverbs 15:3; Psalm 145:18; Exodus 3:14; Isaiah 44:6

WRITERS: Proverbs—Solomon; Psalm 145—David; Exodus—Moses; Isaiah—Isaiah

Proverbs 15:3 'The Lord is watching everywhere. Keeping His eye on both the evil and the good.'

Psalm 145:18 'The Lord is close to all who call on Him, yes, to all who call on Him in truth.'

Exodus 3:14 'God replied to Moses, 'I am who I am. Say this to the people of Israel: I am has sent you.'

Isaiah 44:6 'This is what the Lord says-Israel's King and Redeemer, the Lord of Heavens armies: 'I am the first and the last; there is no other God.

Have you ever been asked the question, 'Who Is God?' If you have been asked, what did you answer? There are no doubt hundreds of names that are shared in the bible such as, Almighty, Sovereign, King, Lord, Master, Holy One, Messiah. God is omnipotent (all powerful), omniscient (all knowing) and omnipresent (everywhere present). God is love. God is just. God is good. God IS.

The Bible teaches that God is so Holy, He is without any darkness or imperfection. He is so perfect that He is completely unlike anyone else, and anything evil, dark, or unclean cannot survive in his presence.

Even though we know God has so many names in his three-fold character. There is only one God, who manifests Himself in three persons, God the Father, God the Son, and God the Spirit. Together, these three persons of God are known as the Trinity.

So, are you and I prepared to answer the question today, if asked? I will answer, He is my Savior, the one who gave His life for a ransom of many. I love Him intimately and I am thankful that He lives in me.

PRAYER: Dear Almighty God, I thank You for all the names that You are known by in our world. To me, You are Father and I praise You today. AMEN

DON'T FORGET!

# GOING AGAINST THE CURRENT—MANAGING YOUR FINANCES

SCRIPTURE: Philippians 4:19

WRITER: Paul

Philippians 4:19 'And this same God who takes care of me will supply all your needs from His glorious riches, which have been given to us in Christ Jesus.'

As I am writing to you today, I just overheard a conversation between an inmate and a correctional officer that he wanted to see an email from an inmate that just got out and is trying to establish himself in the community that he lives in and is trying to adjust financially. While in prison, the hourly wage is between 12 cents an hour to 40 cents an hour based on the level of your position. This inmate sent $400 to make sure that the guys in the camp who are less fortunate and not able to work would have extras. Low wages put you going against the current as long as you are in prison unless you have some assistance from family or friends.

We all have our stories of getting married early in life and having to scrape by from paycheck to paycheck just to get by financially. So, you are probably asking, what in the world is a guy in prison going to be able to share with me about finances. I was blessed and thankful to have been in the financial world for some 28 years. I managed a lot of money for clients, some 3,000 personal relationships that I impacted until the day came that I could not. However, I gained a lot of knowledge and here are just a few to help you if you like:

- Fill out a monthly budget and stick to it.
- Tithe 10% of your income to your local church.
- Save money into an emergency fund – 6 months of income for a rainy day.
- Save money into a pre-tax retirement account, 401K, 403B or personal individual retirement account (IRA).

- Request a yearly Social Security Statement so you can plan for the future.
- Stay on top of your retirement statements quarterly so you know where you stand for retirement. (The day is coming soon)
- Stay out of debt – credit card interest rates can eat your lunch, and your dinner too! If you use a credit card for purchases, pay them off every billing cycle.
- Meet with a local attorney you trust to complete your last will and testament, power of attorney and a living will.

These are but a few of the items that will help you make it through the current of the financial waters of your life. So, show up for work, work hard, but also work smart.

PRAYER: Dear Lord, thank You for what Your Word says about money. Thank You for blessing us and supplying all of our needs, since You know our needs. AMEN

DON'T FORGET!

# IT'S FRIDAY!

SCRIPTURE: Mark 15:34-39

WRITER: Mark

Mark 15:34-39 'Then at three o'clock Jesus called out with a loud voice 'Eloi, Eloi, lema sabachthani?' which means 'My God, My God, why have you abandoned me?' Then Jesus uttered another loud cry and breathed His last. And the curtain was torn in two, from top to bottom. When the Roman officer who stood facing Him saw how He died, exclaimed, 'This man truly was the Son of God!'

It's Friday? Our scriptures today clearly depict for us that Jesus had once and for all gone to the cross after a long walk and a heavy cross on his shoulders to pay the ultimate price for the sin of the world. Many things have happened leading up to this point and it began in Genesis chapter 3 when sin entered the world. It's Friday! He was accused of many crimes that He did not do but He continued the road on our behalf. He was flogged, whipped, mocked, pierced, forced, offended, nailed and crucified based on His deep concern and love for you and me. It's Friday!

I can only imagine that day and what it must have been like for Jesus as He took on the sins of the world. It's hard to comprehend what He was thinking, and the mental anguish His mind went through. He wasn't surprised, but He never backed down from what He chose to face. He knew He would be temporarily separated from his Father and although the physical agony was unimaginable, the spiritual alienation from God was the ultimate torture. It's Friday! Yet, He sacrificed for you and for me, so that we would never have to be separated from a loving heavenly Father. His sacrifice was made so that we would know and understand the greatest love God has for us for all eternity. Guess what? It's Friday!

PRAYER: Almighty God, thank You that It's Friday! You did it for all of us and we thank You. You paid the price so we would not have to and we thank You! AMEN

### DON'T FORGET!

DEVOTIONS FROM OAKDALE

# PRAYER

SCRIPTURES: Colossians 4:2; Matthew 6:6; Joshua 1:8; Philippians 4:6; Ephesians 6:18

WRITERS: Colossians—Paul; Matthew—Matthew; Joshua—Joshua; Philippians & Ephesians—Paul

DEFINITION: prayer—conversation with God-in praise; thanksgiving or intercession; confession,

Colossians 4:2 'Devote yourselves to prayer with an alert mind and a thankful heart.'

Matthew 6:6 'But when you pray, go away by yourself, shut the door behind you, and pray to your Father in private. Then your Father, who sees everything will reward you.'

Joshua 1:8 'Study this book of Instruction continually.'

Philippians 4:6 'Don't worry about anything; instead, pray about everything. Tell God what you need, and thank Him for all he has done.'

Ephesians 6:18 'Pray in the Spirit at all times and on every occasion, stay alert and be persistent in your prayers for all believers everywhere.'

How many times in a day are we able to go to God in prayer? How many times during the day do we have critical events happen and we really need someone to talk to? How many times do we get ourselves in a corner because we made a mistake in our choices and decisions and now there are consequences? What do we do? We pray.

We pray to God for our requests, petitions, thanksgivings, and concerns. Most of the time, we are praying because we are in a jam and we need help and we need it right away. Why is it that we cannot be different in our daily prayer life? Well, it can be different.

Put prayer at the top of your list for the purpose of an ongoing personal relationship that commands the need for that one-on-one that God expects of us to make everything go smoother.

We are all facing trials, struggles, challenges and positive things such as personal victories, blessings, and answers to our prayers. So, why not flip the coin over and take a different approach. Pray consistently first before you need anything. Pray before you are in a jam. Pray because it is out of obedience and faith in the one true God who desires to fellowship with you all of the time.

PRAYER: Most Gracious Lord, I thank You for prayer. For a connection that is so meaningful each and every time we speak. You know our hearts and they are imperfect. However, we have You and that makes all the difference. AMEN

DON'T FORGET!

# YOU CAN DO IT

SCRIPTURES: Hebrews 13:6; II Timothy 1:7; I John 4:18-19

WRITERS: Hebrews—unknown; II Timothy—Paul; I John—John

Hebrews 13:6 'So we can say with confidence, the Lord is my helper, so I will have no fear. What can mere people do to me?'

II Timothy 1:7 'For God has not given us a spirit of fear and timidity, but of power, love, and self-discipline.'

I John 4:18-19 'Such love has no fear, because perfect love expels all fear. If we are afraid, it is for fear of punishment, and this shows that we have not fully experienced his perfect love. We love each other because He loved us first.'

To receive a diagnosis of cancer, word of loss of a loved one, a career change with a demotion can all cause fear. The list can become overwhelming and the fear of what is next looms over you. What fear is it that you have in your life? Aging, health concerns, death, rejection, and criticism are just a few of the topics that sometimes hit us from side to side.

We are in great need of encouraging our kids. Keeping them pumped up and excited about life. They truly are our future for the years to come. Remember to plant positive things in their lives so they can always remember to do wholesome things. Kids don't need to experience fears that keep them from succeeding in life. Help your children to pray, to learn Bible verses and then to memorize scripture so they can have recall in life when they need it the most.

God's word shares with us that we as Christians can have faith in knowing that the Lord is our helper. Also, God's perfect love expels fear. So today, believe in God for all you do and believe fear will stay far away walking your daily walk in Him.

PRAYER: God Almighty, thank You Lord for Your love and for helping us to stay away from fear. Fear of You Lord is a good thing and it keeps us in alignment with where we need to be. AMEN

DON'T FORGET!

# THINGS TO RENEW

SCRIPTURES: II Corinthians 4:16-18; Psalm 23:3; Ephesians 4:23

WRITERS: II Corinthians—Paul; Psalm—David; Ephesians—Paul

DEFINITION: renew—to restore to freshness, vigor or perfection; to make new spiritually

II Corinthians 4:16-18 'That is why we never give up. Though our bodies are dying, our spirits are being renewed every day. For our present troubles are small and won't last very long. Yet they produce for us a glory that vastly outweighs them and will last forever" So we don't look at the troubles we can see now; rather, we fix our gaze on things that cannot be seen. For the things we see now will soon be gone, but the things we cannot see will last forever.'

Ephesians 4:23 'Instead, let the Spirit renew your thoughts and attitudes.'

Today our 'to do' list consists of renewing the magazine subscription, picking up fresh milk, bread and fruit, go to the nursery to get new spring flowers and return home. Oops, have to go back to pick up new makeup for the woman of the house, new nail job to freshen things up and of course, the men need to get a new wash for their vehicle.

When we think about the things that need to be renewed in our personal life, we have a couple of writers that address the things spiritually that need our attention. We need renewal in our Christian life each day. Renewing our mind, spirit, thoughts and actions are a must just like the flowers planted need rain and sunshine. God has given us a heart for his Kingdom and we need to follow suit keeping things in our life sharp for Him. Remember, the small problems we incur from time to time won't last and therefore we need to keep our eyes on Christ.

Think about the things that you desire to renew and pray that God will work mightily in your life.

PRAYER: Most Gracious Heavenly Father, thank You Lord for all You do to remind us about renewal. Help us to identify the things that are of You. AMEN

DON'T FORGET!

# PLANTING FOR THE HARVEST

SCRIPTURE: Hosea 10:1

WRITER: Hosea

Hosea 10:12 'I said, 'Plant the good seeds of righteousness, and you will harvest a crop of love. Plow up the hard ground of your hearts, for now is the time to seek the Lord, that He may come and shower righteousness upon you.

We are merging into Spring as I write to you and the grass is beginning to green up, the clover is all over the surface and against the sidewalks and the majestic colors of greens are upon each of the trees coming back to form their spectacular leaves. Their shapes are so distinct. So much oneness in their buds and pollination that only God can control in his beauty.

In our lives, we pray, we love, we trust, we forgive and all of a sudden, things in the soil changes. Seeds we plant start to open and then with the sun and rain, we see new life. We are called to obedience in our life through each of the changes that we experience. So have the faith that is needed to trust in God.

Things must grow beneath the surface before the harvest comes forth in a new season. Walk in faith and trust in God to see our prayer life grow, the way in which we love those around us and the way in which our hearts are open to forgive. Don't forget that you are planting today for the harvest tomorrow.

PRAYER: Heavenly Father, You are the Master Gardener in life. In You, all things are new, renewing and alive. May we do the things we need to do to produce the right harvest in the lives of others. AMEN

### DON'T FORGET!

# STAY

SCRIPTURE: Matthew 2:13

WRITER: Matthew

Matthew 2:13 'After the wise men were gone, an angel of the Lord appeared to Joseph in a dream. 'Get up! Flee to Egypt with the child and his mother,' the angel said. 'Stay there until I tell you to return, because Herod is going to search for the child to kill Him!'

I read a poem that speaks of staying where you are in life and not moving until God tells you to move. We are inclined to want to follow our peers and to march with the rank and file but God says stay where I put you.

Then, we have our own field and request the seed. We sow it freely without fear to hope someday for rain that produces a crop but God says stay where I put you.

We exclaim, God, I will stay where you put me. We will bear the day's burden and heat while always trusting in God and laying the fruit of our labor at His feet. So, when we know that our work here on earth is ended and done with life's record all closed, we know that it was better to stay than to go.

Allow God to direct all Your days. Have patience and trust even in the midst of monotony of your daily routine. Courageously handle the stress and the strain of each day while leaning on God to help you in every way.

PRAYER: Lord God, we thank You for how Your timing is always perfect. Never too late, never too early, always right on time. Help us to stay put when we need You most and to always understand Your timing is always perfect. AMEN

DON'T FORGET!

# EASTER MIRACLE
# JUST IN TIME

SCRIPTURE: Luke 23:34; Luke 23:43; John 19:26-27; Matthew 27:46; John 19:28; John 19:30; Luke 23:46

WRITERS: Luke—Luke; John—John; Matthew—Matthew

DEFINITION: miracle—an extraordinary event manifesting divine intervention in human affairs

When we think about Easter and the Resurrection of Christ, these seven last words of Jesus from the cross set the scene for us. They are forgiveness, salvation, relationship, abandonment, distress, triumph and reunion. Because of these words, we experience Easter and our greatest possible purpose and know that Jesus is Lord over life and death and that God's grace is greater than our sin and shame.

When I personally think about Easter from a 200-acre prison complex and knowing and understanding things you can and cannot do at Easter. I had to step back and watch as God unveiled His perfect plan for a sunrise prayer opportunity at 6am for an hour along, with a gathering of men to celebrate Jesus' resurrection. He has risen and He lives today!

Planning an Easter Sunday gathering is not easy, it takes careful planning to complete everything for us in Spanish as well as English, music to be used, the Easter story along with communion. You need those elements to break bread and have juice to represent Jesus' blood on the cross. Well, the miracle happened the evening before sunrise. At 5:38pm, a sleeve of crackers was donated and one hour later at 6:38pm, the juice arrived from two donors. Praise God, just in time. The service was awesome and the love of Jesus was glorified!

PRAYER: Almighty God, your timing is always perfect. Thank You for moving the hearts of those who gave along with Your Spirit that filled the room where we gathered. AMEN

DON'T FORGET!

# OBEDIENCE

SCRIPTURES: I John 5:3; James 1:22-23; John 15:10

WRITERS: I John—John; James—James; John—John

DEFINITION: obedience—an act or instance of obeying; the quality or state of being obedient, submission to authority

I John 5:3 'Loving God means keeping his commandments, and commandments are not burdensome.'

James 1:22-23 'But don't just listen to God's word. You must do what it says. Otherwise, you are only fooling yourselves. For if you listen to the word and don't obey, it is like glancing at your face in a mirror.'

John 15:10 'When you obey my commandments, you remain in My love, just as I obey My Father's commandments and remain in His love.'

What things are true when we think about obedience? Obedience is the starting point of true holiness. We are to be obedient, even unto death. Nothing on earth can dare to hinder obedience in the man who has given himself to God. The Christian life is first and foremost, characterized by obedience. Obedience is the secret of a good conscience and the confidence that God hears us. Obedience holds a very high place in scripture.

If we yield ourselves to the searching of God's Spirit, we may find that we never gave obedience its proper proportion in our way and plan of life and that lack is the cause of all of our failures in prayer and work. Therefore, we need full surrender and absolute obedience in all we do.

Other ways that we can follow through with obedience in our daily walk is though daily Bible study, prayer time and fellowship with our neighbors. When we are in God's word, we will find the answers and direction on how to follow in His steps along with seeking God through consistent prayer.

Lastly, we know that the Scripture commands us to love our neighbors above all else along with loving the Lord our God.

PRAYER: Most Gracious Heavenly Father, thank You for obedience to You. We often miss the mark and therefore are able to seek after You for the help and direction that we need. We praise You for who You are and are thankful for Your son Jesus. AMEN

DON'T FORGET!

# UNIQUE

SCRIPTURE: John 14:6

WRITER: John

DEFINITION: unique—being the only one of its kind; unusual, extraordinary

John 14:6 'Jesus told him, 'I am the Way, the Truth, and the Life. No one can come to the Father except through Me.'

We are all unique in how God made us. Think of uniqueness, take a look around at all the examples. It is spring here in Oakdale and I see a blonde squirrel with a foot long tail, elm trees, Bradford pear trees, pine trees that are packed with pollen, new roses budding out, butterflies, baby turtles in a slough soaking up the sun, along with many other natural elements that scream uniqueness.

You and I on the other hand, are unique individuals with many special traits that attract other people around us in our everyday walk. What makes us different and set apart are our actions, our demeanor, our kindness, our attitude along with our Christian spirit that impacts those around us. To the contrary, we impact others in a negative way and treating them in an unkind way which is not what we want to do at all. As you know, a wrong move towards someone and we damage friendship. We speak harshly and we ruin a good opportunity to impact others in a powerful way.

I am currently living with one hundred other unique men here at Oakdale. We all have our own story and our own background. Sometimes we need to step back and recognize that there are good things in each person and their uniqueness is something that can always be added to with the experiences we do daily. What I have experienced here is a group of men that love the Lord and are all working hard to put their best foot forward to do right and live for Christ.

PRAYER: Father God, thank You for how unique You are, having lived a perfect life. You are our God and we praise You for all You do in our life to make us unique. We always want to follow You and bring honor and glory to You. AMEN

DON'T FORGET!

# THE THREE P'S

SCRIPTURES: Romans 5:3-5; James 1:4; Hebrews 10:36

WRITERS: Romans—Paul; James—James; Hebrews—unknown

DEFINITION: patience—longsuffering, enduring hardship, difficulty, or inconvenience without complaint; persevering; constant

Romans 5:3-5 'We can run into problems and trials, for we know that they help us develop endurance, and endurance develops strength of character, and character strengthens our confident hope of salvation. And this hope will not lead to disappointment, for we know how dearly God loves us, because He has given us the Holy Spirit to fill our hearts with His love.'

James 1:4 'So let it grow, for when your endurance is fully developed, you will be perfect and complete, needing nothing.'

Hebrews 10:36 'Patient endurance is what you need now, so that you will continue to do God's will. Then you will receive all that he has promised.'

Pursue, patience and perseverance are today's three P's. There are many times in life when we need to just step back and wait for a situation to unfold and see exactly what God is going to do. Patience is never easy when you are waiting on an unanswered prayer, and diagnosis of cancer, the outcome of a business deal that you spent a lot of time on or even little things like a house closing. Can you think of examples in your life when you were waiting and waiting and no answers are occurring? God's Word clearly states that we will have problems and trials and we will stump our toes but, through all of this, we will build endurance. Once that is done, our character will change and we will then begin to build confidence once again.

What are you going through right now in your life or the life of someone that you are close to? Are you waiting on God patiently or are you giving up and throwing in the towel? Listen, don't do it!! Don't give in to thinking any way other than positive thoughts because God loves you too much for you to quit. Hold you head up and seek God.

PRAYER: Lord God, thank You for Your patience and perseverance in our lives along with the fact that Your Holy Spirit pursues us each day. We want to ask for diligence in our life to be more intentional in all we do. AMEN

DON'T FORGET!

# ALWAYS AROUND

SCRIPTURE: Psalm 139:4,7

WRITER: David

Psalm 139:4, 7 'You know what I am going to say even before I say it, Lord. I can never escape from your Spirit! I can never get away from your presence.'

In today's scriptures, David asked, 'Where can I go from your Spirit?' The more he thought about it, the more he realized the answer was 'nowhere.' God is present everywhere and at all times. This answer causes people to either find comfort in the answer or to find others are filled with bad feelings.

Even when we think that we are going through tough times and that we are experiencing trials and heartaches, God is there with us guiding, protecting and providing for us.

There is literally never a time that we are alone and having to think that we are in situations all by ourselves. This is security we have as believers, so let's rejoice in knowing God is always with us.

I can't tell you how many times I have been in a situation and out of nowhere comes an answered prayer, a divine moment, a wink from God and just the perfect feeling that the Holy Spirit provides to nudge us to have a reminder that God is always around!

PRAYER: Heavenly Father, thank You for always being there for us. We sometimes do not understand everything in life but You help us to remember that You are always around! AMEN

DON'T FORGET!

# WAITING TIMES

SCRIPTURE: Isaiah 64:1-4

WRITER: Isaiah

Isaiah 64:1-4 'Oh that you would burst from the heavens and come down! How the mountains would quake in your presence! For since the world began, no ear has heard and no eye has seen a God like you.'

Our God we serve is a God of action and He is always working regardless of the situations we are in. The relationship we have with God is one of an intimate nature. Even when we experience down feelings or events not going in our direction, we still need to know that God is constantly at work.

God is the one behind circumstances. The one involved in our relationships. We need to remember that we should follow him and choose to trust Him and depend on Him rather that make foolish decisions.

When we have to wait, God is growing us in character, obedience, faith and service. Be encouraged that these are also good times to reflect and remember back to the last time you had to wait upon the Lord. The outcome was one that was instrumental in taking you to a new level in your faith.

PRAYER: Almighty God, we thank You for Your perfect timing in our lives. Sometimes we wonder about Your timing, but we know deep down that it is always perfect. AMEN

## DON'T FORGET!

# BE INTENTIONAL

SCRIPTURES: Romans 12:1-5; Matthew 4:4

WRITERS: Romans—Paul; Matthew—Matthew

DEFINITION: intentional—done deliberately, purpose, goal, objective; signifies a course of action, on purpose

Romans 12:1-5 'Don't copy the behavior and customs of this world, but let God transform you into a new person by changing the way you think. Then you will learn to know God's will for you, which is good and pleasing and perfect. Because of the privilege and authority God has given me, I give each of you this warning: Don't think you are better than you really are. Be honest in your evaluation of yourselves, measuring yourselves by the faith God has given us.'

Can you think of some things that point to how we are shaped in our Christian life and also how we become more like God?

As we know, the more time we spend in God's word, the better things are for us. We stay connected and are fed constantly with His riches and His truths about how to live consistently for Him.

Then, we can also be intentional with how our prayer life is taking shape and the regular schedule that we keep staying in touch with our Lord. Dependence on God allows for our life to experience growth along with a deeper love for the One who died for you and me.

Lastly, being with and around a body of believers in a small group Bible study along with corporate worship will allow us all to continue building relationships, loving our neighbors and finding encouragement in each other.

Therefore, when we have an intentional schedule with God, reading the Bible and spending time with people, He will reshape us exactly like He wants us to be.

PRAYER: Dear Lord, may we find ourselves intentional in all we do with You. Bible study, prayer time and worship time. Help us to always seek You in all we do. AMEN

DON'T FORGET!

# EVERYONE MATTERS

SCRIPTURE: I Timothy 2:1-7

WRITER: Paul

I Timothy 2:3-6 'This is good and pleases God our Savior, who wants everyone to be saved and to understand the truth. For, there is one God and one Mediator who can reconcile God and humanity – the man Christ Jesus. He gave his life to purchase freedom for everyone.'

Everyone wants protection in life, from cars and trucks that keep us safe while driving us to our destinations. We put on sunscreen with a high SPF so we don't do damage to our skin or get skin cancer. If we are going to ride an ATV 4-wheel drive vehicle out in the woods or over rough terrain we will want protection with the right gloves, helmet and plenty of fluids to keep us hydrated. Let's face it, we want to be protected and to be safe.

Most people we come in contact with don't know God and Jesus. I Timothy 2:5-6 clearly states that there is one God, one mediator also known to have given his Son Jesus Christ for the world. Paul encourages intercession on behalf of all people. This is what we as Christians are called to do. That means prayer for them and fellowship for them to let them know we care.

Faith in Christ is the only way to enter into a personal relationship with God. Why not choose to accept the offer that God has given us and follow Christ today.

PRAYER: Most Gracious Heavenly Father, everyone does matter to You and we thank You that You impart responsibility to us as your children. Help us to reach out to those around us and always be willing to share. AMEN

DON'T FORGET!

# THE INVISIBLE
# BECOMES VISIBLE

SCRIPTURE: John 3:8

WRITER: John

John 3:8 'The wind blows where it wishes, and you hear the sound of it, but cannot tell where it comes from and where it goes. So is everyone who is born of the Spirit.'

'We can't see the wind, but we can certainly feel it's effect. The mysterious line between visible and invisible reveals the evidence of the unseen wind. My hair whipping around definitely can feel the effect as the winds grows stronger. There is a greater invisible mystery, that is our invisible God. We can't see God, but we feel His effects. His life and His Spirit have been breathed on us. He changes us, His work in our lives is like the wind that we can't see, but we know it's there, doing an invisible work.

Yes! We believe in a God we can't see. We believe in salvation that is ours because we accepted His free gift of salvation and eternal life by grace through faith in his Son Jesus Christ. We believe in the invisible, the work He does that makes us a new creation.

There are a lot of unseen factors in our Christian walk as the evidence of an unseen God is lived out in our lives every day. The effects of God in our lives are just as real as the wind blowing through our hair and through the leaves of the trees and as it makes ripples on the water. Open your eyes and ears and observe the evidence of our unseen God.'

C. Smith

Can you think of a time in your life when you are impressed with the surroundings that God has created?

Today, I am honored to have my wife share the devotion and impart her heart with you the reader.

PRAYER: Almighty God, You control the wind, the breeze, the rain, the snow, the elements in our world. We thank You for a hint of Your hand each day we live. AMEN

DON'T FORGET!

# ARE YOU GRUMBLING?

SCRIPTURES: Philippians 2:14-15; Jude 1:16

WRITERS: Philippians—Paul; Jude—Jude

DEFINITION: grumble—to mutter discontent

Philippians 2:14-15 'Do everything without grumbling and arguing, so that no one can criticize you. Live clean, innocent lives as children of God, shinning like bright lights in a world full of crooked and perverse people.'

Jude 1:16 'These people are grumblers and complainers, living only to satisfy their desires. They brag loudly about themselves, and they flatter others to get what they want.'

Take a look at your life and check to see if you are in the midst of grumbling. Sometimes it's easy to find ourselves grumbling and complaining about the way the Lord takes us to get us to the place of blessing. We grumble because it's uncomfortable. We grumble because it's difficult. We grumble because we encounter enemies and discouragers along our pathway. We grumble because we believe we are lacking in what WE want or what WE think WE need.

Before long, we miss out on our blessings because of our faithlessness and grumbling against HIS ways and many times end up missing out on our blessings all together.

If we really confess how things are going in our life, we would have to admit that life is pretty good. Family, friends, jobs, successes, fellowship with neighbors and the list goes on and on. Give thanks today for the blessings that God has bestowed upon each of us and then make a difference each day.

PRAYER: Dear Lord, we pray for Your touch in our lives that we will forgo the grumbling that we have in our life. Nothing is so bad that we cannot have plenty to praise You about. AMEN

DON'T FORGET!

# THREEFOLD CORD
## 'DON'T GO IT ALONE'

SCRIPTURE: Ecclesiastes 4:9-12

WRITER: Solomon

Ecclesiastes 4:9-12 'Two are better than one. Because they have a good reward for their labor. For if they fall, one will lift up his companion. But woe to him who is alone when he falls, for he has no one to help him up. Again, if two lie down together, they will keep warm; but how can one be warm alone? Though one may be overpowered by another, two can withstand Him. And a threefold cord is not quickly broken.'

I love those words 'not quickly broken.' That is why we do not have to go it alone in life. We don't have to choose loneliness and yes, I said choose loneliness. Loneliness is a choice that we do not have to make. God has provided us with everything we need in life. First, he has given us his Son Jesus Christ. Second, God has given us His Word, the Bible. Scriptures that are God inspired and perfect for us to live by and live in. We simply have to read, meditate and study independently and will find ourselves growing in Him. Lastly, God has given us Christian brothers and sisters that are the foundation of fellowship.

Now we can see why God works in the world and intertwining each of us together. When we are alone and by ourself, that is when we head towards loneliness. Not a place God wants us to go. God wants us to be part of something exciting, something intertwined with others. Start with yourself, Jesus Christ, the Holy Spirit and God the Father. Don't go it alone.

PRAYER: Dear God Almighty, thank You for the threefold cord approach that you provide each day if we will stay in Your word and look to You. AMEN

DON'T FORGET!

# OVERCOMING WORRY

SCRIPTURES: Matthew 6:25; Philippians 4:6; Luke 14:28

WRITERS: Matthew—Matthew; Philippians—Paul; Luke—Luke

Matthew 6:25 'That is why I tell you not to worry about everyday life-whether you have enough food and drink, or enough clothes to wear.'

Philippians 4:6 'Don't worry about anything; instead, pray about everything. Tell God what you need, and thank Him for all He has done.'

Luke 14:28 'But don't begin until you count the cost. For who would begin construction of a building without first calculating the cost to see if there is enough money to finish it?'

'To take thought' or 'to be careful' is somewhat characteristic of the word worry. Sometimes it leads to a divided mind. Someone who worries has a mind torn between the real and the possible, the immediate and the potential. That person is trying to fight the battle of life on two fronts, and more than likely will lose the war.

Take a close look at the three passages and we will find that 'don't worry' does not mean don't plan. In Matthew 6:34 Jesus says, 'do not worry about tomorrow.' Also, 'don't worry' does not mean don't be concerned. Philippians 4:6 says, 'be anxious for nothing.' This simply means concerns can focus on the present but worry is attached to the future. The present is before us, and there are actions we can take. The future us out of our hands. So, don't be held captive by worry.

PRAYER: Dear Lord, we pray for Your help over worry in our life. We know that when we trust in You and stay close to You that all things will work for our good. AMEN

DON'T FORGET!

# JUST RIGHT

SCRIPTURES: Galatians 2:20; Romans 8:15-17

WRITERS: Galatians and Romans—Paul

Galatians 2:20 'My old self has been crucified with Christ. It is no longer I who lives, but Christ lives in me. So I live in this earthly body by trusting in the Son of God, who loved me and gave Himself for me.'

Romans 8:15-17 'So you have not received a Spirit that makes you fearful slaves. Instead, you received God's Spirit when he adopted you as His own children. Now, we call him Abba, Father.'

When you hear the words, just right, what comes to mind? Today, it is the fact that 'God is just right.' He is the just right one and in Him, He's made us just right. Therefore, we can and are able to now accept ourselves on the basis the same basis God does. Through Jesus Christ, we no longer have to fend for ourselves and take from others. We find our foundation, our identity in Him. Romans shows us who God is and what He has done in Jesus Christ.

Then the question arises, 'If God loves us, then why am I going through this?'

Think about how your life is each day in all the circumstances that you are faced with and then notice that God really is just right. Work, relationships, career moves, medical health changes, loss of a family member and the list goes on and on. Truly, God is always 'Just Right.'

PRAYER: Heavenly Father, thank You for always being just right. We thank You for salvation, faith and love in You. We pray that You continue to bless us in all we do. AMEN

DON'T FORGET!

# FAITH IS IMPORTANT!

SCRIPTURES: Galatians 3:11-12, James 1:3; I Corinthians 13:13

WRITERS: Galatians—Paul; James—James; I Corinthians—Paul

DEFINITION: faith—reliance, loyalty, or complete trust in God; a system of religious beliefs

Galatians 3:11-12 'So it is clear that no one can be made right with God by trying to keep the law. For the scriptures say, 'it is through faith that a righteous person has life.' This way of faith is very different from the way of the law, which says, 'it is through obeying the law that a person has life.'

James 1:3 'For you know that when your faith is tested, your endurance has a chance to grow. So let it grow, for when your endurance is fully developed, you will be perfect and complete, needing nothing.

I Corinthians 13:13 'Three things will last forever—faith, hope, and love—the greatest of these is love.'

How important is faith in your life? Can you do without it? How would you do if you totally removed faith from your life? It is definitely something to think about, the importance of one of the most integral factors that we live with and live by, our faith.

So, let's think about what faith means to you. Men in my Bible study shared the following definitions; obedience, commitment, belief, confidence and reliance on God. Then, how does faith affect our lives? It's about a personal one-on-one with God. A reliance on God and our place to go and know that Christ is there for us no matter what we are experiencing.

Think differently about an all-encompassing, all-in attitude towards how important faith really is to each of us.

PRAYER: Most Gracious Heavenly Father, thank You for faith in You, our Almighty God, Savior, Redeemer and faithful Father. Thank You for what faith really is to each of us each day. AMEN

DON'T FORGET!

# OUR PERFECT GUIDE

SCRIPTURE: Psalm 32:8

WRITER: David

Psalm 32:8 'The Lord says, 'I will guide (instruct) you along the best pathway for your life. I will advise you and watch over you.'

The scripture today is saying God will counsel with us and will have His loving eye upon us. We feel very comfortable in our life sometimes and we know that God prefers our faith. We love predictability; God desires for us to be on this life of adventure. We want a break; God wants a break through. Deep down in every challenge that we experience is an opportunity to experience God and to engage our faith and to see Him in action. So, why are we not asking more of God and having faith that He is there for us? He is greater, bigger, and more magnificent than we could ever imagine.

He wastes nothing and He is truly using every part of our life story to make us someone special and unique that we never dreamed that we could be.

Think big, dream big, take risks and know that Jesus will lead us on the right path for our lives.

I truly believe that in everything we experience in life, God is shaping and molding something wonderful. Something that can only be of Him! Pray to be obedient and trust in Him today.

PRAYER: Most Perfect Lord, Father God, You are perfect in every way. Please help us to always strive to be our best for You. AMEN

DON'T FORGET!

# MASTERPIECE

SCRIPTURE: Ephesians 2:10

WRITER: Paul

Ephesians 2:10 'For we are God's masterpiece. He has created us anew in Christ Jesus, so we can do the good things He planned for us long ago.'

We truly are God's masterpiece. His word says so in Ephesians 2:10. With that comes some of our traits, our smile, gifts, insights and thoughts from our mind that God has so richly blessed us with. Our heart which is in tune with His heart beats in such a way that we move and think and care about others as our Father thinks about us. Our souls long to grow stronger and as we learn to trust Him more, then we can trust ourselves.

God's sense of nearness grows stronger with each day that passes and when we trust Him, He fills us with his joy and peace. We are always upheld by a great God. In Christ, we are secure, loved, called and equipped. May we always stay strong while He writes our earthly story. We are called to love God, love others and also to love ourselves.

Think today about all of the many things in your life that sets you apart from others. For me, it is my height (I'm 6'8"), my baldness, my ears can move up and down if I make them with a special twitch of movement. You are laughing right now and this is good. I love to make people laugh and to be themselves. We are all created differently but we truly are God's masterpiece.

PRAYER: Lord God, I thank you for all of the special traits you have blessed me with in my life. We are all different, made in your image. Help us to be set apart as your Word calls us to be. We love You and thank You. AMEN

DON'T FORGET!

# ROAD TEST OF LIFE

SCRIPTURES: Luke 22:27-28; Hebrews 4:15

WRITERS: Luke—Luke; Hebrews—unknown

Luke 22:27-28 'Who is more important, the one who sits at the table or the one who serves? The one who sits at the table, of course. But not here! For I am among you as one who serves. You have stayed with me in my time of trial."

Hebrews 4:15 'This High Priest of ours understands our weaknesses, for He faced all of the same testing we do, yet he did not sin.'

You leave out of your home or apartment and you board your vehicle. Strap yourself in and prepare for your road test. And yes, this is the road test of life. You begin to see other vehicles just like yours, simply different colors. What you don't know is they too are strapped in for the road test of life. Also, just perhaps a different course than you. So, you continue your life drive and all of a sudden, a slight bump in the road. A little further down the straight road, the road now has bends. That road that was asphalt and smooth becomes rocky and ultimately dirt. Now all of a sudden, you have hair-pin turns and worsen as you are driving overlooking deep cliffs and the road begins to narrow. The driving conditions now experience the elements of rain, possible sleet, high winds and what looks to be a possible storm headed your way.

My friend, welcome to the road test of life. What I have described to you is what others like you and I encounter on a daily basis. Sometimes, the road is smooth sailing and other times we are about to drive off of the cliff.

All selfishness in our life has to go away. We know that Jesus lived a perfect life. As we know, it is the giving that pays; it is the helping that pays; it is loving that pays; it is putting yourself out for another person that pays. We all know that we will have trials in our life and temptation.

Follow Christ in constant regeneration. Every day is a regeneration;

every day is a day of advancement; every day is a place of choice. Today, if you are not on fire for Christ, you are not in a place of regeneration. Allow Christ to navigate you through the road test of life.

Glorious Father, thank You for who You are and how You have set the ultimate standard by which we are to live daily. Help us to attain excellence in all we do for You and to stay on course with our life. AMEN

DON'T FORGET!

# WHEN YOUR CUP SEEMS EMPTY

SCRIPTURE: II Corinthians 12:9-10

WRITER: Paul

II Corinthians 12:9-10 'But He said to me, My grace is sufficient for you, for My power is made perfect in weakness. Therefore, I will boast all the more gladly of my weaknesses, so that the power of Christ may rest upon me. For the sake of Christ, then, I am content with weaknesses, insults, hardships, persecutions and calamities. For when I am weak, then I am strong.'

Perhaps you can recall a time when something happened in your life that just took everything out of you. Then, quickly, you have someone depending upon you and you are thinking, oh my goodness, I cannot pour anything else from this cup. So, step back and take a breather and then try to hit it head on again.

Do you always seem to feel empty yet somehow you are still able to pour from your cup? Sometimes, we pray to God wondering how can I really be expected to do more that I am doing. Well, you are expected to continue pouring because God calls us to continue having faith that there is something in the cup and guess what, He creates it for us.

It is for sure during the times in your life that a crisis is going on, a life event has just taken place or is taking place or is about to take place. Are you ready? Your cup may seem empty and it probably is, but that is right where you need to be. God is able to fill your cup right to the brim just when we need His perfect strength. Turn to God today for all of your needs.

PRAYER: Almighty God, thank You Father for any empty cup where we can continue to give and watch to see just how perfect You're timing really is. It does not matter how much we experience; You are always there for us. AMEN

DON'T FORGET!

# CHOOSE TO SERVE

SCRIPTURE: John 1:29

WRITER: John

John 1:29 'The Lamb of God, who takes on the sin of the world.'

Today, it is on my heart about the many ways in which we can serve others, like mowing a neighbor's yard, getting your neighbor's newspaper and delivering to their front door, getting groceries for a home bound neighbor or friend, going the extra mile when it is unexpected, delivering food when bad weather hits and you know the people do not need to get out in the elements. My good friend Dave, fits the bill for the one who serves all in any need. He is a giver.

So, when is enough, enough? When are you not worried about someone seeing you do something and acknowledging it before others, or you getting credit so you can be seen? I know that we all want to be recognized once in a while but, come on…. serve someone other than yourself.

I forgot to ask a very important questions, how much does it cost to serve in monetary value? Here is your answer…. NOTHING. That's right, no money to serve someone. Now, I do have to tell you that it will cost you some time out of your schedule, but you must invest in others if you want to see what serving is all about.

I must warn you here that if you try it once and I mean serve others, you will be blown away and very much surprised once you experience it. The feelings you will experience will have you coming back time after time to impact the lives of so many individuals.

Accept this personal challenge today and choose to serve someone. May God bless you as you try it. I promise that you will not be disappointed.

PRAYER: Dear Lord, thank You for the awesome opportunity that You provide us with each day when we are in front of people, a smile, a handshake or laughter. These only come from You. AMEN

DON'T FORGET!

# SHOULD WE WORRY?

SCRIPTURE: Philippians 4:6-7

WRITER: Paul

Philippians 4:6-7 'Don't worry about anything; instead, pray about everything. Tell God what you need and thank Him for all He has done.'

The big question on everyone's minds these days is should we worry? Do we worry? Why do we worry? Is worry healthy and does it really get us that far in life? Well, all good questions that lead us back around to the fact that worry is not good, it is a sin and it is very counterproductive in everything we do and think.

Worry seems to divide our minds and just creates issues and takes away from our happiness and never does anything good for us. Worry wastes time, effort and really keeps us from the potential that God has for us in our lives.

Take a minute, take a snap shot of your life and your current situations. See how each of those scenarios got you where you are and how you have been handling those things. As we know when we read through current situations around us, we see increased COVID-19 cases due to spring break, new strands of COVID-19 from different parts of the world, mass murders along with nonsense going on in Hollywood with celebrities doing crazy things in their lives.

I have to share with you that I have had worry in my heart and weighted on my shoulders since my indictment some 3 years ago. It is something I struggled with during many sleepless nights just knowing that my day in prison was on the horizon. That situation shook me worse than anything in my life to date. Perhaps you ask, how are you doing with that worry now that you are in prison and serving your time for what you did wrong. My answer to you is, all of that worry lifted the day I arrived and started serving my sentence here at Oakdale.

What have I noticed with prior worry is that the Devil loves to be in our business and confusing us with temptations to carry things that we do not need to carry? One of those things is worry. Leave it at God's feet and He will give you rest, peace and assurance that all is well.

PRAYER: Most Gracious Heavenly Father, thank You for Your peace that passes all understanding and that we can rest easy in You when there is worry around us. AMEN

DON'T FORGET!

# PEACEFUL PERSEVERANCE

SCRIPTURES: I Peter 3:19; II Timothy 1:12; I Corinthians 15:58

WRITERS: I Peter—Peter; II Timothy—Paul; I Corinthians—Paul

DEFINITION: perseverance—enduring hardships with patience, steadfastness in undertaking in spite of opposition or discouragement

I Peter 3:19 'So He went and preached to the Spirits in prison.'

II Timothy 1:12 'If we endure hardship, we will reign with Him.'

I Corinthians 15:58 'So, my dear brothers and sisters, be strong and immovable. Always work enthusiastically for the Lord, for you know that nothing you do for the Lord is ever useless.'

How in the world do we have hardships, challenges and tough stuff that we are enduring and call it peaceful? The title today is encouragement that perseverance can be peaceful if we are looking to Christ to guide us and to check us along the way.

I know you are probably thinking, how in the world can he talk about perseverance and not know that it is tough. Keeping a busy schedule, working in adverse career situations along with family tensions that can sometimes eat away at all the good.

Prepare yourself for some good news. Enduring hardships with patience, and being steadfast and being fully persuaded that God is with us all the way is all we need to be victorious in this life.

Recently, great news came for many inmates that meet certain criteria and have also served a certain percentage of their prison sentence. This week it got even better for those with ongoing health issues that reach a specific level based on Bureau of Prisons data. Men are going home well before the required percentage of sentence is met.

That, my friend, is peaceful perseverance, God's way!

PRAYER: Dear Lord, thank You for Your hand on Oakdale. You are doing a mighty work in the lives of many men who thought it would be a long time coming for them to finish their sentence and go home. How blessed they are! AMEN

DON'T FORGET!

# DON'T TAKE THINGS FOR GRANTED

SCRIPTURE: Luke 16:19-31

WRITER: Luke

Luke 16:19-31 v.24 'The rich man shouted, Father Abraham, have some pity! Send Lazarus over here to dip the tip of his finger in water and cool my tongue. I am in anguish in these flames.'

Look around and take note of all the many blessings that have affected you in your life. For instance, you never miss the water until the well goes dry. And then, there comes a day when you would give anything you have for just one ordinary day that you had back there – that you took for granted.

Wives and husbands still have that privilege of living another day together, don't take it for granted.

There are times when you are inclined to think this is kind of a dull, boring day, and that life gets sort of ordinary. Don't take it for granted.

We take health for granted until we are in the hospital and then months go by. Don't take it for granted.

You may go to church; you may act and dress the part. You are comfortable, you are satisfied. But if you don't know Jesus, you will be without life in Christ. Don't take it for granted.

The things that come to mind for me at this moment are: freedom, family time, special walks, special talks, morning sunrises with a glass of orange juice and just the little things that sometimes get taken for granted. Be appreciative today for life. It is very precious.

PRAYER: Most Gracious Lord, thank You for everything that You have blessed us with. Most of all, your Son Jesus giving his life on the cross for each of us. May we not take these things for granted. AMEN

DON'T FORGET!

# THE SURVIVOR

SCRIPTURE: II Timothy 4:7

WRITER: Paul

II Timothy 4:7 'I have fought the good fight, I have finished the race, I have kept the faith.'

We all know there is a show titled 'Survivor' and it literally pits competitors to use hard core tactics of finding certain artifacts to be used in the event of a disqualification. Tough situations of survival acts include finding your own food. The rain and weather elements along with getting along and positioning yourself with people alliances are all essential tactics. Today, I share with you a personal survivor story that is real life and not in a jungle for a television show.

We all live in and around people we care about and love. I know someone very special to me that has experienced just that in her life and truly makes her a survivor.

First, I am sharing a direct first-hand story that a first marriage brought forth a gift of a son who means very much to her and whom she loves very much. The marriage also yielded much abuse, mental, physical, emotional and lots of hurt. She didn't know how she would make it sometimes but she always found a way. Feelings of struggle and fight were overwhelming at times but she remained fearless, flawless and faultless. This lady is always real, genuine and authentic….The reason I know is…I know her.

Characteristics of a survivor is loving with all your heart and not doing anything halfway. Having a soul that is full of passion, loving hard and of course, being loved back. Through that, you are capable of conquering anything. It doesn't mean that sometimes your life will be feeling like it is coming off the track. You will always find your way back….The reason I know is…I know her.

So, build up someone's self-image through encouragement, a kind word, a special touch. Tell someone it is possible to do anything. Be a builder through all times. This woman has lost a father to cancer and remained faithful to her Mom, being able to strengthen her through actions and attitudes.

Unconditional, obedient, loving, and caring are all traits to help you stay a survivor. This woman is a person of many talents, qualities and depths. SHE is the one who keeps me going, gives me strength and currently loves me from afar while I am in prison. The reason I know her, she is my wife. Thank you for loving me and making me your survivor.

PRAYER: Most Gracious Heavenly Father, thank You for giving us the survivor spirit of never giving up and always depending on You. AMEN

DON'T FORGET!

# LEAVE TOMORROW ALONE, DON'T DWELL ON TOMORROW'S STRESS

SCRIPTURES: Deuteronomy 33:25; Matthew 6:34

WRITER: Deuteronomy—Moses; Matthew—Matthew

Deuteronomy 3:25 'May the bolts of your gates be iron and bronze, may you be secure all your days.'

Matthew 6:34 'Therefore, do not worry about tomorrow, for tomorrow will worry about its own things. Sufficient for the day is its own trouble.

Sometimes it is said, 'I don't know how I can face it.' The rich practical wisdom of the Bible states to leave tomorrow alone. When the sun comes up each morning, God will give the grace and strength that is needed for the situation.

Don't dwell on yesterday's mess because that is exactly what it is. One thing is always true about yesterday – it's gone. Its complete. It's out of reach for you to be able to go back and retrieve. There is not one thing that we can do about it ever again.

I have spoken with friends that have allowed things from the past to pop up and remind you what you did. Guilt is powerful and you need to remember that God has forgiven us of our past. If you have confessed things in the past, it's been forgiven and it is over. Leave it!

That is why Paul said – 'forgetting what was behind him and pushing forward to the one wonderful thing that was still before him. The high calling of Christ.

An anonymous poet once wrote the following....

My name is I AM. If you live in the past, it will be very hard, for I am not there, my name is not I WAS.

And if you live in the future, it will be very hard, for my name is not I WILL BE, but if you live in the present, it is not hard, for my name is I AM.

PRAYER: Father God, please help us today to leave yesterday alone. May we be thankful for life today and live life to the fullest. AMEN

DON'T FORGET!

# TRUST ME

SCRIPTURES: Psalm 50:15; Psalm 55:22; I Peter 5:7

WRITERS: Psalm—David; I Peter—Peter

DEFINITION: trust—to place confidence or depend on; to commit or place in one's care or keeping; to rely on the truthfulness or accuracy of

Psalm 50:15 'Call upon Me in the day of trouble; I will deliver you, and you shall glorify me.'

Psalm 55:22 'Cast your burden on the Lord, and He shall sustain you; He shall never permit the righteous to be moved.'

I Peter 5:7 'Casting all your cares upon Him, for He cares for you.'

Why are there so many verses in the Bible concerning the issue of trust, not being anxious, casting all of our burdens and cares on God along with many more examples of just bringing everything to God? Wisdom tells us to worry about nothing and pray about everything.

We are in a daily battle and we must guard our hearts and minds and do everything through Christ Jesus.

So, what are you going through today in your life? What challenges have you experienced that put you in a questionable position with what the outcome will look like? There are many things in our world today that can take us in a tailspin and have us questioning why things are happening as they are.

The solution is a daily, intimate walk with Jesus Christ. The choice is taking a stand and following Him in all you do. The direction towards the light of the world shines so bright that there is no question that He is in control. Place your trust, confidence and dependence on Christ today and you will see how precious that relationship is and where it takes you.

PRAYER: Dear Heavenly Father, thank You for always being there for us no matter how many things come against us. May we always trust you in whatever things we experience. AMEN

DON'T FORGET!

# CHOOSE JOY

SCRIPTURE: Ecclesiastes 12:1; Luke 21:28

WRITERS: Ecclesiastes—Solomon; Luke—Luke

DEFINITION: joy—the emotion evoked by well-being, success, or good fortune

Ecclesiastes 12:1 'Don't let the excitement of youth cause you to forget your creator. Honor Him in your youth before you grow old and say, Life is not pleasant anymore.'

Luke 21:28 'And when these things begin to come to pass, then look up and lift your heads; for your redemption draweth nigh.'

Today is the day for each of us to choose joy. We live in a world where people have their heads down and their hearts are downtrodden. We recall that John the Baptist was in prison. Paul was in chains many times and he continued to hold fast to knowing he was walking with and following Christ.

No doubt when we see the frightening headlines on television, the newspapers as well as internet updates, it is viewed differently by the Christian. The Christian does not get caught up in the world's misery but holds his head up because he knows the redemption of this world has been put in place by the blood of Jesus.

John 4:35 says, 'Lift up your eyes and look on the fields; for they are white and ready to harvest.' This is a great reason to choose joy. I am reminded by a number of men in my location that are on walkers and in wheelchairs that they are living with conditions that control their lives. We all have to step back and be thankful of our health, our mind and our Godly perspective of the ability to choose joy. These men who are now my new friends and brothers choose joy no matter what the situation. I have grown from seeing them and appreciate their attitude towards daily life.

PRAYER: Lord God, thank You for the choice that You give us each day to choose joy. To choose a positive attitude. To choose a loving heart and kind heart. AMEN

DON'T FORGET!

# STAY AWAY FROM DEBT

SCRIPTURE: Deuteronomy 15:1

WRITER: Moses

DEFINITION: debt—what is owed; sense of obligation

Deuteronomy 15:1 'At the end of every seventh year you must cancel the debts of everyone who owes you money.'

Debt is not a very good topic around most dinner tables. However, it is a topic that needs to be discussed and held in high regard within our lives every day.

I remember back while growing up how my parents instilled in me the opportunity to make money, to tithe ten percent to God and to wisely spend those hard-earned dollars. I always remember those discussions and I also remember seeing that my parents never extended themselves on their purchases. That is why today while in their eighties, their house is paid for and has been for thirty years along with not having any financial debt and no doubt having the financial means to live comfortably and be able to enjoy life.

Take a blank piece of paper and turn it sideways, draw a line on the left side of the page and connect at the bottom and draw another line from left to right, this second line is time from birth to life expectancy. The bad thing with this drawing is that there is uncertainty in this picture. The left line is earnings over your lifetime with no mention of the debt that you will incur. The other thing is that we know not the time of our passing. We all have to plan our lives financially in a Godly manner and not go crazy with the hi-tech gadgets that are viewed by the world as must have items. God's word states that He will supply our every need and all we have to do is trust in Him. We also have to be obedient in our giving of not only tithes but also the over and above offerings to bless our church and individuals in need.

Stay out of debt and don't let 'things' control your life and how you live it.

PRAYER: Dear Precious Lord, thank You for the financial resources that You bless us with. We mess up numerous times and You continue to forgive and forget. Thank You for Your grace and mercy. AMEN

DON'T FORGET!

# WHAT MATTERS MOST,
# IS WHAT HAPPENS NEXT

SCRIPTURE: Romans 15:13

WRITER: Paul

Romans 15:13 'I pray that God, the source of hope, will fill you completely with joy and peace because you trust in Him. Then you will overflow with confident hope through the power of the Holy Spirit.'

What happens next for someone that has been fighting cancer and continues to have treatments and hang on?

What happens next for the person who is expecting a job promotion and it went to someone else?

What happens next for a child that just lost a parent at a young age and will live the rest of their life without ½ of the support?

What happens next for the couple that has been trying to have a child and it has not happened yet?

What happens next for the person that is unexpectantly in a wreck and it damages property and maybe even hurts someone physically?

What happens next for the person that finds out that he can no longer deal with the sin in his life and is invited to accept Jesus Christ into his heart and turn from that sin and begin the best life ever?

Well, that's where the 'What matters most' phrase comes in. I can promise you as a follower of Christ that having a personal relationship and an intimate relationship is all I need on a daily basis. Why don't you do the same and trust God today?

PRAYER: Father God, thank You for being 'What matters most.' You truly are all we need in life. I love You and praise Your name. AMEN

DON'T FORGET!

# COMEBACK

SCRIPTURE: I Timothy 6:12

WRITER: Paul

I Timothy 6:12 'Fight the good fight for the true faith. Hold tightly to the eternal life to which God has called you, which you have declared so well before many witnesses.'

From where I sit now after my first 120 days in prison, things are settling in, new friendships are being forged and the one constant for me is my walk with Christ. You can go through things in life and your situations, surroundings and circumstances be different but God is always there with us and is our steady rock.

I recently read in USA Today about President Biden and his first 100 days in office and his accomplishments, promises made and promises kept. As I looked at that article, I was reminded for myself of the things I wanted to commit to going into prison as well as my journey and the things I committed to God to accomplish with His help once I leave.

This for me is my comeback and my ability to overcome what I have experienced, my feelings towards my fellow brothers and just how I will be perceived and welcomed back into society once I get home.

For me, I have been showered by personal visits from family and loved ones which is so important for communication. Being able to work through my tenure here in the landscaping area was just what God had directed me towards during my adventure.

What I have learned most during my time so far is that I am not alone. God is with me during everything I experience and He is providing me the strength I need exactly when I need it. Praise God for the Christian men that have entered my life as I entered as well as along the journey. This place is a revolving door of men who have diligently served their sentences, met the requirements to leave and hopefully are taking a relationship with Christ with them. Some will choose differently but I have been called to serve those individuals, impact them in a positive way and to always give a smile of encouragement to kick off their day. We all make a choice each day to either encourage or tear down and for me, God has been staging an unbelievable comeback and I am very thankful and prayerful for the way He is using me.

PRAYER: Most Gracious Heavenly Father, thank You for comebacks in life. You, Heavenly Father are so good and such a great example of comebacks. You impart hope, desire and fortitude right when we need it the most. Help us today. AMEN

DON'T FORGET!

# WOULD YOU SELL IT ALL?

SCRIPTURE: Matthew 19:20-21

WRITER: Matthew

Matthew 19:20-21 'If you want to be perfect, Jesus said to him, go sell your belongings and give to the poor, and you will have treasure in heaven. Then come, follow me. When the young man heard that, he went away grieving, because he had many possessions.'

Wow, I have to say when I read this passage, my heart nearly stops because Jesus is seen sharing with this young rich man that he needed to give his stuff away and follow Him. He was so attached to the 'stuff' that he would miss his opportunity for eternal life.

So, how about you? Where do you stand? You work hard and you may have more 'stuff' than others. The question today is...... would you sell it all to follow Christ if asked?

External obedience is the 'stuff' part. Internal obedience is us trusting God and having a level of full devotion and commitment to Him. We can exhibit those traits by following Him daily and being in a right relationship that does not waiver.

The Bible says nothing about having wealth or accumulating material values. However, God's word directs us not to worship the 'stuff' where it overtakes everything we do in our life. We all encounter wanting to have things but when it overtakes and rules our life, we have a problem.

Step back and take inventory of your material 'stuff' you have been blessed with over time. A home, vehicle or vehicles, furnishings, clothes, career and the list can go on and on. Make sure your priorities have Jesus Christ at the top of the list.

PRAYER: Dear Lord, may we always have our focus on You, not 'stuff.' Nothing else matters when that alignment is correct. AMEN

DON'T FORGET!

# THE 3 S's
# SERVICE, SERVANTHOOD
# AND STEWARDSHIP

SCRIPTURES: Mark 10:45; II Timothy 2:24

WRITERS: Mark—Mark; II Timothy—Paul

DEFINITION: service—to meet the needs of and subject one's will to that of another

Mark 10:45 'For the Son of man came not to be served but to serve others and to give His life as ransom for many.'

II Timothy 2:24 'A servant of the Lord must not quarrel but must be kind to everyone, be able to teach, and be patient with difficult people.'

I have seen many examples of service, servanthood and stewardship over my 60 years of life. Even though we all miss the mark in striving to do all we can to serve those around us, we have to be obedient to our Lord and Savior each day.

There are many different ways in which we can provide great stewardship characteristics and one of those is active devotion serving God through good works. Of course, we know that good works alone will not get us into heaven. Only having salvation through Jesus Christ our Lord will allow that to happen, so we need to keep the right attitude and keep our eyes on Christ.

Serving community through outreach is also a great means of servanthood. Meeting the needs of those less fortunate, those going though family losses or even celebrating events like birthdays and holidays are always great opportunities to do community service and impact our neighbors.

Colossians 3:23-24 shares with us the following: 'Work willingly at whatever you do, as though you were working for the Lord rather than for people. Remember that the Lord will give you an inheritance as your reward, and that the master you are serving is Christ.

The word 'willingly' means from the soul or the inner self. That means to always give everything you have. Always bring your best and your outcome will be service, servanthood and the stewardship of Jesus.

PRAYER: Dear Lord, thank You for giving us the greatest example of service through Your Son Jesus Christ. What an example He exhibited for us through His daily walk and the miracles He performed. AMEN

DON'T FORGET!

# WAIT PATIENTLY

SCRIPTURES: Galatians 5:22-23; II Timothy 3:10

WRITERS: Galatians—Paul; II Timothy—Paul

DEFINITION: patience—the power or capacity to endure without complaint; something difficult or disagreeable; forbearance, long suffering

Galatians 5:22-23 'But the Holy Spirit produces this kind of fruit in our lives: love, joy, peace, patience, kindness, goodness, faithfulness, gentleness and self-control.'

II Timothy 3:10 'But you, Timothy, certainly know what I teach, and how I live and what my purpose in life is. You know my faith, my patience, my love and my endurance.'

I can truly start off by saying that I know a lot of people who find it hard waiting in life and also doing it with patience. I do find myself experiencing those feelings in my current situation from time to time. The definition of patience says enduring without complaint. Something that is difficult. We all have difficulties that we experience and we simply have to be prepared as to how we will handle certain situations. Waiting patiently on God for the things we encounter is truly the way to do it if you so choose.

I am persuaded that you are going through something in your life that you are trying so hard to either let go of or hang on to the hope that a clear answer will be coming soon. Perhaps there is a job interview for something that you have wanted to venture into and try for a new beginning. Perhaps a new relationship will blossom into something meaningful in God's eyes and will be a new start for you. Each of these events come with patience and waiting. Lean on our scriptures today to assure you that God knows exactly where you are and will provide the faith, patience and endurance that you need.

PRAYER: Most Gracious Heavenly Father, thank You for helping us to wait patiently on You during stressful times. Help us to have the right confidence to know You are there for us. AMEN

DON'T FORGET!

# CONTENTMENT

SCRIPTURES: I Timothy 6:6-7; Philippians 4:11

WRITERS: I Timothy—Paul; Philippians—Paul

DEFINITION: contentment—the state of being content, feeling or showing satisfaction with one's status or situation

I Timothy 6:6 'Yet true godliness with contentment is itself great wealth. After all, we brought nothing into the world, and we can't take anything with us when we leave it.'

Philippians 4:11 'Not that I was ever in need, for I have learned how to be content with whatever I have.'

Are you content in your life? Are you satisfied with your current situation? A lot of people are not content and they continue to strive for accumulating more stuff than the Jones' next door and they sometimes find themselves in trouble.

Rewind the movie of your life back 10-20 years and see where you have come from. Look at career, family, marriage, mishaps, slip ups as well as successes. Have you been content with the accomplishments in your life? If not, maybe you need to travel a different path and see what God can do for you in bringing you peace of mind and helping you to be content.

As the scripture says, you will not be taking anything into the grave with you. Your lifetime trophies, your jewelry, your money and all the stuff that means so much to you and me. Guess what, if the stuff goes away, I promise that you will not miss it. It happened to me and I am a totally different person because for once in my life, I am content with where God has me and the accomplishments He has blessed me with in my current situation.

PRAYER: Heavenly Father, thank You for contentment. Help us to always be satisfied with what You give us and exactly where You have us in life. AMEN

DON'T FORGET!

# A LETTER, A WORD, A SENTENCE

SCRIPTURE: Ephesians 4:23

WRITER: Paul

DEFINITION: thought—the action or process of thinking; a developed intention or plan

Ephesians 4:23 'Instead, let the Spirit renew your thoughts and attitudes.'

Sometimes I don't think we give enough value and importance to the letters that become our words that we speak or the sentences that are formed to impact those around us. We have to remember the tongue can sometimes be very sharp and can cut if we are not careful. Today's scripture addresses that the Holy Spirit should renew in us our thoughts and attitudes. No doubt, those thoughts and attitudes should be those of Christ Jesus.

I received the alphabet arranged in a very special way from a very special person and I want to share it with you today. This is the way of life....

**A**lways **B**e **C**ool**, D**on't have **E**go with **F**riends and family. **G**ive up **H**urting **I**ndividuals, **J**ust **K**eep **L**oving **M**ankind. **N**ever **O**mit **P**rayer, **Q**uietly **R**emember God **S**peaks **T**ruth, **U**se **V**alid **W**ords, **X**press **Y**our **Z**eal.

Kind of neat to see how letters become words that turn into sentences that impact others. May God bless you and encourage you as you share with others today.

PRAYER: Father God, thank You for all that You do for us through Your words. We thank You for the ability to think, to speak, to share and to impact. AMEN

DON'T FORGET!

# FRESH VISION

SCRIPTURE: Proverbs 4:11

WRITER: Solomon

Proverbs 4:11 'I instruct you in the way of wisdom and lead you along straight paths.'

We walk along the same pathway so many times thinking that we will see something different. Yes, we travel to work on the same streets, we keep the same friends, we eat at the same places on the same days and maybe even have the same person serving us. You need to shake things up and travel a different route and start new friendships.

We need to allow Jesus to lead us to the edges of our comfort areas and give us a fresh vision for where He wants to direct us. We need to share everything with Him and totally submit to rearrange our lives. We should open our hands look to Him and breathe a prayer of thanks in the midst of uncertain times. We need to be aware that he is far kinder than we can ever understand and far greater than we have ever imagined. Do you sense His invitation to you to join Him on your great adventure of faith? Will we trust Him like we need to? Choose joy today, right now in your heart and every moment after. God is waiting to do a great work in you today if you will simply open up and place your trust in Him. Just know that at the end of the day that our security is found in Him!

PRAYER: Most Gracious Heavenly Father, help us to always trust in You and expect great things because of who You are. AMEN

## DON'T FORGET!

DEVOTIONS FROM OAKDALE

# THE CHAPTER YOU DID NOT SEE COMING

SCRIPTURES: Proverbs 7:3; James 1:12

WRITERS: Proverbs—Solomon; James—James

DEFINITION: reminder—to cause to remember, to keep in mind for attention or consideration

Proverbs 7:3 'Tie them on your fingers as a reminder; write them deep within your heart.'

James 1:12 'God blesses those who patiently endure testing and temptation. Afterward they will receive the crown of life that God has promised to those who love them.'

Over ten years ago, I was blessed to be a first-time author of my first book, 'The Don't Forgets of Life.' On that cover is a number of people's hands with their index finger pointing to heaven and each finger has a bow tied on as a reminder not to forget. You ask, forget what? Years ago, my PawPaw was the one to inspire me to not forget that he was proud to be my PawPaw.

As I have grown up, many great things have occurred to me in my life and when I think back, I am reminded of how I have been blessed.

Now that I am away from my family, friends and loved ones, I want to tell you not to miss the chapter of your life that you did not see coming. For me, thirty-three months of divine intervention of never missing work, continual jobs along with working with some very neat individuals. I just know that I have been truly blessed in my life. Today, I am in prison serving a sentence, but for me, it is temporary. I love the Lord and I am His child and He gives me strength that I need each day. Thank You God for the chapter I did not see coming.

PRAYER: Dear God, You are awesome and I thank You for the chapters in life that You are writing. I love the way in which you move me and impact My life. AMEN

DON'T FORGET!

# A WILLINGNESS TO FORGIVE

SCRIPTURES: Psalm 86:5; Romans 5:15

WRITERS: Psalm 86—David; Romans—Paul

DEFINITION: forgiveness—to pardon or acquit of sins

Psalm 86:5 'O Lord, you are so good, so ready to forgive, so full of unfailing love for all who ask for Your help.'

Romans 5:15 'But there is a great difference between Adam's sin and God's gracious gift. For the sin of this one man, Adam, brought death to many. But even greater is God's wonderful grace and His gift of forgiveness to many through this other man, Jesus Christ.'

When you look at the scripture from Psalm 86:5, one assumes that the verse is a psalm of praise, but the introduction says it is a prayer from someone who is poor and needy. David is begging God to help him in his dark season of his life. But he doesn't stop there. In the midst of his misery, he sings his praise to God. David reminds the Lord of His willingness to forgive. He is faithful to his covenant which is beyond our understanding. And He is faithful to all who call upon Him.

How about you today? Are you going through a dark season of life? Are you facing struggles that you just cannot work your way through? God says to bring all of your worries and all of your sins to God in prayer. His faithfulness is great and He is ready to forgive.

We are all faced with forgiveness in our life. We wrong people and people wrong us and sometimes we find that it is very hard to let go of certain situations and that also means our forgiveness of others.

Turn things over to God today and step aside so He can work through you. He desires to be the Lord of Your life and to have you trust Him and know that e is good. Be willing to forgive someone today.

PRAYER: Most Gracious Lord, thank You for Your forgiveness. You always show us the way if we trust You. Thank You for loving us. AMEN

## DON'T FORGET!

# RECONCILED

SCRIPTURES: Proverbs 14:9; II Corinthians 5:19

WRITERS: Proverbs—Solomon; II Corinthians—Paul

DEFINITION: reconciled—to restore to friendship or harmony, especially between God and human beings

Proverbs 14:9 'Fools make fun of guilt, but the godly acknowledge it and seek reconciliation.'

II Corinthians 5:19 'For God was in Christ reconciling the world to Himself, no longer counting people's sins against them. And He gave us this wonderful message of reconciliation.'

Anytime I see or hear the word reconcile, I think about having done something wrong and because of the Holy Spirit in me, I need to seek someone out to make things right. The word reconcile is to change or exchange. Jesus exchanged for us so He could give His life that we would be made right.

We do have to recognize sin and wrong doings in our life for us to be able to live a victorious life. Recovery and renewal are key for everyone going through life and experiencing things that somewhat set us back.

This topic of being reconciled is a very important party of the Christian life and we cannot take it lightly. We live with and around people that have so many things going on in their lives along with the numerous challenges that they are experiencing. A failed marriage, a diagnosis of cancer, a career that is now on shaky ground and the list goes on and on.

As we go through life and we wrong people, friends and of course family, we must quickly recognize those wrongs and with the help of the Holy Spirit, make things right. That is what God calls us to do and we need to follow Him daily.

PRAYER: Lord God, I thank You for reconciliation and the ability to restore, resolve, and to reestablish relationships and live in harmony. Lord God, You make that happen. AMEN

DON'T FORGET!

# THE CROSS

SCRIPTURES: Galatians 3:1; Colossians 1:20; Mark 8:34

WRITERS: Galatians and Colossians—Paul; Mark—Mark

DEFINITION: cross—an upright post used as an instrument of death in ancient times; the means by which atonement was made between God and humanity

Galatians 3:1 'Oh, you foolish Galatians! Who has cast an evil spell on you? For the meaning of Jesus Christ's death was made clear to you as if you had seen a picture of His death on the cross.'

Colossians 1:20 'And through him God reconciled everything in Himself. He made peace with everything in heaven and on earth by means of Christ's blood on the cross.'

Mark 8:34 'Then, calling the crowd to join his disciples, he said, 'If any of you wants to be My follower, you must give up your own way, take up your cross and follow Me.'

When reviewing today's scriptures, I think about many things as it relates to the cross. I think of a very heavy railroad-tie instrument that Jesus carried which represents my sin, my evil, my wrongdoings and just everything not of God. I also think about foolishness, unkind words as well as paths I chose along life's road that took me in opposite directions of where I truly needed to go.

I also think about a different cross, the one that God calls me to take up on a daily basis. This one is different because Jesus has already paid the price of my sin and He is simply desiring for me as his follower to put my ways behind me, take up my cross daily and then follow Him. That is what I am striving to do.

Lastly, I have shared in a previous devotion that when I self-surrendered to the Federal Prison at Oakdale, Louisiana, as I arrived on the road leading into the two hundred acres there were three crosses on the left. My daughter quickly stated, Dad, you are going to be okay because there are the crosses protecting the entry. God has been good to me each and every day.

PRAYER: Most Gracious Father, thank You for the cross that represents a price paid, a promise kept and a love for a world that is underserving. AMEN

DON'T FORGET!

# ARE YOU DOING YOUR BEST?

SCRIPTURE: Psalm 103:14; II Chronicles 16:9

WRITERS: Psalm 108—David; II Chronicles—possibly Ezra

DEFINITION: commitment—to carry into action deliberately, to obligate or pledge oneself

Psalm 103:14 'For He knows how weak we are; He remembers we are only dust.'

II Chronicles 16:9 'The eyes of the Lord search the whole earth in order to strengthen those whose hearts are fully committed to him. What a fool you have been! From now on you will be at war.'

Have you ever had a day when a lot of things just went all wrong? Perhaps it was even hard for you to pray that night. Finally, you gave up and gave in and committed everything to God. God knows the messes we get into and exactly the ones that we cannot get out of as well. Amazing how God takes the jagged edges and smooths them out and makes things whole and complete again.

The question today is 'are you doing your best?' Perhaps you stand back and quickly say, 'well of course I am' when you are really missing the mark by a long shot.

How committed to Jesus Christ are you at this time in your life? We have to remember that God knows the heart's intent and credits the soul's sincere desire though sometimes our deeds are poorly expressed. We just have to remember to always do our best and He will perfect it himself.

Just remember, others on the outside are watching your every move and they need to be seeing you giving and doing your best. God expects our best, not mediocrity.

PRAYER: Father God, thank You for all You do for us each day. Please always help us to do and give our best so we glorify You. AMEN

DON'T FORGET!

# MOVE OVER

SCRIPTURE: II Corinthians 1:9

WRITER: Paul

II Corinthians 1:9 'We had the sentence of death in ourselves, that we should not trust ourselves, but in God which raiseth the dead.'

There are a lot of times in life that challenges come our way and we just know without reservation that we can't fix it. We have to get self out of the way and deny ourself.

So few Christians ever get out of themselves and into Him. They live a changed life but not and exchanged life. We have to leave our experiences, our successes, our prayers, our seeking and striving, and settle down with God. We need to move over and allow God to work in us and with us.

Think for a few moments of times that you can identify as being in complete control. God was nowhere in your life or your situations and basically you were doing things on your own. Today, life is so busy with the internet, e-commerce purchases, cell phones, making deals, getting greedy and just living for the moment.

Don't think for a second that those times won't eventually mount up and weigh on your heart in a very heavy way. Be careful not to push God out of the way when He provides His strength, His perfect nature and His overall aura of our Savior all in one. God loves you and cares for you no matter what you have done or what you are going through. Simply move over and allow Him to work beside you.

PRAYER: Most Gracious Father, thank You for all You have done for us and what You continually do. Please help us to move over and allow You to be in charge. AMEN

DON'T FORGET!

# SMILE
## 'STIR IT UP'

SCRIPTURES: Psalm 4:6; Psalm 7:1

WRITER: David

DEFINITION: smile—to bestow approval

Psalm 4:6 'Many people say, 'Who will show us better times? Let your face smile on us, Lord.'

Psalm 7:1 'May God be merciful and bless us. May his face smile with favor on us.'

I am about to issue a small challenge to anyone reading this devotion, along with anyone you know that you can share this with. Ready? Here we go.....STIR IT UP! By that I mean, take the time to be proactive and smile at people and see what reaction you get. I truly believe you will be surprised at the number of people you will actually affect for good.

Of course, when I came to Oakdale, I did not know a soul. Now, after having been here nearly six months, I know most people personally and I have also stirred it up by simply being kind to people, treating them the way in which I want to be treated and also smiling at them. Smiling is a very powerful trait to have and I know a lot of people that are moved by a kind gesture such as a smile.

Perhaps you are going through some very different situations in your life and you just say Greg, I just cannot make a smile happen because everything has me in a valley. Bad things are happening to me and time after time I keep getting knocked down. Keep your chin up and look to God for help in STIRRING THINGS UP to impact others around you.

PRAYER: Lord God, thank You for the touch of a smile. A glistening of beautiful eyes and a demeanor that points people to You Lord. AMEN

### DON'T FORGET!

# FROM GETTERS TO GIVERS

SCRIPTURES: Philemon 1:6; II Corinthians 9:10

WRITERS: Philemon and II Corinthians—Paul

DEFINITION: generosity—the quality or fact of being magnanimous, kindly, or openhanded abundance

Philemon 1:6 'And I am praying that you will put into action generosity that comes from your faith as you understand and experience all the good things we have in Christ.'

II Corinthians 9:10 'For God is the one who provides seed for the farmer and then bread to eat. In the same way, He will provide and increase your resources and then produce a great harvest of generosity in you.'

Grace is attractive. It is energizing and a true inspiring force. That happens when we give and share with others. Today we are talking about moving from the getters to the givers for a couple of reasons.

First, we have always heard that it is better to give than to receive. You especially hear that at Christmas time. Secondly, giving is what we are called to do in life. Not always worrying what we will receive in return.

Image your life in a giving mode rather than a getting mode. Always trying to serve others either through mowing a neighbor's yard, cutting a tree for a neighbor, delivering a gallon of milk and a loaf of bread just at the right time, right when someone needs it most. Be creative and pray to God for opportunities that will really shake things up on a good note. People love to be on the receiving end of a great giver. Try it today and see how you bless others.

PRAYER: Heavenly Father, thank You for Your love for me as a sinner saved by Your grace. Thank You for the act of giving your Son Jesus for my life and my sins. AMEN

## DON'T FORGET!

# ARE YOU GROWING?

SCRIPTURE: I Peter 2:1;4-5

WRITER: Peter

I Peter 2:1;4,5 'So get rid of all evil behavior. Be done with all deceit, hypocrisy, jealousy, and all unkind speech. You are coming to Christ, who is the living cornerstone of God's temple. He was rejected by people, but was chosen by God for great honor. And you are living stones that God is building into His spiritual temple. What's more, you are His holy priests.'

Are you growing in your faith? Does it really matter to you? Are you satisfied with just enough Bible knowledge to have conversations with friends? Are you still feeding on spiritual food that directs you to continue the desire to live a stronger life for Christ? Do you look for God's grace in places where you are really in need or are you living a complacent life that is just burning time?

Does your relationship with God really shape the way you think about and act in your marriage, in your friendships, in your parenting, in your job, in your finances, as a citizen or neighbor, in your private pursuits, or in the thoughts you have when you are alone? So, again, examine yourself and see exactly where you are with God and will you decide to work on you to be a better you.

Be honest today and truly evaluate where you are in your growth with Christ. It calls for a daily reunion, a committed prayer life, continual Bible study and then just allowing God to work through you to impact those people you are around. Remember that it takes grace to admit how much you still need grace. That grace is yours in Jesus.

PRAYER: Gracious Father, thank You for Your grace and mercy in our lives. Please continue to work in each of us to strive to grow more like You. AMEN

DON'T FORGET!

# GOD'S AGENDA

SCRIPTURE: James 1:12-15

WRITER: James

James 1:12-15 'God blesses those who patiently endure testing and temptation. Afterward they will receive the crown of life that God has promised to those who love Him. And remember, when you are being tempted, do not say, 'God is tempting me.' God is never tempted to do wrong, and he never tempts anyone else. Temptation comes from our own desires which entice us and drag us away. Those desires give birth to sinful actions.'

What is God doing in the here and now? How should I respond to it? Do you ever struggle with God's love, faithfulness, wisdom and goodness? Do you feel alone today? Do you feel as if you are trying to accomplish things on your own?

Remember this today, God isn't so much working to give you your perfect schedule of happiness. He's not committed to give you a predictable schedule, awesome relationships, comfortable surroundings without issues.

No, God has promised you Himself and what it brings to you in an unbelievable zest and his transforming grace. God is committed to your holiness. Through grace, God is wanting to deliver you from your biggest issue, sin. He provides much grace that takes control over any situation and provides eternal value.

The hardships you may be facing are exposure, forgiveness, liberation and transforming grace. In summary, rough moments aren't a part of your life because God is distant and uncaring, but rather because He loves You so much.

PRAYER: Lord God Almighty, help us not to be worried about our own agenda when we need to keep our focus on You. AMEN

DON'T FORGET!

# GOD GIVES US CHOICES

SCRIPTURES: Luke 9:23; Proverbs 10:9; John 8:12

WRITERS: Luke—Luke; Proverbs—Solomon; John—John

DEFINITION: follow—to pursue or run after; to imitate; to obey

Luke 9:23 'Then He said to the crowd, 'If any of you want to be My follower, you must give up your own way, take up your cross daily and follow Me!'

Proverbs 10:9 'People with integrity walk safely, but those who follow crooked paths will be exposed.'

John 8:12 'Jesus spoke to the people once more and said, 'I am the light of the world. If you follow Me, you won't have to walk in darkness, because you will have the light that leads to life.'

To follow Him or not, that is the question. Do you run after God? Do you pursue God? Do you even try to imitate and obey God? These are just a few questions that come to the surface of the topic today. God gives us choices. We do not have to follow Him and we can choose to go the other way. However, is that really what you want to do?

Look at the scriptures today and take note of exactly what God is giving us the opportunity to do. To give up our own way and choose to take up our cross and follow Him. You know that we are faced with the yellow sign of the fork of the road and yes, you will make a choice to follow.

Make a search around you and take note of all the things that are going on and how fast time is moving even in a pandemic like COVID-19. Today, I saw that 585,000 people have lost their lives to this terrible virus. We have to realize just how important life really is and say thank you God for who You are and how You move.

PRAYER: Dear Lord, I say thank You for the choice to follow You and the ways in which You call us to imitate You. AMEN

DON'T FORGET!

# LOVE YOUR ENEMIES

SCRIPTURE: Luke 6:27-30

WRITER: Luke

Luke 6:27-30 'But I say to you who listen; love your enemies, do what is good to those who hate you, bless those who curse you, pray for those who mistreat you. If anyone hits you on the cheek, offer the other also. And if anyone takes away your coat, don't hold back your shirt either. Give to everyone who asks you, and from someone who takes your things, don't ask for them back.'

Well, well, well....What a great topic. So, who is your enemy? Is it someone on the other team that perhaps is undefeated and you can never win a competition against them? Is it someone who harmed you or a family member and you view them as a threat? Good questions to ponder and they all have merit but don't forget that Satan is our enemy and he wants to destroy each of us with his lies and persuasion. Don't allow it!

Jesus calls us to a different approach. A radical approach that is to love, serve, bless and pray. That all sounds good but what about when we come in contact with our enemies-the ones that cut us to the core and the ones that trash us?

We are called to forgive the person, do good to the person and bless the person, if we are going to be unconditional about our calling. So this is our test on a daily basis.

The Christian life is a life of sacrifice. Sacrifices may be in the areas of money, time, schedules, energy, goals or expectations.

Let's remember that in John 13:34, we are given a new commandment: Love each other. Just as I have loved you, you should love each other. Your love for one another will prove to the world that you are my disciples.

PRAYER: Lord God, please help us work on us and not have enemies. Through You we can make relationships work and live in love with our neighbors. AMEN

DON'T FORGET!

# BE AN OVERCOMER

SCRIPTURE: John 16:33

WRITER: John

DEFINITION: overcome—to get better of; to overwhelm

John 16:33 'I have told you all this so that you may have peace in Me. Here on earth, you will have many trials and sorrows. But take heart, because I have overcome the world.'

I often share with those closest to me that we haven't come this far just to come this far. I heard that statement during an ESPN interview of a professional baseball player who nearly passed away with a bad illness. He rose to the occasion through faith in God and the necessary medical attention that he needed.

You don't fight the good fight hard day in and day out to just give up regardless of whatever you are experiencing. You also don't survive that which was meant to destroy you by chance. The devil will come to do everything he can but he will not be allowed to prosper.

So, I say to you today, never back down from anything you are going through just because it may seem too hard. Look to the cross and see Jesus. Jesus did not take Himself off the cross when things got tough. He endured and kept His commitment to his Father to see things through. He simply asked and called upon his Father. Push through the rubble of life, the losses and the pain, because on the other side of the mess and stuff are the promises God has just for you. If Jesus could die to deliver them, we can fight to receive them.

Push through whatever you are going through and know Jesus is there waiting with open arms.

PRAYER: Dear Father, thank You for overcoming the world. We thank You for helping us each day to look to You for our best. AMEN

DON'T FORGET!

# DOES GOD STILL HAVE A PLAN?

SCRIPTURES: I Corinthians 9:17; II Corinthians 5:8; II Peter 3:9

WRITERS: I & II Corinthians—Paul; II Peter—Peter

I Corinthians 9:17 'If I were doing this on my own initiative, I would deserve payment. But I have no choice, for God has given me this sacred trust.'

II Corinthians 5:8 'Yes, we are fully confident, and we would rather be away from the earthly bodies for then we will be at home with the Lord.'

II Peter 3:9 'The Lord isn't really being slow about His promise, as some people think. No, He is being patient for your sake. He does not want anyone to be destroyed, but wants everyone to repent.'

Do you have a plan in your life and for your life? More specifically, do you believe God still has a plan for you? If you say yes, how do you know and what do you look for to know it?

Let's take a step back and see what God is doing in your life and how exactly it fits into your life and into his plan. Let's start at looking at your relationship with God first. Do you have a personal relationship that you strive to live for each day? Are you where every waking moment is about that relationship and how you wish to develop that relationship to the fullest? If not, this is a great time to make a personal commitment and follow Christ.

Secondly, let's take a look at a few other areas in your life, like your family, your career, and the friends that you hang out with each day. Who is in control of those relationships and how are they prompted by God each day?

When we look at God's Word, we see that when we are in Him, things work for us. We have to be patient, depend on Him and trust Him to work in us and our relationships. God truly does have a plan for each of us.

PRAYER: Dear Heavenly Father, breathe on us for all that we do and experience. We love You and trust you for everything. AMEN

DON'T FORGET!

# REMEMBER

SCRIPTURE: Daniel 2:22

WRITER: Daniel

Daniel 2:22 'He knows what is in the darkness, and light dwells with him.'

How important is life to you? Have you ever known of someone that had such a close call and how life could have gone either way? I experienced that with my middle daughter during her time in college. I remember the call so vividly. I was told my daughter had been in a wreck and not just an ordinary wreck, a motorcycle wreck. I had had many conversations with my three daughters concerning ever being on a motorcycle. If nothing else, make sure to wear a helmet for protection. I quickly went to the hospital to find the EMS vehicle pulling in and rolling my daughter out on a stretcher. I did not know what to think other than Dear God, please spare my daughter's life. When she passed by me to enter the hospital, she looked at me and said, Hey Dad, I'm sorry that I didn't mind you and went against what you told me. I told her that I was glad she was alive and that we could work through anything for her recovery. I remember....

Our journey on her rehab for the next 100 days was just beginning. A broken pelvis from being thrown some 20 feet in the air and landing on the asphalt on her right shoulder, right side of her face and top side of her feet. By the grace of God, a plastic surgeon was with one of my physician friends and set up an appointment at his office after the first 24 hours so he could make sure the process went well and was handled properly. I remember....

We moved her from her apartment into our sunroom and I took time off from work the next 100 days to take care of her and love on her. I often shared with her, 'It's Dad, you are not alone and God is with you too.' I held onto the thought that our lives were not out of control, just a period of time during life that we needed to really trust God and lean on Him. I remember....

Remember today that there is one who looks at what you see as

340

dark and sees light. And as you remember that, remember too, that He is the ultimate definition of everything that is wise, good, true, loving, and faithful. Trust in Him for all you do. My daughter made a full recovery and looks as beautiful today as she did before her accident. I remember....

PRAYER: Dear Lord, I am thankful for my children, their health, their safety, their life and just how proud I am of each of them in all they do. I remember.... AMEN

DON'T FORGET!

# SEEK STEADFASTNESS

SCRIPTURE: James 1:2-12

WRITER: James

DEFINITION: steadfastness—faithful, strong, keeping the faith

James 1:1-12 'Count it all joy, my brothers, when you meet trials of various kinds, for you know that the testing of your faith produces steadfastness. And let steadfastness have its full effect, that you may be perfect and complete, lacking in nothing.'

What is God doing in your life now? He is impacting the difficulties of life as a means of grace to produce character in you that would not grow any other way. Remember God has not forgotten you and He is committed to His grace and will not forsake it – it will complete its work in you.

James says, 'remain steadfast under trial.' Don't become discouraged and give up in anything you are experiencing. Don't listen to the lies of the devil. Don't forsake your good habits of faith. Don't question God's goodness. When you look at your trials, you will see grace.

We serve an awesome God who is steadfast in every area of life. The question is, whether or not we will recognize what He is doing around us for us to truly see his works in us. We will have difficulties and our Redeemer will show us he is completing his wonderful work.

Be thankful today for the trials and challenges that you experience and know they will make you stronger.

PRAYER: Father God, thank You for helping us to seek steadfastness in our life always looking to You for our strength. AMEN

DON'T FORGET!

# CAN YOU FIGURE IT OUT?

SCRIPTURE: Isaiah 26:3

WRITER: Isaiah

Isaiah 26:3 'You keep him in perfect peace whose mind is stayed on you, because he trusts in you.'

Are you discouraged today? Do you have a lot of things on your mind? Are you trying to take care of understanding things all on your own without God? Even though you may have a lot of biblical knowledge, sometimes we become confused with everything that we face in life. There are perhaps times when you just notice that you are doing everything you can do but just cannot figure things out.

How is your faith today? Is it strong or is it weak and needing a lot of help? The right avenue and answer for you is true Biblical faith. You need to be in the loving hands of Jesus each day and that happens with true peace and lasting faith in the one who loves you the most.

God understands where you are and He also knows that you are trying to be in control and also solving things on your own terms. Why? Why do you want to put yourself through that when you have a choice? Sometimes we make things a lot harder than we really need to.

I am reminded of a church acquaintance that was always on the cusp of figuring things out in his life but never could. He could talk a great game and sound very smart but ultimately, he could not ever figure things out. He would always blame others for where he was and his situation because, he really was not trusting God and depending on Him.

Lean on God today to help you in figuring things out in this very important Christian walk.

PRAYER: Most Gracious Lord, we thank You for all You do in our lives and ask for rest and peace in the moments that we face things that we don't understand. AMEN

DON'T FORGET!

# ALWAYS LOOKING FOR MORE

SCRIPTURE: Genesis 1:2

WRITER: Moses

When was the last time that you were disappointed? Maybe a job position, an achievement, a personal relationship or even a start-up idea you had and perhaps someone rained on your parade. I am here to share with you today that life is about making a difference. Always looking for more in life is okay if it is in the right context.

Let's take a walk today. We are going to climb Mt. Everest. The reason I am qualified to share with you about Mt. Everest is because I have a close friend that became the youngest to climb all seven of the toughest climbs and live to share about it.

I knew Jobie when he was just in grade school and he would come and watch me play basketball in high school and then in college. He always had high aspirations to be great and I can for sure share with you that Jobie was always looking for more. Always inspired to tactfully think out the next big climb, the timing, the risk, the wind factors, the base camp locations, his guides and the unexplainable 'what ifs' that might occur during the climbs.

Attitude as we know is always so important in life. It carries us from good times through rough times back to the top of the mountain to be able to share our story.

What I appreciate most about Jobie is his steadfastness in his Christian walk as well as the daily pressure that is upon him each day with timing and precise movements that are so important to every step along his journey.

My friend, the Christian life for us is no different. We too, have daily pressure, timing of relationships and precise movements with our tongue when we speak to our neighbors and our friends. We experience valleys and mountaintops but we also have great experiences along the way through the faith that

God gives us. My challenge today for you is always look for more in Christ.

PRAYER: Most Gracious Lord, thank You for helping us to always look for more in this life through You. AMEN

DON'T FORGET!

# UNDER THE SHADOW
# OF THE CROSS

SCRIPTURES: Psalm 130

WRITER: David

Think about where you are. Think about what you will think and say. You are in the shadow of the cross. This is the place that Grace arose for our sins and transgressions.

What are you bringing with you today on your shoulders that you cannot carry any longer? Is it guilt, blame, anger, shame, envy, ill will or just good ole mediocrity? What sins are mounting up and weighing heavy on your heart that you just need to gently unload at the foot of the cross and say, Lord, please take all of this and deal with it for me. I just can't do it without You.

You know that God awaits you each day for you to join Him in the shadow of the cross and to share your heart in a very intimate way. A way that can only be through God's unexplainable grace that covers everything, all the time in every instance. That should give each of us the confidence we need to trust in Him.

Are you running as fast as you can away from God or are you fighting for the finish line because He is waiting on you to greet you and congratulate you for trusting in him to be right there by your side?

What are some specific things in your life that are keeping you from the shadow of the cross? Are these things material things or spiritual things? Allow God to help you identify them so you can work through those items so you can begin again to live for Him.

PRAYER: Most Gracious Heavenly Father, thank You for Your shadow that gives us shade from the tough things in life. We are not worthy of all You do for us but we thank You. AMEN

DON'T FORGET!

# BRIGHTER COLORS EXIST

SCRIPTURE: Hebrews 4:16

WRITER: unknown

Hebrews 4:16 'So let us come boldly to the throne of our gracious God. There we will receive His mercy, and we will find grace to help us when we need it most.'

# A PRAYER

Dear God,

I love you because....in a world that only sees what is wrong with me, you choose to always see what is right with me. All my life, people try to make me conform to their standard of what is right and how we should be. They tell you to be yourself then judge you if they don't approve of your choices.

For so long, that's just how I thought everything and everyone would always be....UNTIL YOU

You didn't criticize my flaws; you celebrated my imperfections. You saw the person that I stowed inside and slowly began to win my trust, my heart, and my soul. You didn't push, force or overwhelm. You just let me be myself, loved me for everything I am in a way that I had never know.

In an instant you changed the story of my life with a chapter I couldn't have seen coming. You sent Godly parents and grandparents to impact wisdom, love and knowledge moving forward that would mold me into the person I am today. I thought the world was full of the same people doing the same things and thinking the same way.

You proved me wrong and I have never been happier to be wrong. It is so much more than just love too. You have accepted me unconditionally from the moment I was born. All my jagged edges and broken pieces, you accepted without question or hesitation. You hugged them tightly and made me realize that everything will be okay. You have shown me that love isn't a word, it's a power that escapes definition and changed my world, my heart and my mindset. You, God, love me in such a way that it empowers me to love myself, my life, my future and my neighbor as You love us all.

I've found that the darkness that sometimes comes allow for me to take Your hand and be shown the way exactly through Your eyes. Then, all things exist in a much brighter color because of you. AMEN

DON'T FORGET!

# ARE YOU WILLING TO
# SETTLE FOR LESS?

SCRIPTURE: Matthew 4:8-11

WRITER: Matthew

Matthew 4:8-11 'Next the devil took to the peak of a very high mountain and showed Him all the kingdoms of the world and their glory. 'I will give it all to You,' he said, 'if you will kneel down and worship me.' 'Get out of here, Satan,' Jesus told him. For the scriptures say, 'You must worship the Lord your God and serve only Him.' Then the devil went away and angels came and took care of Him.'

Ever have one of those moments when you remember a time from your past that was a teaching moment? I had a terrific PawPaw who instilled in me to always impact your neighbor. So, off I go to start mowing between my home and my next-door neighbor, Mr. Red. Mr. Red was a large burley, strong fellow and up until now, I had only seen him in his front yard. I would greet him with a wave, he never waved back.

As I am mowing my first strips, my head is down concentrating on keeping my lines straight. All of a sudden, out of the corner of my eye, I see a large man standing in my mowing line. I could go no farther and he has his arms folded and stopped me dead in my tracks. I turn off my mower and he informed me that I was mowing on his side of the yard and I better not do it again. He left and went back in his house. I could only think that his coming out as a brand-new neighbor was to get me to stoop to a low point and say something negative. I chose to settle for more rather than less and recall the instruction from my PawPaw had given me to strive to keep my witness strong.

Time went on and years passed. I always showed respect to Mr. Red. We never became close neighbors until an event occurred. I began to miss seeing Mr. Red and eventually his wife came over and told my family that Mr. Red had stage 4 cancer and was not expected to live. At that point, the Holy Spirit prompted me to ask if I could have the honor of mowing the yard and keeping the yard up indefinitely. She said yes and I now went back to the area where Mr. Red had stopped me and I thanked God that I did not settle for less.

I had the opportunity to visit Mr. Red in the hospital and just as I walked in, I guess his wife had shared with him that I committed to take care of the yard. He broke down and cried, he then offered his hand in friendship and apologized. I accepted and shared Christ with him and he died literally days later and is in heaven today. What about you today? Will you settle for less or strive for all you can give?

PRAYER: Dear God, thank You for that special day at the hospital with Mr. Red. Thank You for friendship and forgiveness. AMEN

DON'T FORGET!

# WITH CHRIST – A, B, C's

SCRIPTURES: Romans 6:23; I Corinthians 10:4

WRITER: Romans—Paul; I Corinthians—Paul

Romans 6:23 'For the wages of sin is death, but the free gift of God is eternal life through Christ Jesus our Lord.

I Corinthians 10:4 'And all of them drank the same spiritual water. For they drank from the spiritual rock that traveled with them, and that rock was Christ.'

Able, Abundance, Acceptance, Advocate, Alive, Almighty, Always, Ambition, Attitude, Assurance, Beautiful, Beginning, Believe, Belonging, Blessed, Born, Branch, Brightness, Building, Called, Care, Carried, Celebrated, Changed, Cheerful, Chosen, Character, Christlike, Church, Cleansed, Comforted, Commanded, Committed, Compassion, Complete, Confidence, Content, Converted, Cornerstone, Courageous, Covenant, Covered, Created, Cross, Crown, Cultivated, Cared.

These are but a few of the A, B, Cs with Christ.

I begin by sharing that we are able to live in abundance because of Jesus' acceptance in our lives. He is our advocate because He is alive and Almighty God. He always shares for us to have ambition in our life and exhibit an attitude that shows assurance in Him. His love for us is beautiful and is only the beginning of what He has in store for us. I believe that belonging to Christ, I am blessed. I have been born and am a branch that can reach others with a brightness that only comes from Him. He is building me because I am called to care for others because He carried me through my transgressions. I have celebrated a changed life in Christ and now, I am cheerful and I have chosen to follow Him all the days of my life. As we know, character is an important trait to be Christlike and the church shares with us we must be cleansed by the blood of Jesus.

I am comforted daily to know that God has commanded me to be committed and to have compassion for my neighbor. I am complete in Christ because He gives me the confidence, I need to be content in Him. I have been converted because Jesus is the cornerstone. He lived a courageous life and has given each of us His new covenant. He covered our sins and created a newness of life after paying the ultimate price on the cross. He wears a crown today because his Father cultivated in Him a perfect life and therefore, we are cured by acceptance and following Him.

May I challenge you to take the same A, B, C's and build your own story of what it means to you to be with Christ.

PRAYER: Dear God, it does not matter how we use the words, it all points to you. AMEN

DON'T FORGET!

# WHO IS HOLDING YOU?

SCRIPTURE: I Corinthians 10:12-13

WRITER: Paul

I Corinthians 10:12-13 'If you think you are standing strong, be careful not to fall. The temptations in your life are no different from what others experience. And God is faithful. He will not allow the temptation to be more than you can stand. When you are tempted, He will show a way out so that you can endure.'

What is holding you? Is it a situation of grip that will not let you go? Is it something that you have been trying to break away from and for some reason, you can't? Think for a moment and ponder the answers to these questions.

Is your happiness in question in your life? Is God present or absent in your daily walk of life? Is money so important to you that buying your way in and out of things might be where your wallet and your heart are at this time?

If you remember, the rich young man that was striving to follow all of the commandments, do the right things and complete good deeds to get him where he felt he needed to be. Once he approached Jesus about following Him, He told him to sell everything he owned and give the money away and follow Him. The rich young man balked and chose not to follow Him due to having to give up his assets.

I hate to say it but a lot of people are in the position of the rich young man. They are holding on for dear life not to let go of the 'stuff' of life and therefore, going all over the board when it comes to living a fulfilled life in Christ.

Are there things in your life that you can't live without? If you experienced a loss, what would it do for you in your normal daily life? Lastly, and more importantly, where does God fit in to all you are doing? Is stuff holding you or is God holding you?

PRAYER: Most Gracious Father, thank You for Your love and Your watchful care over my life. May I always be in tune with You and keep my focus obediently following You. AMEN

DON'T FORGET!

# HEARTBEAT OF THE CROSS

SCRIPTURES: Deuteronomy 6:5; Romans 2:29; I Timothy 1:5

WRITERS: Deuteronomy—Moses; Romans—Paul, Timothy—Timothy

Deuteronomy 6:5 'And you must love the Lord your God with all your heart, all your soul, and all your strength.'

Romans 2:29 'No, a true Jew is one whose heart is right with God. And true circumcision is not merely obeying the letter of the law; rather, it is a change of heart produced by the Spirit. And a person with a changed heart seeks praise from God, not people.'

I Timothy 1:5 'The purpose of my instruction is that all believers would be filled with love that comes from a pure heart, a clear conscience, and genuine faith.'

I have recently been given a battery of tests for updated bloodwork, EKG, and normal routine checkups. It came to mind while sitting in the chair watching the monitor as the lines went up and down with each heartbeat that Jesus is the heartbeat of the cross. Deuteronomy 6:5 clearly states that we must love the Lord your God with all your heart, all your soul, and all your strength. Are you truly giving all you have to give each and every heartbeat? Does it make sense that we do not want to miss one beat? That means one opportunity to share the gospel with someone that you have been meaning to speak with as it hit your heart.

The lines on the machine are bright just like the light of Christ in our lives. Our hearts flutter each beat as we are impressed to follow the direction of our Lord in all that we do.

As you go about your normal workday, be looking for the next beat that God is providing. Each day that we are blessed to have life, we should be so thankful and be able to share with others how precious life really is. I challenge you to be the Heartbeat of Christ today.

PRAYER: Dear God Almighty, thank You for all of Your blessings each day. May our heartbeat be constant in me in all that I do. AMEN

DON'T FORGET!

# CONDITIONS TO APPRECIATE

SCRIPTURE: Galatians 5:22-23

WRITER: Paul

Galatians 5:22-23 'But the Holy Spirit produces this kind of fruit in our lives; love, joy, peace, patience, kindness, goodness, faithfulness, gentleness, and self-control. There is no law against these things.'

I want to introduce you to my friend Ron. Ron is seventy years old and a co-worker with me in the landscape area here at Oakdale. Ron is about to exit the federal system and go home to his two sons and his thirteen-year-old granddaughter. She has Asperger's, on the autistic spectrum, and he is really looking forward to spending time with her.

Ron has made me feel very welcome at work and we both together lead our group of seven each work day. He always has each of the kinds of fruits in the scripture reading. He is always smiling, cutting up and showing out in a good way. He has served 50% of his sentence along with having some fairly extreme health issues such as open-heart surgery, diabetes, high blood pressure just to mention a few.

I was able to hear the rest of the story the other day as to how he is a POW-Prisoner of War from the Vietnam war. He was a platoon leader that was captured and served time under some very dire situations. He along with the rest of his rifle team was tortured and made sure he could not move around and flee captivity. Food was scarce, the living conditions for 9 months were very strenuous and the idea of survival was in every thought of every minute. The two governments finally worked out an agreement that released my friend, Ron.

I think about how we each have conditions in life to deal with and I thanked Ron for his service to our country and to his platoon in the Marines. Think about the conditions that you work in and live in today and strive to be happy with where God has placed you and blessed you.

PRAYER: Dear God, thank You for men and women like Ron who willingly gave a commitment to serve our country. Help us to do likewise in serving You our mighty God! AMEN

DON'T FORGET!

# LORD

SCRIPTURES: Deuteronomy 6:5, Psalm 23:1

WRITERS: Deuteronomy—Moses; Psalm—David

DEFINITION: Lord—highest one, honored one, master, God or Jesus

Deuteronomy 6:5 'And you must love the Lord your God with all your heart, all your soul, and all your strength. And you must commit yourselves wholeheartedly to these commands that I am giving you today.'

Psalm 23:1 'The Lord is my shepherd; I have all I need.'

What a great honor to bring to you today the greatest of all times. My Savior, Jesus Christ, My Lord, My Heavenly Father. Let me share with you that our small group Bible study had the topic of Lord and I decided to carry it a step farther and write a devotion for us to share about.

We see 'Lord' used a number of times in the Bible as in 'Lord Bless you and protect you' which by the way, He has and does. Psalm 100:5 says 'For the Lord is good. His unfailing love continues forever, and his faithfulness continues to each generation.' Then Psalm 121:2 says 'My help comes from the Lord, who made heaven and earth! He will not let you stumble.'

We have so many great promises from our Lord that we just have to step back and look at his faithfulness and just ways.

I want to share with you today that the Lord is first and foremost in my life and has been for now fifty years. My parents were instrumental in leading me to the Lord at First Baptist Church in Hobbs, New Mexico under Pastor Bailey Smith. Being in prison I am so thankful to have a personal relationship with Christ and know that He is with me every step of my life.

Miracles are happening here at Oakdale with inmates going home at 50% of their statutory sentence. That means if their sentence is five years, they leave after two and a half years of time served. That is a blessing only from the Lord.

PRAYER: Dear God, thank You for all You do in my life. I call you Lord because You are my Savior, my God, and my life. Because of You, everything else is blessed in my life. AMEN

DON'T FORGET!

# GOD WON'T FORGIVE THIS SIN

SCRIPTURE: Matthew 12:22-23

WRITER: Matthew

Matthew 12:22-23 'Then a demon possessed man, who was blind and couldn't speak, was brought to Jesus. He healed the man so that he could both speak and see. The crowd was amazed and asked, 'Could it be that Jesus is the Son of David, the Messiah?'

Question......Growing up, what was the 'unforgivable sin' in your home?

Answer.........Lying and not minding my parents.

What was it for you when you were young? The answers will vary but I can tell you having three daughters, the same held true in our home. I wanted my girls to mind, be respectful and to always tell the truth.

The setting in Matthew is an occasion of Jesus healing the man who suffered from 3 distinct ailments—blindness, mute, and demon possessed.

Attention....here is not so much the miracle itself, but the attention of what would follow.

We assume that this man used all available resources to him to try and remedy his situation. Only until Jesus saved him did he get healed. Others brought him to Jesus – they heard, believed, and knew he was the only one to change and heal him.

Verses 30-22 of Matthew addressed straight forward that our relationship to Jesus can have no neutrality. Jesus is the one who will harvest in the last days.

Blasphemy was viewed as extreme slander – speaking against. Blasphemy against the son of man is forgivable, but blasphemy against the Holy Spirit, is not.

Thoughtfully, willingly, self-consciously rejecting the work of the Spirit even though there can be no other explanation of Jesus exorcisms. For such sin, there is no forgiveness either in this age or the age to come. Since it is only by being drawn by the Spirit that a person can be drawn to God, to blaspheme and grieve away the Holy Spirit leaves that person forever guilty. Keep your eyes on Jesus each and every day and be obedient to Him.

PRAYER: Most Gracious Lord, thank You for forgiveness each day. We always want to strive for excellence in You. AMEN

DON'T FORGET!

# THERE IS NO SAFETY IN SIN

SCRIPTURES: I Peter 4:8; Psalm 86:5; Romans 5:8

WRITERS: I Peter—Peter; Psalm 86—David; Romans—Paul

DEFINITION: sin—moral evil, transgression of or rebellion against God's law; separation, disobedience, missing the mark

Romans 5:8 'But God showed his great love for us by sending Christ to die for us while we were still sinners.'

Psalm 86:5 'O Lord, You are so good, so ready to forgive, so full of unfailing love for all who ask for Your help.'

I Peter 4:8 'Most important of all, continue to show deep love for each other for love covers a multitude of sins.'

The topic of 'SIN' is a very broad topic in our world today. It first started with Adam and Eve; they disobeyed God. Not much has changed over all of these years as it relates to sin. They are all listed in the Bible from gossiping, lying, cheating, lusting, stealing, murdering, selfishness, envy, and the list is very long as it continues.

There is not one thing good about sin other than recognizing it in our life and us bringing it to Jesus and asking for forgiveness.

Sin affects family, friends and relationships in so many ways because of the negative effect it as associated with it. It breaks down everything it touches and it truly swarms like a host of bees looking for honey or something sweet. However, there is nothing sweet about sin.

Why are we drawn back to sin time and time again? Why are we selfish when it comes to thinking about ourself and not avoiding sin?

Isaiah 41:10 says, 'Don't be afraid, for I am with you. Don't be discouraged, for I am your God. I will strengthen you and help you. I will hold you up with My victorious right hand.'

Do we really need anything more instructional? God is with us regardless of what we encounter.

PRAYER: Dear Lord, we pray today for forgiveness of sin in our lives. Help us to keep our heart, mind and soul on You. AMEN

DON'T FORGET!

# WHAT IS IT WITH CANCER?

SCRIPTURE: I Corinthians 6:7

WRITER: Paul

DEFINITION: cancer—something foreign in the body that endangers life

I Corinthians 6:7 'Even to have such lawsuits with one another is a defeat for you. Why not accept the injustice and leave it at that? Why not let yourselves be cheated?

I remember very vividly in May 2010 having completed my first book, "The Don't Forgets of Life.' The project had basically gone on for some three years and I just could not rest on the completion for one reason or another. I had moved some content around, more specifically in different headings like, wisdom, love, perseverance and friendship, just to name a few. However, once I had completed the book, the book publisher asked when I would be writing my second book. I wished I had looked in the mirror at my facial expression when I was asked that question! I told them quickly that it would not be anytime soon since the last one lasted some three years. As we finished our discussion and just as I was getting off of the phone, I was asked to pray about my next book and the title so it could be printed on the last pages to promote what was coming next. I agreed and told him I would pray about it and get back in a few days or weeks, however long.

The timing actually was one day. I called the guy back and told him, 'Cancer, The Don't Forgets of Cancer.' This title was burning in my heart. Literally a couple of months later when the book came out and I was sending copies to my family and friends, I received a call from my oldest daughter. She said, 'Dad, I have this funny feeling in my throat and it hurts.' I told her to go to the doctor and she literally did the next day. She called me back and told me, 'Dad, I have cancer of the thyroid. It took three surgeries and aggressive treatment to get rid of it. That is one of the main reasons I dislike cancer and everything that goes and comes with it. It's like sin which is out to destroy our body, our witness, our adventure in life and what far reaching touch it has.

By the way, my daughter had a full recovery and two years ago was blessed to have a son that is 100% healthy today!

DON'T FORGET!

# SECRET INGREDIENT

SCRIPTURES: II Corinthians 9:8; II Corinthians 1:24

WRITERS: Corinthians—Paul

DEFINITION: secret ingredient—surprise

II Corinthians 9:8 'And God will generously provide all you need. Then you will always have everything you need and plenty left over to share with others.'

II Corinthians 1:24 'But that does not mean we want to dominate you by telling you how to put your faith into practice. We want to work together with you so you will be full of joy, for it is by your own faith that you stand firm.'

We all have special recipes that we love to cook and when we do, we want to add in the special ingredient that makes the dish all worthwhile. I love cooking on the grill and trying new things to spice up and tenderize the meats I cook and I also have lots of cannisters of mixes, rubs, etc. to try out.

What is your special ingredient that comes to mind for you in any dish? It is listed as a secret ingredient because you don't tell many people, right? Some people I know will never share that information.

Is it like that for you in your daily walk? Do you keep things to yourself about Christ or are you willing to share with others what He is doing in your life? Are you excited to the point in life where people have to know that the secret ingredient in the equation for you is that personal one on one with Christ? Be willing to share with others so they may experience the secret in your life.

PRAYER: Lord God Almighty, thank You for Your love and watchful care in all that we do. Help us to be vocal about You and what You mean to us. AMEN

DON'T FORGET!

# IMPORTANCE OF THE LORD'S SUPPER

SCRIPTURE: Luke 22:14-16

WRITER: Luke

Luke 22:14-16 'When the time came, Jesus and the apostles sat down together at the table. Jesus said, 'I have been very eager to eat this Passover meal with you before my suffering begins. For I tell you now that I won't eat this meal again until it's meaning is fulfilled in the Kingdom of God.'

I cannot think of a more honoring observance than that of the Lord's Supper. Today, I am going to share with you my view points from a couple of different angles only because the angles have occurred in my life as one being served the Lord's Supper as well as one serving the Lord's Supper.

First, let me say that I recently had to opportunity to lead the Easter Service here at Oakdale Federal Prison at the Camp location. Preparation time throughout the week I thought was on tract until I found out that due to the COVID-19 protocol, there would be no serving of elements as in the juice for representation of Jesus' blood shed for our sins as well as the bread to represent the breaking of Jesus' body for our sins. I have to say it was a big letdown for everyone because Easter and Resurrection Sunday is engrained in every believer's heart.

I think back to times that I sat in the pew, listening to the Pastor prepare each person for the serving of the elements. Jesus spoke about making ourselves right with Him and a clean heart before taking the Lord's Supper. This is a great reminder for each of us to step back quietly and pray for a real clear picture of our heart and the preparation of respectfully worshipping in the right way.

Back to our Easter service, the night before our service the Holy Spirit prompted me to locate the grape juice and the crackers and we respectfully moved forward to honor God in serving the Lord's Supper and not following man. We serve a risen Savior and He said it was worth it for our sins and we need to say He is worth it for us.

PRAYER: Dear Father, thank You for how the Lord's Supper renews our daily commitment of our walk with You. May it always glorify You. AMEN

DON'T FORGET!

# GATHERING OR SCATTERING?

SCRIPTURE: Mark 4:4-9

WRITER: Mark

Mark 4:4-9 'As he scattered it across his field, some of the seed fell on a footpath, and the birds came by and ate it. Other seed fell on the shallow soil with underlying rock. The seed sprouted quickly because the soil was shallow. But the plant soon wilted under the hot sun, and since it didn't have deep roots, it died. Other seed fell among thorns that grew up and choked out the tender plants so they produced no grain. Still other seeds fell on fertile soil. And they sprouted, grew and produced a crop that was thirty, sixty and even a hundred times as much as had been planted? The he said, 'Anyone with ears to hear should listen and understand.'

Listen and understand is the command here in these very important verses. The footpath where some of the seed falls is the person who is busy with life. The person that falls into the category is not involved in a lot of sin, just too busy for God and has a hard heart. They are involved in church activities but they are too occupied with everything else in their life.

Ultimately, we see a footpath where seed falls and we have a different outlook because this person is viewed as the fertile soil. They are growing and producing a crop so to speak because they have God involved in their life on a regular basis. God is the daily focus and very few things distort this pathway. Here we see the gospel getting through.

Maybe this is a great time for you to look inside and see whether or not you are gathering or scattering.

PRAYER: Most Gracious Lord, thank You for our daily journey. It is sometimes overwhelming to see when we question things, He becomes the answer. Thank You for your perfect timing. AMEN

DON'T FORGET!

# UPROOTING OF THE OLD
# AND PLANTING OF THE NEW

SCRIPTURES: I Corinthians 3:6; II Peter 3:18

WRITERS: I Corinthians—Paul; II Peter—Peter

DEFINITION: grow—to become; to spring up and develop to maturity

I Corinthians 3:6 'I planted the seeds in your hearts, and Apollos watered it, but it was God who made it grow. It's not important who does the planting, or who does the watering. What's important is that God makes the seed grow.'

II Peter 3:18 'Rather, you must grow in the grace and knowledge of our Lord and Savior Jesus Christ. All glory to Him, both now and forever! Amen'

Do you have a green thumb when it comes to gardening? I know a very special Master Gardener that has just uprooted the old plants from last fall and has recultivated the soil and pulled all the weeds. Once having finished doing those things, the soil is turned and new landscape mix fertilizer is added to prepare to plant new plants. New color brings about a new life for flower beds and also makes the front of your home look beautiful.

Once the beds are ready, new plants and bushes are ready to be set in and then lastly, watered in to begin the growing process.

Think about what I have shared with you and how it correlates with cleaning out our old habits, reading God's word to help cultivate our hearts and the fertilizer is how we feed our minds with Godly intake each day. This makes our life look beautiful being in harmony with Christ.

God no doubt makes everything grow for us but we do have to choose to uproot the old and plant the new to make that happen.

PRAYER: Father God, You are the Master Gardener in our lives. Help us to rid ourselves of the weeds and trash that we need to clean out. Plant in us a newness that others may see. AMEN

DON'T FORGET!

# PATIENCE PLEASE

SCRIPTURES: Revelation 14:12; I Corinthians 13:4; I Thessalonians 5:14

WRITERS: Revelation—John; I Corinthians—Paul; I Thessalonians—Paul

DEFINITION: patience—the power or capacity to endure without complaint, something difficult or disagreeable; forbearance, longsuffering; bearing pains or trials calmly or without complaint, steadfast despite opposition, difficulty, or adversity; not hasty or impetuous

Revelation 14:12 'This means that God's holy people must endure persecution patiently obeying His commands and maintaining their faith in Jesus.'

I Corinthians 13:4 'Love is patient and kind. Love is not jealous or boastful or proud or rude.'

I Thessalonians 5:14 'Brothers and sisters, we urge you to warn those who are lazy. Encourage those who are timid. Take tender care of those who are weak. Be patient with everyone.'

Wow…I have to share with you that this topic is one that I really have challenges with from time to time. No doubt now, more than ever before in my life primarily due to the personal things that have gone on with my indictment, through my sentencing and now being away from loved ones, family and friends.

So, what does patience mean to you in the fast-paced world that we live in? Off the cuff, my definition was kind of hard to express but here it is: standing back and allowing things to happen in God's timing; one's ability to patiently wait. Not to rush, understanding and being still.

I think the few interesting words in the definition to me were WITHOUT complaint and also STEADFAST despite opposition and difficulty. Those are very interesting words to piece together in the midst of having to be patient.

Look at the three scripture references for today and take note how the writers encourage patiently obeying God's commands, maintaining faith and being patient with everyone. Let me encourage you today to do the same.

PRAYER: Almighty God, thank You for Your patience in my life. I don't deserve the second chances but I thank You and praise You. AMEN

DON'T FORGET!

# A GOOD DEED THAT
# CANNOT BE RETURNED

SCRIPTURES: Luke 9:23; John 12:24; Romans 12:1

WRITERS: Luke, John, Paul

Luke 9:23 'And [Jesus] said to all, 'If anyone would come after Me, let him deny himself and take up his cross daily and follow Me.'

John 12:24 'Truly, truly, I say unto you, unless a grain of wheat falls into the earth and dies, it remains alone; but if it dies, it bears much fruit.'

Romans 12:1 'I appeal to you therefore, brothers, by the mercies of God, to present your bodies as a living sacrifice, holy and acceptable to God, which is your spiritual worship.'

I am often reminded how awesome I have been blessed to have Christian parents who brought me up in a Christian home, took us to church when the doors were open and ministered to us at home on how to become a Christian and then finally, to see my parents live it out each day. I am most thankful to God above for that blessing. I am also thankful that there are grandparents and great grandparents and yes, they are impacting each of them in a special way as well even as I write this devotion. A good deed that cannot be returned.

I also look back to early years in my life growing up and not only having Godly parents but I also had a PawPaw and MeeMee that instilled in my parents the Godly traits that have ultimately impacted my life and thereby being able to impact my children and my grandchildren because of them. A good deed that cannot be returned.

Lastly, yet most importantly in my live is that of my Lord and Savior, Jesus Christ doing what He did for me on Calvary's cross. Paying not only for my sins but the sins of the world. My life has meaning and value to a God who created me and provides a beautiful world to have meaningful love relationships and also neighbors that we are call to love as well. This is a good deed that cannot be returned.

PRAYER: Heavenly Father, I am so moved and so thankful for You. You gave the deed that cannot be returned. You gave Your all and I wish to always give my all. AMEN

DON'T FORGET!

# ARE YOU READY?

SCRIPTURE: Genesis 32:12

WRITER: Moses

Genesis 32:12 'You said, I will surely treat you well.'

The couple gathered on the couch to began planning their trip out of town and now it was time to do the detailed part of the trip…book the flight. The couple worked diligently to make sure the seats they selected has extra leg space, an exit row has extra space to move around. Then, hit select to purchase the upgrades. Then, reserving the lodging for the days they were planning and lastly to select the right clothes for the weather that was expected. A backpack to have as a carry on and then to make final plans on what time to arrive at the airport for check in.

Are you ready for takeoff in life? The Lord says that He will treat us well. He needs nothing, His purposes in life are settled and we are the ones that need to ask the question, 'Are We Ready?' As we see from the dialogue above that we spend a lot of our time planning and preparing for one trip out of town for a week. We spend a lot of money, stress and strain and then of course things are subject to change once we get to the airport. Flights are delayed; weather occurs along the string of flights that we are catching, as well as having a flight totally canceled.

So, the question today is, Are You Ready? As we know, we cannot take earthly possessions with us when we die. So, what are you packing and placing in your heart? Are they wholesome thoughts and actions or those of deceit? Is your attitude daily that of Christ or are they attitudes of negativity and downer moods? As you know, this is a one-way ticket on this trip of life. God gives us and encourages us for a personal relationship with Him. Get your stuff, plan your trip and commit to a lifetime of eternity with Christ.

PRAYER: Lord Jesus, thank You for the time to plan in life. We know not the time or the hour, so prepare us for today. We love You and adore You. AMEN

DON'T FORGET!

# THE PROMISES OF PRAYER

SCRIPTURE: Matthew 6:9-13

WRITER: Matthew

Matthew 6:9-13 'Pray like this: Our Father in Heaven, may Your Name be kept holy. May Your Kingdom come soon. May your will be done on earth, as it is in heaven. Give us this day the food we need, and forgive us our sins, as we have forgiven those who sin against us. And don't let us yield to temptation, but rescue us from the evil one.'

Paul Tripp in his book 'Journey to the Cross' says that prayer is abandoning our own righteousness, admitting our own need for forgiveness, and resting in the grace of the cross of Jesus Christ.' He also goes on to share that prayer is one of God's sweetest gifts to us.

Prayer is where Christ welcomes us as his children to talk to Him, commune with Him and abide with him. This is where we are able to be very intimate in our confessions and know that He is loving us and hearing out heart.

The heart of prayer is worshipful confession to Him which results in gratitude, humility, vision as well as willingness in us.

As we know, prayer is spiritual warfare. Get ready when you pray to have the devil coming after you and seeking you out. When prayers are answered by God, the devil is going to be chasing your heart. So, take time to meditate, examine and consider changes you need to make in your life. Thank God for what He has done in sending His Son Jesus for our sins. Confession with our mouth allows accuracy of our wrong doing and then submission is giving our requests to God's plan. Lastly, supplication is having submitted ourselves fully to God's will and knowing our prayers are heard.

PRAYER: Most Gracious Lord, thank You for how important prayer is to us and for us. May we always stay in close communication so we can love like You. AMEN

DON'T FORGET!

# FISHING SPOTS

SCRIPTURE: Mark 1:17

WRITER: Mark

DEFINITION: fishing—'a fun time to grab some bait, a fishing pole and sit by the edge of a pond or lake and just enjoy God's creation. It matters not whether the fish are biting or not.' (Greg's definition)

Mark 1:17 'Jesus called out to them, 'Come, follow Me, and I will show you how to fish for people!' And they left their nets at one and followed Him.

When I think of fishing, I always go back to the times that my PawPaw would take us out to Gus' Marina on Lake Whitney, Texas. My PawPaw would of course grab all of the necessities that we would need, such as a case of Dr. Pepper, a second case of Dr. Pepper, some rods and reels, tackle box and some worms from Gus' personal stash. Oh, the fun we had with our PawPaw just watching him love up on his grandkids.

I am amazed at when I read in the gospels how when Jesus called out or requested that the future disciples come and follow him, just how quick they were to literally drop and go. First of all, I know that the fishermen's nets they left were commercial nets and were expensive. I know as a business owner; equipment is important and had to be taken care of daily.

Fishing for people definitely has a different viewpoint than that of fishing for fish. The analogy from Jesus was that people are the reason for everything He has created. The goal is for us to be successful fishers for Jesus. We must always work and serve under divine anointing, always depending on the Holy Spirit.

PRAYER: Most Gracious Lord, help us to always follow You as You have commanded, with a Godly attitude and a humble spirit. AMEN

DON'T FORGET!

# GENTLENESS

SCRIPTURES: II Timothy 2:24; Galatians 5:22-23; Colossians 3:12-13

WRITER: Paul

DEFINITION: gentleness—kind, mild mannered, disposition

II Timothy 2:24 'A servant of the Lord must not quarrel but must be kind to everyone, be able to teach, and be patient with difficult people.'

Galatians 5:22-23 'But the Holy Spirit produces this kind of fruit in our lives: love, joy, peace, patience, kindness, goodness, faithfulness, gentleness and self-control.'

Colossians 3:12-13 'Since God chose you to be the holy people He loves, you must clothe yourselves with tenderhearted mercy, kindness, humility, gentleness, and patience. Make allowance for each other's faults, and forgive anyone who offends you. Remember, the Lord forgave you, so you must forgive others.'

I love being able to write about Gentleness and how it truly fits into our daily life. We are called to treat others with gentleness. As we know, sometimes it is not always easy to do that but we are called and instructed to look past people's faults because we also have some of our own.

I acknowledge my sweet mother on how she raised my two sisters and my brother and me. She was always very patient, loving and gentle in her approach that she took in growing us as a family while my dad was away working in the oil fields.

Think back on specific instances when perhaps you were short with someone and you snapped over something that did not really make a lot of sense. We are called to go make it right and fix it before the sun goes down.

It is interesting how we are not to quarrel, we are to overlook faults, be tenderhearted and basically seek the good in people regardless of the situation. Let me challenge you to always be your best, strive for the excellence of Christ and always have a gentle spirit.

PRAYER: Father God, thank You for who You are each day in our life. May we always be gentle in spirit toward others so they may see You in our hearts. AMEN

DON'T FORGET!

# WORK HEARTILY

SCRIPTURE: Colossians 3:23-24

WRITER: Paul

Colossians 3:23-24 'Work willingly at whatever you do, as though you were working for the Lord rather than for people. Remember that the Lord will give you an inheritance as your reward, and that the Master you are serving is Christ.'

Paul says to 'work willingly' which really means 'from the soul' or 'from the inner self.' We are called to work always giving our all and representing Christ in everything we do. So, the question today is, are you giving your all from your soul?'

The definition for heartily is: in a friendly, sincere, cordial way; with zest, enthusiasm and a good attitude.

What kind of work and willingness are we demonstrating? Our daily work that we do is definitely a reflection of how we place our trust and faith in God. We are called to work for God rather than for people and we are blessed as we serve others.

I recently read an article of a football player who grew up in a hard life scenario with very limited resources yet had grandparents that loved him and his mother regardless of their situation. This football player was born with ABS-Amniotic Band Syndrome. This syndrome is a condition where the blood circulation is cut off during the pregnancy process and stunts the growth of the fingers, and sometimes hands and arms. This young man ended up having surgery to remove his hand and yet, he never gave up. He was drafted into the NFL and he, works soulfully everyday striving to exceed what is expected of him because he does not want to fail.

My encouragement to you is to always give yourself mightily to everything you do in life. God will handle the rest.

PRAYER: Lord Jesus, thank You for work and the fact that You give us healthy bodies to get up and show up for work. May we glorify You in everything. AMEN

DON'T FORGET!

DEVOTIONS FROM OAKDALE

# IS EIGHT ENOUGH?

SCRIPTURE: Isaiah 45:3

WRITER: Isaiah

Isaiah 45:3 'I will give you hidden treasures from dark concealed places and riches waiting in secret sites so that you recognize me, for it is I, Yahweh, the God of Israel who calls you by your name.'

I received a special note back in April and I wanted to share the contents because it fits with today's topic. 'Rest assured that God is using all your past experiences to prepare you for this moment – NOW – you are not who you once were. You are wiser, stronger, and more resilient, shake off yesterday's regrets, fears and worries and lay hold of faith, hope and love. Jesus will not fail you now or ever. You will have what you need in the days ahead. He has your back. He has gone before you. See your current trial as a time to declutter your soul, renew your mind and grow your faith. God has something for you in the here and now. Listen for His voice and accept the treasures He has to offer you.

Even though we go through unusual trials during our lifetime, God is always with us and gives us the strength to make it just when we think that we cannot hold on any longer.

In Romans we are told that, 'we can rejoice, too,' when we run into problems and trials, for we know that they help us develop endurance. And endurance develops strength of character, and character strengthens our confident hope of salvation. And the hope will not lead to disappointment. For we know how dearly God loves us, because He has given us the Holy Spirit to fill our hearts with His love.'

So, you are probably wondering where and how the title fits in today on 'Is Eight Enough?' It is because the unusual trials we encounter in life are not one or two or even eight. Paul said that we would face things throughout our life and then the challenge begins to decide how we will try to handle those trials. Our hidden treasures and riches waiting in secret sites are searching and longing for Yahweh, our Lord and Savior. Trust God and be obedient to Him each and every day.

PRAYER: Almighty God, You are my rock and my fortress. Thank you for the stability that You give me each day of my life. AMEN

DON'T FORGET!

# BEING FRUITFUL

SCRIPTURES: II Peter 1:8; Philippians 1:22

WRITER: Peter

DEFINITION: fruitful—bearing fruit (product of a tree or plant); abundant (at producing) work or in bearing children

II Peter 1:8 'The more you grow like this, the more productive and useful you will be in your knowledge of our Lord Jesus Christ.'

Philippians 1:22 'But if I live, I can do more fruitful work for Christ. So, I really don't know which is better.'

Having had some experience in the landscaping and tree business, I have been able to see trees and bushes that are producing new growth as well as new fruit. I remember one particular property that me and my crew were cleaning up. We each looked at one another and said, this is going to take a lot of work, a lot of trimming, so new growth can come about.

We began by raking out all of the many dead leaves that had fallen during the off season. We then shoveled around and dug out old dirt. We fertilized and began trimming back so new growth could take place in the upcoming season. It was amazing to see when all the trashy stuff was removed and specific attention was given to the soil and with the proper trimming, new life could flourish and new growth could once again bring forth fruit and beautify the landscape.

I believe it is the same with each of us if we truly look within our own life. Life rolls on and we have a lot of clutter that builds up and trashes our surroundings. It is not until we give the needed attention that we start cleaning up and making things look like they need to, so we can glorify God. We all need to produce fruit so others see just how powerful God's love is for us. Fruit is the overflow of life and we must be full before we can flow over.

PRAYER: Holy God, thank You for Your master gardener touch. A touch that pulls back old stuff and cleans out to make room for new beautiful blooms. AMEN

DON'T FORGET!

# TOTAL TRUST

SCRIPTURES: Psalm 33:21; Philippians 1:29; Psalm 62:8

WRITERS: Psalm 62—David; Philippians—Paul

DEFINTION: trust—assured reliance on the character, ability, strength, or truth of someone or something; hope—to place confidence or depend; to commit or place in ones keeping

Psalm 33:21 'In Him our hearts rejoice, for we trust in His Holy Name.'

Philippians 1:29 'For you have been given not only the privilege of trusting in Christ but also the privilege of suffering for him. We are in this struggle together.'

Psalm 62:8 'O my people, trust in Him at all times. Pour your heart to Him, for God is our refuge.'

Have you ever told someone that you totally trust them? Most of us know that specific one or two close friends that we would share that information with and know that it is in good hands. The basis for faith is what allows us to go deep in our soul to share something and to know that it is locked down and going no place outside of that confidence.

When I research the definition of trust and see the words character, ability, strength, hope, confidence, depend and commit, I know that it really does mean something to me.

Total trust is that of Christ. We can meditate on His Holy Name both day and night. He is in character holy, just, true, gracious, faithful and unchanging. Jehovah Jireh will provide; Jehovah Shalom will send peace; Jehovah Tsidkenu will justify, Jehovah Nissi will conquer every foe. They who know the name of Jesus will trust in Him and will also rejoice in Him.

PRAYER: Father God, thank You for the trust we have in You.

You are our great Redeemer, the finisher of everything. Help us to build our character upon your foundation each and every way possible. AMEN

## DON'T FORGET!

# GIVING IS ALWAYS BETTER

SCRIPTURES: Matthew 5:7; Psalm 112:9; II Corinthians 3:6

WRITERS: Matthew—Matthew; Psalm—David; II Corinthians—Paul

DEFINITION: give—to grant, to bestow, convey, offer, provide, or designate; to yield or produce

Matthew 5:7 'God blesses those who are merciful, for they will be shown mercy.'

Psalm 112:9 'They share freely and give generously to those in need. Their good deeds will be remembered forever. They will have influence and honor.'

II Corinthians 3:6 'He has enabled us to be ministers of His new covenant. This is a covenant not of written laws, but of the Spirit.'

Have you ever been in a position where someone would not forgive you? It is not right that a person who will not forgive should be forgiven, nor shall that person not give to the poor and have their own wants relieved. God will measure to us with our own bushels. Judgement is without mercy to the one who has shown no mercy. Giving is always better.

Today, let us try to give and forgive. Let us mind the two bears – bear and forbear. Let us be kind, gentle, and tender. Let us not drive hard bargains or pick foolish quarrels, or be difficult to please. We all want to be blessed. Let us be merciful, that we have mercy. Giving is always better.

Giving is something I remember my PawPaw always doing. I am reminded when I would go on the weekends to his house in Lubbock, Texas, each morning he would take me to deliver the newspapers to each of the neighbors. We would go and place the paper literally on their doorstep out of the rain where when they opened the door, surprise. Morning paper is ready to read.

Other occasions during the summer months, I remember my PawPaw going to the deep freeze and getting a box of popsicles and giving them out to neighbors that were outside mowing, painting or just enjoying the day. This is the true description of giving and my PawPaw set a terrific example for this grandson. That's why giving is always better.

PRAYER: Dear Heavenly Father, thank You for Godly grandparents that impact us in such special ways. My PawPaw, MeeMee and Betty were always so kind and understanding to me and my siblings. AMEN

DON'T FORGET!

# A VISION OF GREATNESS

SCRIPTURES: Ephesians 2:10; John 3:30; John 15:13

WRITER: Paul

DEFINITION: greatness—huge, remarkable in strength, magnitude, degree or effectiveness

Ephesians 2:10 'For we are God's handiwork, created in Christ Jesus to do good works, which God prepared in advance for us to do.'

John 3:30 'He must become greater and greater, and I must become less and less.'

John 15:13 'There is no greater love than to lay down one's life for one's friend.'

What kind of person do you want to be? One that follows everyone else's lead or will you follow the direction of Christ? No one can make you want to be the kind of person perhaps that others want you to be – it is on you and no one else in the end.

Remember that we don't do good works to gain salvation in life, we do them out of love for our heavenly Father. Hear the word early and continuously and then it sinks in and paves the way to success in life.

We have to remember that we are all created on purpose, for a special purpose and then we have to live it out to impact those around us.

For me each and every day, I am called to greatness with the work I do at Oakdale. I am up at 5:45am shaving and preparing for my day, checking communications and then at work at 6:30am. I am called to:

- Perform at my best – take pride
- Impact others around me
- Do my best taking care of 200 acres at Oakdale

Today.....this is my vision of greatness

PRAYER: Most Gracious Father, thank You Lord for all you do. Thank you for vision to see opportunities that are sometimes very close at hand. Help me to be a difference maker. AMEN

DON'T FORGET!

# SPECIAL TIME WITH THE FATHER

SCRIPTURES: I Corinthians 7:29; Psalm 62:8

WRITER: I Corinthians—Paul; Psalm 62—David

DEFINITION: time—occasion; an opportune or suitable moment; an appointed, fixed or customary moment or hour for something to happen

I Corinthians 7:29 'But let me say this, dear brothers and sisters: The time that remains is very short.'

Psalm 62:8 'O my people, trust in Him at all times. Pour out your heart to him, God is our refuge.'

When was the last time you made a concerted effort to spend special time with the Father? Was it today? Was it last week? Was it last year? Whatever you answer, God waits at all times for a simple knock so He can quietly say, come in.

Special time alone with the Father offers some of the following points:

| | |
|---|---|
| It quietens your spirit | Gives insight and instruction |
| Renews your energy | Prepares us for conflict |
| Strengthens your faith | He is our hiding place |
| Refreshes your emotions | He is a source of Joy |
| Enlarges your view of God | God is sitting on 'ready' to forgive and save us |
| It purifies your heart (purification causes pain) | You never lose by making God #1 |

Now you know that I am blessed when today, my mother sends me the above attributes of special time with the Father. Thank you Mom, I love you.

PRAYER: Dear God, thank you for Godly parents that when prompted by the Holy Spirit, put pen to paper to impact a son like me in prison to continue to show her love. AMEN

DON'T FORGET!

# A NAIL AND A HAMMER

SCRIPTURE: Luke 23:32-33

WRITER: Luke

Luke 23:32-33 'Two others, both criminals, were let out to be executed with him. When they came to a place called the Skull, they nailed Him to the cross. And the criminals were also crucified – one on his right and one on his left.'

I have a question for you to consider as you read the title today and as you read today's text. Did you pick up the nail and the hammer? Don't be too quick to answer because I feel like you have a lot of things on your plate right now and you have been very busy wondering what else in life is going to happen to you next.

Perhaps you are facing some really tough times in your world. A job just went away or a promotion did not occur and you got passed over. Maybe a severe health situation has just been brought to your attention from your most recent annual exam and now, you do not know what to do. Turn to Christ and let Him be there for you.

Your children are growing up and making decisions that do not always mirror what you would want them to do.

These are but a few of the many challenges that we experience in this trying life that we live in. How are you really doing in life? Are you looking for more out of life? Why are you trying to do things on your own? Did you pick up the nail and the hammer?

Jesus Christ, our Lord and Savior gave his life on Calvary's cross because of my sin and your sin. Sin is bad and it separates us from God and everything He has for us that is good. Walk outside this evening and watch the sunset or tomorrow morning and catch the sunrise and see just how great He is. Put down the nail and hammer because Jesus paid the price for you and me.

PRAYER: Father God, thank You for Your love for each of us. We all picked up the nail and the hammer by way of our sin. Father forgive us. AMEN

DON'T FORGET!

# BOOMERANG

SCRIPTURES: John 14:26; I Thessalonians 5:11; Proverbs 22:23

WRITERS: John—John; I Thessalonians—Paul; Proverbs—Solomon

DEFINITION: boomerang—a flat, curved stick that can be thrown so that it will return to a point near the thrower; something that goes contrary to expectations and results in disadvantage or harm to the person doing or saying it

John 14:26 'But when the Father sends THE ADVOCATE as my representative – that is the Holy Spirit – He will teach you everything and will remind you of everything I have told you.'

I Thessalonians 5:11 'So encourage each other and build each other up, just as you are already doing.'

Proverbs 22:23 'For the Lord is their defender. He will ruin anyone who ruins Him.'

There was a store in Hobbs, New Mexico I remember well even though it has been about 50 years ago. Down the aisle there was a bunch of original toys and this happened to be aisle for boomerangs. Nice white oak with many coats of polyurethane and a very nice red and blue stripe that made it look like an airplane wing. I had a number of friends that had either gotten them for a birthday or Christmas and even though I did not have one I tossed theirs. I could not believe how fast it sailed, hissed and flew effortlessly and returned within feet of the one who tossed it.

As I thought about the boomerang and how I felt when I finally got one of my own. I was reminded how we as sinners are like the boomerang. Our life, trouble, challenges and short comings throw us all around and we hiss and moan but the winds of God's touch brings us right back to his side. Paul said that we would experience rough patches, yet it would pass.

How about you, anything slinging you around? Do you sometimes wonder if you will return to God's side or not? Don't ever doubt that God is not patiently awaiting your safe landing.

PRAYER: Most Gracious Lord, may we always stay close to You and return just as that of a boomerang. We need You every second of every day. AMEN

DON'T FORGET!

# GRACE TICKETS FOR LIFE

SCRIPTURE: Isaiah 43:4; Proverbs 3:4; Philippians 1:7

WRITER: Isaiah—Isaiah; Proverbs—Solomon; Philippians—Paul

DEFINITION: grace—God's free unmerited favor toward sinful humanity
favor—gracious kindness; approval from a superior; a special privilege or right granted or conceded

Isaiah 43:4 'Others were given in exchange for you. I traded their lives for yours because you are precious to me. You are honored, and I love you.'

Proverbs 3:4 'Then you will find favor with both God and people, and you will earn a good reputation.'

Philippians 1:7 'So it is right that I should feel as I do about all of you, for you have a special place in my heart. You share with me the special favor of God.'

Today, I am thankful for all of the Grace tickets that have been graciously placed in my life. God continues to place them in my life every day. Each of us is truly special in God's sight and He loves us.

So, perhaps you ask what a Grace Ticket is and how it works. Well, my sister Donna Kay has been such the encourager to me throughout my entire life. Back in 2010 when I wrote 'The Don't Forgets of Life,' she made sure to always stay in touch with me and build me up. Knowing that I would be serving a prison sentence, she casually mentioned that she was sending me something in the mail. I could not believe my eyes, she actually sent me actual Grace 'tickets.' A grace ticket to me was and is so powerful and a terrific reminder that God is bringing about special moments for me all along the way.

I have shared many grace 'tickets' with other men here at Oakdale.

Just a reminder to them God is always there for them and that He would never let them go.

Check out our definitions today for grace and favor and realize just how powerful these two words are. I notice 'free' and 'unmerited favor,' gracious and kindness along with privilege. Wow, what powerful words to know that God has us in his arms forever.

PRAYER: Most Gracious Lord, thank You for the Grace ticket moments that You always give me. I am blessed and thankful for what You mean to me in my life. AMEN

DON'T FORGET!

# PROPER DIRECTION

SCRIPTURE: Proverbs 4:23-27

WRITER: Solomon

Proverbs 4:23-27 'Guard your heart above all else, for it determines the course of your life. Avoid all perverse talk; stay away from corrupt speech. Look straight ahead and fix your eyes on what lies before you. Mark out a straight path for your feet; stay on the safe path. Don't get side tracked; keep your feet from following evil.'

How hard is it for us to go the proper direction in life? Sometimes it can really be a challenge. Our scripture today addresses our heart, mouth, eyes, and feet. We are in Proverbs so we are gaining and growing in wisdom. We all experience situations that sometimes put us in a corner and then we then we have no way out.

As far as the heart, Solomon speaks as if it is so important that it determines the course of our life. Therefore, we should watch what we pour into our heart and the things that we allow to affect our heart. Secondly, our mouth is the next topic and wow how we can spew off at the mouth so fast and before we know it, we hurt someone's feelings. We lose a friend or injured a spouse just because of the words we say to people. How about straying eyes? That can sometimes create a problem because our sights are not set on Christ. This can turn into something major if we don't watch out and pay careful attention. Lastly, our feet are to mark a straight path for us and keep us from getting side tracked. By the time you couple all of the important items, it will definitely keep us on our toes and pushing to always do our best.

Are you at a fork in your life today? Do you have important decisions that need to be made? Are you at a place in your life where you are more willing to ask and listen or are you going to make it on your own? Choose Christ today and let Him be part of what you do.

PRAYER: Almighty God, thank You Father for all You do and all You stand for in our lives today. God, we make plenty of mistakes but we want to travel in the proper direction with You. AMEN

DON'T FORGET!

# HE WILL

SCRIPTURE: Matthew 6:24-25

WRITER: Matthew

Matthew 6:24-25 'No one can serve two masters. For you will hate one and love the other; you will be devoted to one and despise the other. You cannot serve God and be enslaved to money. That is why I tell you not to worry about everyday life, whether you have enough food and drink, or enough clothes to wear.'

We all have plenty of unknowns going on in our life. It is hard not to be anxious about the things we cannot control. The appeal to God for help, strength, obedience, and timing is not ours. God's Word says therefore, I tell you, do not be anxious about your life.

We can't control how God blesses us, all we know is that He will. We don't know how He will meet our needs; all we must know is that He will. We don't know how He is going to get us from where we are right now to where He wants us to be in life. All we must know is that we prayed, He has heard us. It is His timing, His plan, and His perfect will that is in effect for us. When we stop trying to figure out how and when, we will be able to rest in His immense love and receive His grace that is apportioned to us and for us today. Anxiety builds in our hearts when we concern ourselves with things beyond our control. God's grace builds in our lives when we walk in what He has set before us today.

Are you teachable? Are you willing to learn new things? Are you patient, open to hear and open minded? Have you ever thought that you knew more than you really knew? We probably all fall into that category at some point in time. Are you asking God when? When will you get to move into a new home, get a new job, excel in your sport abilities that you do for fun? God points out that we are all important to Him and we all matter to Him. He will bless you, He does love you and He gave His life as a ransom for many. Trust Him with your life today.

PRAYER: Lord Almighty, You know what Your will is for us every day. Thank You, Father, for Your unfailing love. AMEN

DON'T FORGET!

# TRUST HIM MORE

SCRIPTURES: Psalm 31:5; Psalm 56:3; Proverbs 29:25; Philippians 1:29

WRITERS: Psalm 31 and 56—David; Proverbs—Solomon; Philippians—Paul

DEFINITION: trust—assured reliance on the character, ability, strength, or truth of someone or something; hope, to place confidence or depend; to rely on the truthfulness or accuracy

Psalm 31:5 'I entrust my spirit into your hand. Rescue me Lord, for you are a faithful God.'

Psalm 56:3 'But when I am afraid, I will put my trust in You.'

Proverbs 29:25 'Fearing people is a dangerous trap, but trusting the Lord means safety.'

Philippians 1:29 'For you have been given not only the privilege of trusting in Christ but also the privilege of suffering for Him.'

Trust comes with rescue. When you have faced an obstacle and overcome it with God's help, you will trust Him more. As we learn more and more about God, we will realize that He always acts first. God sent Jesus as an act of love. He took the first step in his relationship with us. Because God acted first, he started the conversation. God is always waiting for you to invite Him to talk to you. He is truly available around the clock. When we begin with discussions with God, then things start to happen. When God moves in your heart and your life, you know it is Him.

In our lifetime, we will experience many unusual things with God and we cannot take the credit. What we do know is that God is always moving in every area of our life.

I have found that my time here at Oakdale is definitely one that I have really had to trust in God. There is not a day gone by that I have not called on Him for everything that I am experiencing from meeting new men to jobs being completed to programming classes that help integrate inmates back into society once their sentence has been completed. Trust also comes into play daily when thinking about one's sentence and the time involved and just exactly how one will spend their time. For us at Oakdale, thankfully, there are two prayer times for the group each day for those who choose to participate along with Wednesday evening and Sunday morning Bible study. These opportunities allow for us to trust Him more.

PRAYER: Almighty Father, thank You for trust. Thank You for the times that we face obstacles and for some crazy reason, we wonder what to do. We need only to trust in You. AMEN

DON'T FORGET!

# WHEN YOU NEED STRENGTH

SCRIPTURES: Ephesians 6:10; Hebrews 11:34; Psalm 46:1

WRITERS: Ephesians—Paul; Hebrews—unknown; Psalm—David

DEFINITION: strength—capacity for exertion or endurance; support; the power of a person or of God, measured in terms of wealth, wisdom, military might or physical prowess

Ephesians 6:10 'A final word: Be strong in the Lord and in His mighty power.'

Hebrews 11:34 'They shut the mouth of lions, quenched the flames of fire, and escaped death by the edge of the sword. Their weakness was turned to strength. They become strong in battle and put whole armies to flight.'

Psalm 46:1 'God is our refuge and strength, always ready to help in times of trouble.

The scripture states, 'God is our refuge and our strength.' It also goes on to say something else very important, and is ALWAYS ready to help in times of trouble. As we know, we are going to be in trouble during our life and no doubt, be looking for help. So, when things get jammed up you need the strength.

Think about times that you need strength the most. I recently had the opportunity to work out with one of the guys who was introducing me to free weights just to have a tune-up work out periodically. He tried different weights just to see what my maximum limits were before I would basically tire out or my body give in. Once that was done, I was then challenged with four sets of twelve lifts, presses, etc., and frankly my arms were feeling like jelly in the end. Much of the Christian life is like weight lifting exercise for me. We do things in life over and over again and a lot of times, they are wrong things. Sin is what it is called. Our heart and mind tire out and we give in because it is more than we can handle. Allow God to spot you on your personal lifting and turn everything over to Him. Life presses us sometimes but when we need the strength, we have to lean on Christ.

PRAYER: Most Gracious Father, thank You for always providing the strength for us exactly when we need it. You know exactly what we can handle and it simply needs to be Your will. AMEN

DON'T FORGET!

# OUR GUIDE

SCRIPTURE: Psalm 32:8

WRITER: David

Psalm 32:8 'The Lord says, 'I will guide you along the best pathway for your life. I will advise you and watch over you.'

It is summer and it is time to take a trip to a new place that you have never been before. Perhaps it is a place of adventure and the places you go might be a little dangerous and the activities will take some specific planning or else things could go wrong.

How about having a personal guide that is from the particular area, has been around over the years to know the pitfalls and problem areas so your trip can go very well without issues. This personal guide will also be able to factor in with maps, the best routes to travel and just kind of add that special touch that you need for an adventure trip.

I did a trip like this not too long ago and it was nice having guys that knew all the ins and outs to make it a trip to never forget, in a good way!

Shift over now to life for you and me. We are on this adventure of a lifetime traveling through a maze of unknowns and we really don't need to or have to go it alone. God is there for us and wants to guide us along the right pathways of life and He has it all planned out for us. You see, our God knows every hair on our head and every thought we will have from being a youngster until we take our last breath. So why don't we trust Him now and allow him to guide us in the right direction, making the right decisions and enjoy life to the fullest.

PRAYER: Heavenly Father, thank You Lord for having the map to our lives and knowing exactly the roads we need to take to be safe and secure. AMEN

## DON'T FORGET!

# IN AMAZEMENT

SCRIPTURES: I Chronicles 16:24; Psalm 126:2-3

WRITERS: I Chronicles—Ezra; Psalm 126—The seventh psalm of ascent from the priests returning from captivity in Babylon

DEFINITION: amazed—to fill with wonder, causing amazement, great wonder, or surprise

I Chronicles 16:24 'Publish his glorious deed among the nations. Tell everyone about the amazing things he does.'

Psalm 126:2-3 'We were filled with laughter, and we sang for joy. And the other nations said, 'What amazing things the Lord has done for them. Yes, the Lord has done amazing things for us! What joy!'

I had a terrific day yesterday, writing and studying. I waited until evening before getting outside to walk on the track. As I made the turn, I saw the sun going down behind the clouds. All I could do was stop and stand in amazement. I have to say that it was a walk that I have not experienced since I have been here only because of all the storms that have made their way through here over the last few days. Again, for me, with each step taken, the sun opened up more and more until the entire look of the clouds and sun was stunning.

Have you ever had days when things are just clicking along and then something happens and you can't really do anything but stop and thank God for the awareness that He gives us about His presence? Call it an 'aha' moment, a spiritual moment. I do know they are always special when they happen.

When we look at the definition of amazed, which is to fill with wonder, it is very easy to see how God, who created the universe and everything in it can be making things like rainbows, rainstorms, tornados, hurricanes and yes, bright sun shiny days. That's when we know just exactly who brings about things of amazement, Jesus.

PRAYER: Most Gracious Lord, thank You for always amazing us with Your great wonders. I am thankful because You bring them about for me often. AMEN

DON'T FORGET!

# THE MOST IMPORTANT
# COMMANDMENT

SCRIPTURE: Romans 5:8; I Thessalonians 5:13; Luke 10:27

WRITER: Romans—Paul; I Thessalonians—Paul; Luke—Luke

DEFINITION: neighbors—one living or located near another; fellow human

love—the ultimate expressions of God's loyalty, purity, and mercy extended toward his people; to be reflected in human relationships of brotherly concern, marital fidelity, and adoration of God; a beloved person

Romans 5:8 'But God showed his great love for us by sending Christ to die for us while we were still sinners.'

I Thessalonians 5:13 'Show the great respect and wholehearted love because of their work and live peacefully with each other.'

Luke 10:27 'The man answered, 'You must love the Lord your God with all your heart, all you soul, all your mind; and love your neighbor as yourself.'

We all want to follow the rules and not just any rules. We want to follow God's rules, His commandments. One of His commands to us is to love our neighbors and also to invest in them. Spending time with them, doing things for them, caring for them, reaching out and so much more. We just have to do it and not put if off when things are busy for us in our lives.

Perhaps you might say that you have too many things going on and you are very busy and it might be stepping out of your comfort zone more than you wish to do. That is okay because the Holy Spirit will open up doors for you to make it easier for you.

So, how important is this calling for us concerning our neighbors? Well, God ranks it up there with 'Love the Lord your God with all your heart, mind, soul and body.' If that is the case, then we need to take heed that neighbors are the life blood of how Jesus views relationships and how we are to live around one another each day caring and being interested and serving one another.

Do you know the names of your neighbors left and right, across the street and where you walk or drive? Well, go meet them and smile and follow the most important commandment.

PRAYER: Dear God, it seems so simple but sometimes can be so hard to meet new people and live with and around our neighbors. Open the doors for us today. AMEN

DON'T FORGET!

# WHAT ACTIONS DETERMINE

SCRIPTURE: Philemon 1:6-7; I Peter 1:13

WRITER: Philemon—Paul; I Peter—Peter

DEFINITION: action—a thing done, deed, an exercise of will

Philemon 1:6-7 'And I am praying that you will put into action the generosity that comes from your faith as you understand and experience all the good things we have in Christ. Your love has given me much joy, and comfort, my brother, for your kindness often refreshed the hearts of God's people.'

I Peter 1:13 'So prepare your minds for action and exercise self-control. Put all your hope in the gracious salvation that will come to you when Jesus Christ is revealed to the world.'

A friend shared the other day with me the following:

'What I read determines the way I think. The way I think determines what I do. What I do determines the way I live my life. The way I live my life determines how I am following God.'

I had an early morning Bible study this past week and I had someone in my study share the above excerpt about what actions determine. It got me to thinking just how important my actions are each day and just exactly what kind of impact they are having on other people.

How about my attitude? Is it an attitude that is encouraging others or is it a drag to people? How about my facial expressions and are they positive or are they negative?

I get it…everything I do determines something positive, encouraging, uplifting, championing or quite possibly tripping someone up due to my negative actions.

Challenge yourself today to notice your actions and to always push for them to impact those that you come in contact with today. You never know what others around you are needing and it might just be your kind words that determines their next move. Make it a positive one for Christ.

PRAYER: Almighty God, may our actions always be determined by things that are of You Lord may they be positive, ground breaking, mood awakening and love shaking words that pierce and move the heart for Christ. AMEN

DON'T FORGET!

# A LIGHT IN THE DARKNESS

SCRIPTURES: Isaiah 42:6; John 1:9; I John 1:7

WRITERS: Isaiah—Isaiah; John—John; I John—John

DEFINITION: light—daylight, brightness, illumination; celestial body; spiritual enlightenment; exposure to the truth and justice

Isaiah 42:6 'I, the Lord, have called you to demonstrate my righteousness. I will take you by the hand and guard you and I will give you to my people Israel, as a symbol of my covenant with them. And you will be the light to guide nations.'

John 1:9 'The One who is the true light, who gives light to everyone, was coming into the world.'

I John 1:7 'But if we are living in the light, as God is in the light, then we have fellowship with each other, and the blood of Jesus, his Son, cleanses us from all sin.'

Today, I want you to think about those individuals that bring light into the lives of others. I am speaking of a person that when things are going on in the lives of those who are troubled, down in the dumps and just going through the stuff of life. Those people I am referring to are the ones that I have written about in previous devotions

Perhaps you are that person that has a lot of things going for you such as a good career, perhaps a good family but something is missing in your life. You have very little to hope for in your day to day. Your group of friends are off doing things without you and it does not give you a great feeling about life. Think about how you can get out of the rut you are in and be about being the light in a dark world.

Scripture shares with us that Christ is the one true light and he does give light to everyone. Then the word also shares that if we are living in the light, which is Christ, then we will desire to have fellowship and impact those around us.

Regardless of what you have on your mind, in your heart or in your day to day, you can trust Christ to be the light that you need.

PRAYER: Most gracious Lord and Savior, thank You for being the light that we so desperately need. Help others to always see You in us. AMEN

DON'T FORGET!

# I HOPE

SCRIPTURES: Jeremiah 29:11; Romans 15:13

WRITERS: Jeremiah—Jeremiah; Romans—Paul

DEFINITION: hope—confident trust with the expectation of fulfillment

Jeremiah 29:11 'For I know the plans I have for you,' says the Lord. 'They are plans for good and not for disaster, to give you a future and a hope.'

Romans 15:13 'I pray that God, the source of hope, will fill you completely with joy and peace because you trust in Him. Then you will overflow with confident hope through the power of the Holy Spirit.'

I hope I get the new job. I hope the trip we take is a fun trip. I hope the summer days don't get too hot. I hope that God hears my prayers. I hope she is not angry. I hope we are on time. I hope he is not mad. I hope, I hope, I hope. These are but a few of the I hopes that are thought and voiced a lot in life.

I imagine that we are all alike in that we have our list of things that we hope for. I know that from where I sit in prison, that there are things that I hope for and pray for as I serve my sentence. I cling to God's Word every day that He does have plans for me and my life. I truly believe that He will continue to prosper me and by that I do not mean financially. I mean that with the relationships He connects me with while I am here at Oakdale as well as when I am released.

For each of us, hoping is natural and frequent and it keeps us in the ballgame of life because God wants us to depend on Him in this process.

The Bible warns us that if our hope disappoints us, it is because our hope rests on the wrong things.

What are things you hope for today? Our hope ultimately only needs to be in Christ. No one else. Our hope is seeking God, finding God and communicating with Him. That is where our hope should be daily.

Finally, take a piece of paper out and list all of the things that you are hoping for today and in the future.

PRAYER: Dear God, thank You that our hope is in You. Thank You that life with Christ is all we need.

DON'T FORGET!

# EXPECT BIG THINGS

SCRIPTURE: Lamentations 3:22-23

WRITER: Jeremiah

Lamentations 3:22-23 'The faithful love of the Lord never ends! His mercies will never cease. Great is His faithfulness; His mercies begin afresh each morning.'

What is a faithful love? We see in the book of Lamentations even in the midst of destruction and problems Jeremiah saw an opportunity of hope with and in the character of God. As we know, God's compassion and love never ends and never ceases. His love is always faithful and does not go away. His mercy on our lives is always great. Oh, how I am so thankful for that fact.

God is always faithful to us even when we are doing sinful things that move us away for Him as well as the times that we are in tune and walking hand in hand with Him. Expect big things......

How do you start your day each morning? Is it with a great attitude knowing that you have many opportunities before you because God is good? Or, do you get up and have a mile long list of so much stuff that you cannot even enjoy life? Expect big things......

You know, God wants you to be great in all that you think, all that you imagine, all that you believe. The real question is..... how about you and your expectations in life? Are they big, small, imaginable, visible or do those thoughts not exist for you? Expect big things......

No one should every stop you from believing in yourself and the great things you are capable of doing in life. Dream big, think big, expand your beliefs, do things you have never done before but above all else trust God and expect big things!

PRAYER: Heavenly Father, thank You Lord for belief in You. For Your faithful love and kindness for each of us. Your tender mercies do bring about freshness each day. AMEN

DON'T FORGET!

# READY FOR YOUR NEXT TRIAL?

SCRIPTURE: I Peter 1:6-7

WRITER: Peter

DEFINITION: a legal proceeding based in court; a test of faith, patience, or stamina through subjection to suffering or temptation

I Peter 1:6-7 'So be truly glad. There is a wonderful joy ahead, even though you must endure trials for a little while. These trials will show you that your faith is genuine. It is being tested as fire tests and purifies gold – though your faith is far more precious than mere gold. So, when your faith remains strong through many trials, it will bring you the most praise and glory and honor on the day when Jesus Christ is revealed to the whole world.

Did you see the word trial? A trial is not something that is viewed as being positive. A trial is something that is challenging and something that most want to overcome. What trials have you undergone in your life? Are they trials that you were able to overcome? Were they the type of trials that continue and they are not going away? I just happen to have a list to help us out today beginning with debt, faith, faltering health, cancer, death of a loved one, an accident, a stroke, a lost job or even a career and the list can go on and on in the category of 'trial.'

A trial puts us personally in a challenging position. Once faced with a trial, we have to decide whether or not we will accept the challenge and hit it head on or whether we will allow it to overtake us. God's Word says that we are to count it all joy when we encounter trials. Basically, it puts us in a place where we get to depend on Christ for our strength and not try to accomplish it on our own. So, when your next trial comes calling, be ready with Christ.

PRAYER: Most Gracious Lord, trials are nothing for You. You provide all the strength we need if we simply call upon Your name. AMEN

DON'T FORGET!

# POOR IN SPIRIT

SCRIPTURES: Matthew 5:3; Psalm 37:5, 23-24

WRITERS: Matthew—Matthew; Psalm—David

Matthew 5:3 'God blesses those who are poor and realize their need for him, for the Kingdom of Heaven is theirs.'

Psalm 37:5 'Commit everything you do to the Lord. Trust Him, and He will help you.'

Psalm 37:23-24 'The Lord directs the steps of the godly. He delights in every detail of their lives. Though they stumble, they will never fall, for the Lord holds them by the hand.'

I love to read through the Beatitudes. All eight of them have a special character trait that can definitely show us the way in which to live authentically. Here we see Jesus on the mountainside with his disciples and once again, he is about to impact them and teach them.

Today we focus on the first of the Beatitudes and that is 'Poor in Spirit.' It simply means that we are poor in our lives without Christ. They key word that jumps out at me is 'realize.' We have to first realize we need Christ or things will not happen for us.

Each of these character traits make us a better servant for Christ as long as we implement them in our life each day. Mourning, being humble, being hungry and thirsty for his word, being merciful, working for peace and lastly to understand that we will sometimes be persecuted for our stance on our beliefs in Christ.

Remember, the scripture says, 'God blesses those who are poor and realize their need for Him, for the Kingdom of Heaven is theirs.' That means they will one day be with Christ for eternity. Seek Christ today and be complete.

PRAYER: Almighty Father, thank You for making us complete in You Lord. We pray for each of these character traits to be developed in our life so we may serve You better. AMEN

DON'T FORGET!

# FREE FROM SIN

SCRIPTURE: Romans 8:1-2

WRITER: Paul

DEFINITION: sin—moral evil; transgression of or rebellion against God's laws

Romans 8:1-2 'So now there is no condemnation for those who belong to Christ Jesus. And because you belong to Him, the power of life-giving Spirit has freed you for the power of sin that leads to death.'

The topic of sin is one that hails all the way back to Adam and Eve. Sin occurred in the early beginning of the world and it is still in our world today and has grown out of control. The real question is how can we strive to be free from sin? Well, saddle up and read on.

In Romans 7:7-25, one can easily see the negatives in sin. Those actions mentioned are struggles, coveting, sin taking advantage, sin living in our lives, sinful nature and ultimately, the power within is sin. Then, when we become a slave to sin, we are then miserable. We then have weakness in our life and are dominated with a sinful nature. Because of the sinful nature, we then have no inclination to follow.

So, what do we know about God's law in scripture? The law shows us our sin and also states that we don't understand the law. The law is holy, right and good and our answer in life is Jesus Christ our Lord. We belong to him and through him, we have a life-giving Spirit that frees us from sin. The solution is therefore God sending Jesus for us.

The Holy Spirit controls our mind and leads us to a life with peace and He joins with our spirit so we can be heirs of God's glory. Always looking to Christ for a true one-on-one relationship with Him along with daily Bible study will allow us to deal with the sin we have in our life. Because of our salvation through Christ, we are able to be forgiven of our sins when we mess up.

PRAYER: Lord Jesus, thank You for Your Son, Jesus Christ our Lord and Savior. Because of your love for us, we are redeemed from our filthy sin. AMEN

DON'T FORGET!

# THE TRASH PILE

SCRIPTURES: Romans 7:5; I John 3:6; Numbers 32:23

WRITERS: Romans—Paul; I John—John; Numbers—Moses

DEFINITION: sin—moral evil; transgression of or rebellion against God's laws

Romans 7:5 'When we were controlled by our old nature, sinful desires that produced a harvest of sinful deeds resulting in death.'

I John 3:6 'Anyone who continues to live in Him will not sin. But anyone who keeps on sinning does not know Him or understand Him.'

Numbers 32:23 'But if you fail to keep your word, then you will have sinned against the Lord and you may be sure that your sin will find you out.'

I remember continually going to the city trash pile, also known as the dump. We had to discard trash, old plants, concrete, dead tree limbs and the likes. Trash is something that you do not want. There is no place to keep it without starting to smell like it from the rubbish and the stench. Of course, you wore boots and had to get out of your vehicle to dump your vehicle, you get back into your clean ride and now you stink it up because you are living in it and around it.

Sin is often the same way as the trash pile. We are not in it until we take a trip to be around it. We continue to go back and forth and before long, we smell like it. Sin building upon sin does nothing good for us but push the trash to an area where they can later put more trash and keep compacting it down. We don't have to do that with our sin. Christ is the great healer and with each dump at the site, he makes our sins disappear.

Take a hard look at our verses today....1) anyone who continues to live in Him, 2) when we were controlled by our old nature, 3) but if we fail to keep Your Word, are but a few things that need our attention to make sure that we are living in Christ.

PRAYER: Almighty Father, today we pray that You will keep us white as snow and not filthy like the trash pile. We don't need to be in or around it. AMEN

DON'T FORGET!

# KEEP PRIDE ON THE SIDELINE

SCRIPTURES: Psalm 101:5; Proverbs 6:3; Mark 7:22; I John 2:16

WRITERS: Psalm 101—David; Proverbs—Solomon; Mark—Mark; I John—John

DEFINITION: pride—inordinate self-esteem or conceit; disdainful behavior or treatment of others

Psalm 101:5 'I will not tolerate people who slander their neighbors. I will not endure conceit and pride.'

Proverbs 6:3 'Follow my advice and save yourself, for you have placed yourself at your friend's mercy.'

Mark 7:22 'For from within, out of a person's heart, come evil thoughts, sexual immorality, theft, murder, adultery, greed, wickedness, deceit, lustful desires, envy, slander, pride and foolishness.'

I John 2:16 'For the world offers only a craving for physical pleasure, a craving for everything we see, and pride in our achievements and possessions. These are not from the Father, but are from this world.'

I have been fortunate over my lifetime thus far to have experienced some great athletic events both on the field, on the court and then as a coach on the sideline. Referee's jobs are to keep order as well as the game flowing smoothly. Things such as loud attitudes and disruptiveness are for the sideline and if you go too far, you might be asked to leave the game.

That is also where pride in our lives needs to remain. On the sideline where it is not a distraction and the game of life can move forward without worldly things taking over.

I have to say for myself that I indulged and participated in the game of pride for most of my life. Because of my involvement in sports and activities, I was drawn to trophies and accolades and really anything that drew attention to how good I was and my success. It was so wrong for me not to have learned that lesson so many years ago. Then as I continued to grow up and in college, it happened again with getting a college scholarship. Then, I was big man on campus. Pride once again was in the way. I got married while in college and began to start my career in the oil business and later into financial services. Financial services took me down a road of high-pressure sales, yearly trips and awards that would take over my life for the next 28 years. During this sales position tenure, I was very blessed but also made plenty of mistakes. Pride was always in the way to some extent and it mostly just got covered up. That is something I had to confess and ask for forgiveness.

Always strive to keep pride on the sideline and keep your eyes on Christ.

PRAYER: Most Gracious Lord, forgive me Father for the pride I have had in my life over the years. It was wrong and I thank You for the forgiveness of that sin. AMEN

DON'T FORGET!

# WHAT I DO HAVE

SCRIPTURE: Acts 3:6

WRITER: Luke

Acts 3:6 'But Peter said, 'I don't have silver or gold for you. But I'll give you what I have. In the name of Jesus Christ, the Nazarene, get up and walk.'

In a recent Bible study, four very amazing words popped up and stuck with me as well as prompted what would become today's devotion. 'What I Do Have' are those four words.

In Acts 3:1-8, we see Peter healing a crippled beggar. This particular lame man had to be carried wherever he wanted to go since his birth. He was placed at the temple gate and would beg for money as people were going in each day. This one particular day, Peter and John gave an intent look to be specific this time because there was more to give today than material wealth for the one who was begging. No, today it would be different. Today, Peter would share they had no silver or gold for him BUT, I will give you what I do have.....and that was Jesus!

Think for a moment about all of the relationships you have and those that need what you do have...and that is Jesus. How about being concerned for others and about others in all aspects of their lives?

This scripture reading really challenged me to check into my heart and see the opportunities at hand that God gives us to share with others. For some, it may be at work, church or even in a restaurant or on a vacation trip. You just never know but, we do need to always be prepared to share.

PRAYER: Almighty God, thank You for the opportunity that we have in You to always share the good news about You. Thank You for what I do have and that is a personal relationship with You. AMEN

DON'T FORGET!

# BOLDNESS IN BELIEVING

SCRIPTURES: Acts 4:13; Philippians 1:20; Ephesians 3:20

WRITERS: Acts—Luke; Philippians—Paul; Ephesians—Paul

DEFINITION: boldness—fearlessness before danger; self-assurance, confidence, prominence

Acts 4:13 'The members of the council were amazed when they saw the boldness of Peter and John, for they could see that they were ordinary men with no special training in the scriptures.'

Philippians 1:20 'For I fully expect and hope that I will never be ashamed, but that I will continue to be bold for Christ, as I have been in the past. And I trust that my life will bring honor to Christ, whether I live or die.'

Ephesians 3:20 'Now all glory to God, who is able, through his mighty power at work within us, to accomplish infinitely more than we might ask or think.'

When I focus in on the word boldness, I think about taking a stand for something. A belief, a prompting, a no fear attitude in making an important decision. For me, I want to make good decisions in every aspect of my life. No doubt we all make mistakes and are sorry for those mistakes which are sins. The following 'Being Bold Statements' are a good start for things that we want to be bold about....

- Being bold in our daily walk
- Being bold in our prayer life
- Being bold in the selection of our friends
- Being bold in our convictions from the Holy Spirit
- Being bold believing that Christ will give us the strength we need
- Being bold to share the good news of Jesus Christ to others
- Being bold enough to follow Christ
- Being bold in asking for forgiveness when we do wrong and sin

- Being bold in our desire for spiritual growth
- Being bold in asking for patience
- Being bold in using our spiritual gifts
- Being bold to be good parents

We know there is boldness in following Christ and the work he calls us to do. We are called to take a stance for Christ daily and when we are faced with doubt or lack of faith, we need to step back and pray for boldness.

PRAYER: Most Gracious Heavenly Father, thank You for the right amount of boldness that You give us and the timing with which You place it in our hearts. AMEN

DON'T FORGET!

# YOU LOST IT

SCRIPTURES: Matthew 19:26; Mark 10:27

WRITERS: Matthew—Matthew; Mark—Mark

DEFINITION: possible—being within the limits of ability, capacity, or realization

Matthew 19:26 'Jesus looked at them intently and said, 'Humanly speaking, it is impossible. But with God everything is possible.'

Mark 10:27 'Jesus looked at them intently and said, humanly speaking, it is impossible. But not with God. Everything is possible with God.'

You will not find happiness in the place that you lost it! Move on and make God your true source. Stop engaging in things that bring negative energy into your life. Why? Because God is the author of your story. You are the editor. You have the power to edit and change the story line. Re-write, rearrange, and re-invent.

Listen…when you start to appreciate, you will begin to elevate!

Repeat: In a month from now, I will be in a better situation with people, places and things!

Remember, if a situation has not worked out for you, rejoice. That just means that God has something bigger and better for you. When one door closes, an even better door will open.

I have a close friend that I worked for and with and he had a relationship that just teetered back and forth all of the time and he just could not get off of the merry-go-round. All kinds of issues and problems continued to follow him with no other reason than the wrong company and wrong initiatives. Find yourself today in a true relationship with Jesus.

PRAYER: Almighty God, thank You for do overs when we fall short. May we always look to You for a new start in life. AMEN

DON'T FORGET!

# THE PROMISE OF THE HOLY SPIRIT

SCRIPTURES: Acts 1:2; Acts 2:4

WRITER: Luke

Acts 1:2 'Until the day He was taken up to heaven after giving His chosen apostles further instructions through the Holy Spirit.'

Acts 2:4 'And everyone present was filled with the Holy Spirit and began speaking in other languages, as the Holy Spirit gave them this ability.'

The book of Acts gives us a nice jump start to what the Holy Spirit is doing and the effect it had on many people.

1:2 'After giving his chosen apostles further instructions through the Holy Spirit.'

1:5 'But in just a few days you will be baptized with the Holy Spirit.'

1:8 'But you will receive power when the Holy Spirit comes upon you.'

1:16 'Concerning Judas, who guided those who arrested Jesus. This was predicted long ago by the Holy Spirit.'

2:4 'And everyone present was filled with the Holy Spirit and began speaking in other languages, as the Holy Spirit gave them this ability.'

2:17 'In the last days, God says 'I will pour out my Spirit upon all people.'

2:33 'And the Father, as He had promised, gave Him the Holy Spirit to pour out on us, just as you see and hear today.'

2:38 'Peter replied, 'Each of you must repent of your sins and turn to God and be baptized in the name of Jesus Christ for the forgiveness of your sins. Then you will receive the gift of the Holy Spirit.'

We see what was happening according to Peter was to pour out of the Spirit of God. Due to the Spirit being poured out, prophesy was occurring. Visons and dreams were revealed by the Spirit.

Peter quoted Joel 2:28-32 which confirmed this day was fulfillment of the scripture.

Aren't we thankful for the outpouring of the Holy Spirit from God in our lives? Be thankful to Christ today for the promise of the Holy Spirit.

PRAYER: Dear Heavenly Father, thank You for the Holy Spirit in our lives and the moving in and through us to help guide our lives. AMEN

DON'T FORGET!

# GOD ALWAYS ACCEPTS US BACK (FORGIVENESS)

SCRIPTURES: Mark 2:7; Luke 6:37-38; II Corinthians 2:10

WRITERS: Mark—Mark; Luke—Luke; II Corinthians—Paul

DEFINITION: forgiveness—to pardon or acquit of sins

Mark 2:7 'What is he saying? This is blasphemy! Only God can forgive sins.!'

Luke 6:37-38 'Do not judge others, and you will not be judged. Do not condemn others or it will all come back against you. Forgive others, and you will be forgiven. Give and you will receive. Your gift will return to you in full, pressed down, shaken together to make room for more, running over, and poured into your lap. The amount you give will determine the amount you get back.'

II Corinthians 2:10 'When you forgive this man, I forgive him too. And when I forgive whatever needs to be forgiven, I do so with Christ's authority for your benefit.'

We all go through things in life that we look back at and think, I should not have done that. A bad word or action toward someone that actually took them down or maybe an action that caused someone to stumble. God always accepts us back....

If you have been in a marriage where challenges arose and very unusual circumstances occurred that takes the marriage to a divorce, there can still be forgiveness. If there has been abuse, addictions, infidelity, broken hearts and plenty more to the point that you wonder about forgiveness....Guess what? God will always accept us back if we repent....

You are in a business deal and you understand that everything seems to be all on the table and you later find out that was not the case. In some instances, things can be resolved and not end up in court. For others, the end result is far extreme and indictments come, plea bargains or trials take place and ultimately, sentencing to jail time or prison time occurs. God always accepts us back....

Always remember that it does not matter and I repeat does not matter what you are going through or gone through that may be so bad you just can't imagine God forgiving you for the wrong. God forgives and always accepts us back...

PRAYER: Heavenly Father, thank You for forgiveness, mercy and grace. Your death on the cross exclaims Your love for us daily. AMEN

DON'T FORGET!

# PATIENCE PLEASE

SCRIPTURES: Revelation 14:12; Romans 12:12-13

WRITERS: Revelation—John; Romans—Paul

DEFINITION: patience—the power or capacity to endure without complaint something difficult or disagreeable, forbearance, longsuffering

Revelation 14:12 'This means that God's holy people must endure persecution patiently, obeying His commands and maintaining their faith in Jesus.'

Romans 12:12-13 'Rejoice in our confident hope. Be patient in trouble, and keep on praying. When God's people are in need, be ready to help them. Always be eager to practice hospitality.'

Patience is not always easy. We are to do things without grumbling and to do things with a good attitude. Patience has to always include the spiritual, mental and physical aspects of life. Spiritual patience is resting in Jesus Christ. The physical and mental is having total reliance in Christ.

We are always tested in our life and sometimes, it is more than we think we can handle. We normally want something; we want it now and please hurry. The question is always, 'I wonder when XX will happen?' We need to be content in life and have trust in Christ.

Titus 2:2 states, 'Teach the older men to exercise self-control, to be worthy of respect, and to live wisely. They must have sound faith and be filled with love and patience.'

We also gain encouragement from Paul in Romans 5:3-5 where we see the following, 'We can rejoice, too, when we run into problems and trials, for we know that they help us develop endurance. And endurance develops strength of character, and character strengthens our confident hope of salvation. And this hope will not lead to disappointment. For we know how dearly God loves us, because He has given us the Holy Spirit to fill our hearts with His love.'

Remember, we have Christ that is there for us in all we are going through. We are not alone and just have to be patient and wait on Him.

PRAYER: Heavenly Father, thank You for Your never-ending love for us. Thank You that You help us work through times that we are not so patient. AMEN

DON'T FORGET!

# GOD IS OUR HEARTBEAT

SCRIPTURES: I Corinthians 13:4-7; Deuteronomy 6:5; Proverbs 4:23

WRITERS: I Corinthians—Paul; Deuteronomy—Moses; Proverbs—Solomon

DEFINITION: heartbeat—a single complete pulsation of the heart; a vital force or driving impulse

I Corinthians 13:4-7 'Love is patient, and kind. Love is not jealous or boastful or proud or rude. It does not demand its own way. It is not irritable, and it keeps no record of being wronged. It does not rejoice about injustice but rejoices whenever the truth wins out. Love never gives up, never loses faith, is always hopeful and endures through every circumstance.'

Deuteronomy 6:5 'And you must love the Lord your God with all your heart, and all your soul, and all your strength.'

Proverbs 4:23 'Guard your heart above all else, for it determines the course of your life.'

The anatomy of the heart is one that is very complex. The superior vena cava, the pulmonary aorta, the left atrium, left ventricle, right ventricle, inferior vena cava, right atrium and the aorta make up the physical, muscular organ. It pumps blood received from the veins into the arteries, thereby maintaining the flow of blood through the entire circulatory system. Oh, what a wonderful illustration of a God who created each one of us with such spectacular detail physically.

There are also more facts about the heart that deal with the spiritual. It is the vital center and source of one's being, emotions, and sensibilities. It is the place for our deepest and sincerest feelings and beliefs. It also makes up our intellect and imagination, love and affection along with courage, resolution and fortitude.

That is why God is our heartbeat. He has brought about in us a central innermost physical part that affects our thoughts, expressions and just our innate ability to impact our neighbors. To love and be loved as well as to be patient while also being understanding.

Protect your heart and give all you have to loving Jesus and above all else doing it with all you have.

PRAYER: Lord God, thank You for ways to monitor our hearts physically. We pray that You can help monitor our hearts spiritually through a daily walk with You. AMEN

DON'T FORGET!

# WHAT IS DOCTINE?
# WHAT IS THE BIBLE?

SCRIPTURES: Titus 2:1; Psalm 107:1-2; II Timothy 3:16

WRITERS: Titus—Paul; Psalm 107—David; II Timothy—Paul

Titus 2:1 'But as for you, speak the things which are proper for sound doctrine.'

Psalm 107:1-2 'Oh, give thanks to the Lord, for He is good! For his mercy endures forever. Let the redeemed of the Lord say so.'

II Timothy 3:16 'All scripture is inspired by God and is useful to teach us what is true and to make us realize what is wrong in our lives. It corrects us when we are wrong and teaches us to do what is right.'

Today….some facts about how important the Bible is in our lives along with that of doctrine. The word says that whoever transgresses and does not abide in the doctrine of Christ does not have God. He who abides in the doctrine of Christ has both the Father and the Son.

> 'Doctrine without duty is a tree without fruit.
> Duty without doctrine is a tree without root.'

'Ho Bilblos' – The Book – 66 books of which 39 are Old Testament and 27 are New Testament. A very human book, written by men from all walks of life, prince and pauper, the highly intelligent as well as the very simple. Called the Canon of Scriptures; canon means rule or measurement in Latin.

- Revelation – 'God has spoken' God has revealed himself
- Inspiration – guarantees what God has said – reliable, accurate, without error
- Illumination – must have for the Holy Spirit to teach you
- Preservation – God so watching over His Word that He has preserved it

While reading and studying God's Word you will find the 'Fire within my bone,' Jeremiah 20:9. 'But if I say I'll never mention the Lord or speak in His name, but His Word burns in my heart like a fire. It's like a fire in my bones! I am worn out trying to hold it in! I can't do it!'

Be excited to have Christ in your heart and let it out to share with everyone.

PRAYER: Dear Lord, thank You today and every day for Your Word. Our guide for instruction, our roadmap for life and just the love that is shared from You to us Your children on exactly how much You sacrificed for us all. AMEN

DON'T FORGET!

# A NEW PLATEAU

SCRIPTURES: Romans 5:10; I Peter 5:10

WRITERS: Romans—Paul; I Peter—Peter

DEFINITION: plateau—an elevated, level period, or state – to reach a stable level

Romans 5:10 'For since our friendship with God was restored by the death of his son while we were still his enemies, we will certainly be saved through the life of his Son.'

I Peter 5:10 'In his kindness God calls you to share in His eternal glory by means of Christ Jesus. So, after you have suffered a little while, He will restore, support, and strengthen you, and He will place you on a firm foundation.'

Tuning out distractions in life has to sometimes happen for us to have the opportunity to reach a new level in life. A renewal, a new beginning, a new start. I recently read about Hall of Fame golfer Phil Mickelson and his return to major PGA title matches. He states that he loves the unique opportunities provided by hard work and practice along with luck has focused him once again after thirty years on the tour in search of his first Grand Slam by winning the PGA U. S. Open. Again, through his entire career, never a winner of the U. S. Open.

Are you searching for a new plateau in your life? Have things been so mundane in your life that you need new opportunities, a new breath of fresh life, a new beginning? You can have that with Christ if you simply come and follow Him. God restored everything for us in life when He gave his life.

Life for us is a test unlike any other situation. Peer pressure, job situations, management pressure for more production, family situations, cancer, addictions. All of a sudden, you find yourself plummeting into a dark hole and going the wrong direction in life. My friend, you have the answer to reaching a new plateau in life and that is only with Christ. Seek Him today so you can reach a higher level and allow things to click.

PRAYER: Dear Heavenly Father, thank You for opportunities whereby we can be at a new plateau or be able to see the one that we are headed towards. May we always be seeking You for a better life with You day to day. AMEN

DON'T FORGET!

# THE CLAY

SCRIPTURES: Jeremiah 18:6; Romans 9:21; Isaiah 45:9

WRITERS: Jeremiah—Jeremiah; Romans—Paul; Isaiah—Isaiah

DEFINITION: clay—used for modeling; moist sticky earth; used for brick, tile, and pottery

Jeremiah 18:6 'Oh Israel, can I not do to you as this potter has done to his day? As the clay is in the potter's hand, so are you in My hand?'

Isaiah 45:19 'What sorrow awaits those who argue with their Creator. Does a clay pot argue with its maker? Does the clay dispute with the one who shapes it, saying, 'Stop, you're doing it wrong!' Does the pot exclaim, 'How clumsy can you be?'

Romans 9:21 'When a potter makes jars out of clay, doesn't he have a right to use the same lump of clay to make one jar for decoration and another to throw garbage into?

When I think about clay, I think back when I was a young boy and we had Silly Putty. It had elasticity and would roll up and stretch until it popped. You could also press it over the funnies in the newspaper and get an exact copy of the ink and would look pretty cool. Later on, you could get clay or Play Doh and be able to shape and mold things that you wanted to make.

Our examples in scripture of clay are that our Creator, Jesus Christ, is the one who we desire to mold us and make us into the image He wants us to be. Jesus has just the touch for everything that He is making us into. For some, that is a better husband, a better parent, a better co-worker, a better pastor or even a better child. Jesus has put His mark, His stamp on us as he presses us down to imprint His blood on us.

Are you moldable? Can you be shaped as Christ wants to shape you or are you not available? Think about where your life is today and ask God to make you in his image. We are the clay and He is the hand that makes everything just like it needs to be.

PRAYER: Father God, take us and make us exactly how You want us to be. It is not about the physical mold; it is what You do to our hearts. AMEN

DON'T FORGET!

# ALWAYS ABOUT OTHERS

SCRIPTURE: Mark 12:30-31

WRITER: Mark

Mark 12:30-31 'And you must love the Lord your God with all your heart, all your soul, all your mind, and all your strength. The second is equally important; 'Love your neighbor as yourself.' No other commandment is greater than these.'

Life should always be about others. Scripture is very clear about how we are to live our life and who to live our life for. Our neighbors and loving them is equally important as loving the Lord our God. Listen...do you hear that? Pay careful attention as we scroll forward to life's situations that we will encounter.

You are out mowing your yard and you notice that your neighbor's grass is getting out of hand. The lawn is definitely not looking as well as your yard does and it has become a bit of an eye sore. You approach your neighbor only to find out that the man of the house has had a stroke. By the way, the stroke occurred over a month ago and that is the reason for the tall grass. Now it is up to you to apologize for not being more in touch and only living apart by a five-foot setback between houses. Come on, you can do better.

You also hear about a co-worker, someone you are not real close to, but you pass them every day going down the hall. For some reason, you have not seen this person for some time, but today you hear that this person has been diagnosed with lung cancer. What do you do? What do you say? How will you feel if and when that person returns to work? How about really taking a genuine interest in caring about this person and getting to know them better? Maybe asking to pray for them and helping them to trust in Jesus. Our number one purpose on earth, as Christ followers, is to love God, and love others. If we want to find meaning in our life, start doing what God commands

PRAYER: Lord God Almighty, we pray to You today for being about others. Help us to seek out our neighbors and let them know we care about them and love them. AMEN

DON'T FORGET!

# DISCONTENTMENT IN LIFE

SCRIPTURES: I Samuel 22:2; II Corinthians 13:5; Romans 9:2

WRITERS: I Samuel—Samuel; II Corinthians—Paul; Romans—Paul

DEFINITION: discontentment—unhappy at the conditions of things

> fallen—to collapse, to drop down, to descend, to stumble

> fail—to disappoint, to fall short

I Samuel 22:2 'Then others began coming-men were in trouble or in debt or who were just discontent-until David was the Captain of about 400 men.'

II Corinthians 13:5 'Examine yourselves to see if your faith is genuine. Test yourselves. Surely you know that Jesus Christ is among you; if not, you have failed the test of genuine faith.'

Romans 9:2 'My heart is filled with bitter sorrow and unending grief.'

So, we see David has lost everything: his job with Saul as a commander in the army, his wife, his home, his closest friend Jonathan, and finally his self-respect and pride. It was the lowest moment in his life.

Our life is not one day of sunshine after another. No, it is not. We all experience valleys a lot of our life. Maybe you are in a valley. The space is dark and dismal, disillusioned and desperate. Perhaps you cannot share with anyone how dark your situation is and you just keep it to yourself. A lot of times, these dark places are part of God's strategy for our lives. Far from harsh punishment, valleys can be used by God to bring about some of the greatest moments of your life. God is not giving up on you ever so don't give up on yourself.

Sometimes we have negative thoughts because things are happening to us and we feel sorrow, down-trodden, disappointed and we really don't know where to turn or how to ask for help. Remember, God is there for us and He will never let us down or be in a position to fail us. Continue to depend on Jesus for everything you do and victory will be won.

PRAYER: Dear Lord, thank You for Your saving grace and mercy in our lives. When we face discontentment in our lives and we are unhappy with choices, may we turn to You for direction we need. AMEN

DON'T FORGET!

# WHAT A FATHER MEANS
## TO YOU
## THE ROCK OF MY SALVATION

SCRIPTURES: Exodus 20:12; Psalm 89:26; Ephesians 6:4

WRITERS: Exodus—Moses; Psalm—David; Ephesians—Paul

DEFINITION: father—male parent, characteristic of a mentor or provides relationship; name and role for God in relation to the children he fosters/adopts; originator or creator

Exodus 20:12 'Honor your father and mother. Then you will have a long, full life in the land your God is giving you.'

Psalm 89:26 'And he will call out to me, 'You are my Father, my God, and the Rock of my salvation.'

Ephesians 6:4 'Fathers, do not provoke your children to anger by the way you treat them. Rather, bring them up with discipline and instruction that comes from the Lord.'

Wow....what a topic we have today. To have the honorable pleasure and request to speak about our Heavenly Father and my Earthly Father. There is no doubt it is very emotional to speak of both because of the unbelievable relationships. It starts with my own earthly Father who led me to my Heavenly Father. What a blessing for my own father to have the belief in the Heavenly Father that he would lead and share with me. I am now that same father to my daughters, and I don't ever want to take anything for granted in being the best dad I can be to them.

As a son, I always want to follow God's commands in honoring my mother and my father. My relationship with my father has always been very wholesome. My father was always involved with me in sports either as a coach or as a spectator in the stands. My dad was always present in my life and that has always meant a lot to me.

Lastly, concerning my father, he loves me and has shown love to me all of my life. When I learned about my indictment and my sentencing, my own dad at 84 years old offered to serve my sentence for me. That is true love.

As for my Heavenly Father, I am so thankful daily for His grace, mercy, love, kindness that is extended to us each day. To know that God loved us so much to send His Son Jesus to pay a harsh price for our sins. Today and every day, I am thankful for two Godly Fathers.

PRAYER: Almighty God, Father, Creator of All, thank You for Fathers who lead us and direct us on the right paths in life. AMEN

DON'T FORGET!

# THINGS TO BE THANKFUL FOR TODAY

SCRIPTURES: I Thessalonians 5:16-18; Psalm 107:1

WRITERS: I Thessalonians—Paul; Psalm—David

DEFINITION: thanks—kindly or grateful thoughts; gratitude

I Thessalonians 5:16-18 'Always be joyful. Never stop praying. Be thankful in all circumstances, for this is God's will for you who belong to Christ Jesus.'

Psalm 107:1 'Give thanks to the Lord, for He is good! His faithful love endures forever.'

Rather than a one-page devotional on the topic of being thankful, we could use reams of paper to describe all of the many things that we are thankful for today. Since today is Father's Day, I begin with thanksgiving for a Christian earthly Father as well as the ultimate, my Heavenly Father, my God, Jesus Christ my Lord and Savior.

Having a personal one on one relationship with Jesus Christ sets the landscape for the list I am about to share:

# THINGS TO BE THANKFUL FOR TODAY

| | | |
|---|---|---|
| Relationship with a spouse | Relationship with a parent | Work |
| Relationship with children | Father's Day | Ability |
| Relationship with siblings | Mother's Day | Teamwork |
| Relationship with friends | Friendships | Attitude |
| Hope | Health | Dreamwork |
| Love | Communication | A Smile |
| Forgiveness | Trust | A Handshake |
| Gentleness | Tenderness | Prayer |
| Humbleness | Bible Study | Humility |

Think about things today that you would place on your 'Thankful List' and keep adding to it daily and watch how it expands. A daily walk with the Holy Spirit will reveal a lot of those things that are so vital to our lives today.

PRAYER: Dear Lord, thank You for Your greatness and Your goodness. We do have so many things to be thankful for each day of our lives. AMEN

DON'T FORGET!

# PRAYING FOR UNCTION

SCRIPTURES: Psalm 137:17; Hebrews 1:9; I John 2:20,27

WRITERS: Psalm—Paul; Hebrews—unknown; I John—John the Apostle

DEFINITION: unction—the act of anointing, anything that soothes or comforts, fervent or earnest quality; to give hope

Psalm 137:17 'Here I will increase the power of David; my anointed one will be a light for My people.'

Hebrews 1:9 'You love justice and hate evil. Therefore, I God, your God has anointed you, pouring out the oil of joy on you more than anyone else.'

I John 2:20, 27 'But you are not like that, for the Holy One has given you His Spirit, and all of you know the truth. But you have received the Holy Spirit, and He lives within you, so you don't need anyone to teach you what is true.'

I have a Bible study group that I participate with weekly and the word 'unction' came up so I wanted to dig deeper. It is defined as an anointing of the Holy Spirit. I believe we all would be okay to have a little extra anointing in our lives.

There are many great examples around us of the anointing of the Holy Spirit and I am reminded of the lives of many great men of God but one especially stands out and that is Billy Graham. Billy Graham was a terrific leader for the cause of crusade and so many lives being changed because he was specific in his goals. Billy Graham was an author, evangelist, spiritual advisor to a number of Presidents as well as a Godly husband, father, grandfather and mentor to many.

Let's think about other leaders in our world that have been blessed with unction in their lives. Max Lucado is another author that comes to mind. He is a Christian writer who has sold millions of books just by allowing the Holy Spirit to speak through him and put pen to paper to express his thoughts and to prick the hearts of many to be challenged with following Christ as Savior. Will you follow Christ today and start a new life for yourself?

PRAYER: Dear Lord, we need Your Holy Spirit in our lives so bad each day. We pray for the unction, the anointing that only You can give us. AMEN

DON'T FORGET!

DEVOTIONS FROM OAKDALE

# WHAT IS YOUR PARADISE?

SCRIPTURE: Matthew 5:4; Revelation 21:1-7

WRITERS: Matthew—Matthew; Revelation—John the Apostle

DEFINITION: paradise—an intermediate place where the souls of the righteous await resurrection and the final judgement; a state of delight; the abode of righteous souls after death; heaven

Matthew 5:4 'God blesses those who mourn, for they will be comforted.'

Revelation 21:1-7 'Then I saw a new heaven and a new earth; for the old heaven and the old earth had disappeared. And the sea was also gone. And I saw the holy city, the new Jerusalem, coming down from God out of heaven like a bride beautifully dressed for her husband. I heard a loud shout from the throne, saying, 'Look, God 's home is now among his people! He will live with them, and they will be His people. God himself will be with them. He will wipe every tear from their eyes, and there will be no more death or sorrow or crying or pain. All these things are gone forever.' And the One sitting on the throne said, 'Look, I am making everything new!' and then He said, 'Write this down, for what I tell you is trustworthy and true.' And He also said, 'It is finished! I am the Alpha and the Omega – the Beginning and the End. To all who are thirsty I will give freely from the spring of the water of life. All who are victorious will inherit all these blessings and I will be their God, and they will be My children.'

What is your paradise today? Going to the beach or a property that you own someplace secluded in the woods. Maybe, the setting is quiet and serene with lots of lavish things to compliment the property and the area. Everyone has their own definition of paradise. The Bible clearly defines paradise as our souls are awaiting the final judgement. Heaven is our paradise and we need to be prepared in all that we do to be ready. Revelation 21:1-7 clearly defines and describes that Jesus is waiting for us and will be with us. Are you ready? Are you prepared? Will you be in paradise once you die?

PRAYER: Dear God, help us to be prepared for the one true paradise which is heaven. Please prepare our hearts today. AMEN

DON'T FORGET!

# JESUS, OUR CORNERSTONE

SCRIPTURES: Psalm 118:22; Ephesians 2:20

WRITERS: Psalm—David; Ephesians—Paul

DEFINITION: cornerstone—a stone forming a corner or angle in a wall; foundation

Psalm 118:22 'The stone that the builders rejected has now become the cornerstone.'

Ephesians 2:20 'Together, we are His house, built on the foundation of the apostles and the prophets. And the cornerstone is Christ Jesus Himself.'

We are always in the process of growing in our life. You grow up as a child, then to a teen, and then to an adult. Thinking all along, WOW I can't wait for college and then to get married and have a family. Growth along the way is always good.

Paul uses the scripture in Ephesians to speak of 'becoming.' God's house is always becoming because when people trust and follow Christ, everyone is joined together, the house of God is in the process of being built. God's work is still going on.

We, my co-workers in landscape at Oakdale are in the process of building a memorial to honor a thirty-year marker of individuals that were affected by the fire that destroyed the prison before it was rebuilt. We have a thirty-foot-by-thirty-foot area that we have removed two dead tree stumps, removed all debris, dug out for the proper steel footing and formed up with 2X6 boards in preparation for cement work. Once the cement is poured, we will begin building a concrete block wall that has to be level on a solid foundation before completion of the wall. The cornerstone brick will set the proper angle and course of everything we do. Don't forget that is exactly what Christ is to us in our lives. We are to build everything in our life from the foundation He provides for us.

PRAYER: Dear Heavenly Father, thank You for being our foundation. Our cornerstone that puts everything in motion for a life lived in You. AMEN

## DON'T FORGET!

# RESTORATION

SCRIPTURES: I Peter 5:10; Psalm 14:7

WRITERS: I Peter—Peter; Psalm—David

DEFINITION: restore—to give back, return, to renew

I Peter 5:10 'In his kindness God called you to share in his eternal glory by means of Christ Jesus. So, after you have suffered a little while, He will restore, support, and strengthen you, and He will place you on a firm foundation. All power to Him forever! AMEN'

Psalm 14:7 'Who will come from Mount Zion to rescue Israel? When the Lord restores His people, Jacob will shout with joy, and Israel will rejoice.'

A good example of restoration comes in the scriptures when we see Peter addressing the elders in the churches. He was letting them know of the challenges and sufferings that were taking place. He lets them know also that he is a fellow elder and he is understanding of what they are going through. He continues to let them know that he cares about them and for them. He challenges them to watch over their flock and take care of their calling as leaders of the church more so than worrying what they would gain from it personally.

Peter also shared with them to be humble and to always be alert. The great enemy which is the devil will always be present and prowling around to devour those whom are not standing firm.

Once we have experienced and suffered for a while, restoration will occur and we will receive the strength needed to maintain a firm foundation. As we know, a firm foundation is so important to relationships with those at church, extra-curricular events, work place and most importantly, our home with family.

Perhaps there are things that have happened to you in the past or maybe even some extreme circumstances that have rocked your life. Hold on and hang in there for restoration. Continue to trust in God and allow his Holy Spirit and faithfulness to work in you.

PRAYER: Magnificent Master, thank You for restoration in life. Just when we need it the most, You know the precise timing. AMEN

DON'T FORGET!

# TIME TO BLOOM

SCRIPTURE: Psalm 65:11

WRITER: David

DEFINITION: bloom—the flower of a plant; a condition or time of vigor, freshness, and beauty, to shine, to glow, to cause to flourish

Psalm 65:11 'You crown the year with a bountiful harvest, even the hard pathways overflow with abundance.'

We don't determine the seasons of our lives. God does. We need a faith perspective in every season. We have times when we feel we are walking through a time when we feel undone, exposed and scattered. Our once well-defined boundaries have been replaced with holes in the ground, dirt mounds and even boulders that have surfaced. We wonder what in the world happened in our tidy lives. It is during these seasons that God sets the plow a little deeper into the soil of our hearts because He is about to do a new thing.

Beneath the surface, we have buried hurts, embedded lies, and weeds that choke the life out of us. It's a messy process, and the enemy wastes no time in leveraging his lies to make us feel worse than we already did. But if we look up and listen for the Lord, we will hear him say, 'My dear child, this isn't about who you are; it's about who you are becoming. Your great unearthing will soon be the devils undoing. Hold on, listen for my voice, and know that this season will not last forever.' A time of blooming is ahead for you. Believe it, you will get through whatever you are going through!

Of course, the focus verse takes your mind to the garden. And it is so true, He wants to cultivate a heart of joy, love, trust, and most of all, patience. Much like when planting our flowers, we trust the rain and the sun to help them grow and patience to see them bloom. God wants to see us grow, we just have to be patient and listen for His perfect instruction.

PRAYER: Father God, thank You for the Master gardener that You are. Always showing us the weeds in our life, which is sin. Help us to keep a clean garden and always bloom for You. AMEN

DON'T FORGET!

# THE AMAZING SOMETHING

SCRIPTURES: Matthew 5:3; II Corinthians 8:9

WRITERS: Matthew—Matthew; II Corinthians 8:9

DEFINITION: Amazing Something—Jesus

Matthew 5:3 'Blessed are the poor in spirit, for theirs is the Kingdom of Heaven.'

II Corinthians 8:9 'You know the grace of our Lord Jesus Christ, that though he was rich, yet for your sake he became poor, so that you by His poverty might become rich.'

I have heard it many times in my lifetime, 'If I just had_____, then I would be so happy.' One has to ask the question and that is: On a daily basis how aware are you of your spiritual bankruptcy apart from Christ? How might you grow in this awareness? Maybe even the question of how would your friends characterize you as spiritually self-sufficient or as one who knows the blessing of spiritual poverty?

Everyone in this world needs the 'Amazing Something' and His name is Jesus! Our world we live in is over taken by riches and wealth. That is why we find ourselves interested in others who have wealth.

We all need bankruptcy so God can work grace in our lives. We need to be on empty so we can realize that everything about us is unrighteous. It is recognizing and admitting that we have nothing and then it causes us to reach for the 'Amazing Something,' Jesus.

It is only in that time that we recognize and are willing to confess how poor we actually are, daily seeking and celebrating the vast wealth that is ours because of the life, death and resurrection of Jesus.

PRAYER: Almighty Father, You are the 'Amazing Something' that we have in our lives through Your Son, Jesus Christ. We love You and adore You. AMEN

## DON'T FORGET!

# BENEDICTION

SCRIPTURE: Numbers 6:24-26

WRITER: Numbers—Moses

DEFINITION: benediction—a blessing, an invocation of divine blessing, an expression of good wishes, the placement of blessings

Numbers 6:24-26 'May the Lord bless you and protect you. May the Lord smile on you and be gracious to you. May the Lord show you His favor and give you His peace.'

Have you ever thought of what 'Benediction' really means? Typically, we think of the benediction coming at the end of a service and a song is sung and then the congregation is released to depart the sanctuary. Benediction actually means the placing of blessing. When Jesus said, it is finished,' it was the benediction of placing the ultimate blessing over us. Is there something we need to lay at the feet of Jesus to be finished and the blessing of freedom in Christ received? What needs to be finished? Is there some guilt lingering, some habits, some hurt feelings, some anger?

Today, search your heart and see if there is something that needs to be laid down so you can freely receive your blessings. Perhaps you have not forgiven someone that has wronged you or crossed your pathway with wrong intentions. Don't keep putting things off saying that you will do it tomorrow because that might not happen. Did you do today what you need to do in order to be placing a blessing on the life of someone else?

PRAYER: Most Gracious Heavenly Father, thank You for what benediction really means to us in our lives. A divine blessing, a pouring out, an expression of Your love for us. We continue to ask You to bless us, protect us, smile upon us and show Your favor upon our lives. AMEN

## DON'T FORGET!

# DAILY DON'T FORGETS

SCRIPTURE: I Corinthians 13:4-7

WRITER: Paul

DEFINITION: love—the ultimate expression of God's loyalty, purity, and mercy extended toward His people; to be reflected in human relationships of brotherly concern, marital fidelity and adoration of God; a beloved person

I Corinthians 13:4-7 'Love is patient and kind. Love is not jealous or boastful or proud or rude. It does not demand its own way. It is not irritable, and it keeps no record of being wronged. It does not rejoice about injustice but rejoices whenever the truth wins out. Love never gives up, never loses faith, is always hopeful, and endures through every circumstance.'

When I think of the adjectives that make up the list for me as a writer for the 'driving force' behind my life, I also think about the don't forgets in my life. My PawPaw instilled in me the don't forgets and the way in which he treated me and my siblings throughout our life until he passed with a heart attack. I would have to say the don't forget from my PawPaw really screamed 'love.' So today, my daily don't forget is that of love.

I circle back to the love chapter which is I Corinthians 13 and I get something new from those verses each time I take a trip that way and camp out in these four specific heart felt verses. As we all know and have heard, love makes the world go around. Relationships need love, churches need love, presidents need love, spouses and children need love. Also, workers spending much of their day with one another also need love.

Just like baking a cake as a dessert, you must have all of the right ingredients or it isn't a cake, it is a flop. Such is the case without love in our lives. Love is not just an emotion or a thought. Love has to be put into action. Not just kind thoughts and emotions but a real demonstration. What is your don't forget today that you wish to work on?

PRAYER: Lord God Almighty, thank You for don't forgets like love. I am thankful for Your love for me through Your Son Jesus Christ. AMEN

## DON'T FORGET!

# DRIVING FORCE

SCRIPTURES: Psalm 95:3; Nehemiah 1:5; I Peter 2:9

WRITERS: Psalm—David; Nehemiah—Nehemiah; I Peter—Peter

Psalm 95:3 'For the Lord is a great God, a great King above all Gods.'

Nehemiah 1:5 'Then I said, 'O Lord, God of Heaven, the great awesome God who keeps His covenant of unfailing love with those who love Him and obey His commands.'

I Peter 2:9 'But you are not like that, for you are a chosen people. You are royal priests, a holy nation, God's very own possession. As a result, you can show others the goodness of God, for He calls you out of the darkness into his wonderful light.'

One of my readings recently took me to the two words 'driving force.' A driving force in my book is something you are moving toward in your heart, convictions, beliefs and perhaps attributes you want to seek out. So, here is my short list that means a lot to me. When you are viewing each word, think about where you are in life. What drives you and where do you want to place your inner thoughts and beliefs?

My List

Holy Spirit, love, friendship, giving, bearing fruit, forgiveness, blessing, actions, character, courage, discipleship, encouragement, faith, family, fellowship, grace, growth, honesty, humility, integrity, Jesus, joy, kindness, life, marriage, memories, ministry, mercy, miracles, obedience, opportunity, peace, patience, perseverance, perspective, praise, prayer, preparation, promises, privilege, relationships, provision, purpose, reconciliation, repentance, restoration, resurrection, revelation, sacrifice, strength, transformation, thankfulness, trust, truth, unction, victory, vision, wisdom, work, worship....

I challenge you today to put together your own list of things that drive you and are important to your focus of life and how you live it. Think hard. Think deep. Give the topic your undivided attention.

PRAYER: Lord God, thank You for being the driving force in my life. I pray that You would continue to add things to my driving force list. AMEN

DON'T FORGET!

# DON'T LOOK BACK

SCRIPTURES: Isaiah 41:10; 41:13; Joshua 1:5

WRITERS: Isaiah—Isaiah son of Amoz; Joshua—Joshua

DEFINITION: abandon—to defeat or forsake

Isaiah 41:10 'Don't be afraid, for I am with you. Don't be discouraged, for I am your God. I will strengthen you and help you. I will hold you up with my victorious right hand.'

> 41:13 'For I hold you by your right hand- I, the Lord your God. And I will say to you, 'Don't be afraid. I am here to help you.'

Joshua 1:5 'No one will be able to stand against you as long as you live. For I will be with you as I was with Moses. I will not fail you or abandon you.'

Look back to your past week and think about how things look in your rearview mirror. Yes, it is the past, and for some of us, we would like to quickly forget certain things that have occurred and look forward to new opportunities and new highways so to speak.

This is a new day full of new mercies. Yesterday, with all of its ups and downs, is truly a thing of the past and now new hope is on the horizon. God has already gone before us and prepared the way so there is no step we will take today that our Heavenly Father has not already walked through.

Always remember to look up, don't look back, look to Him, for He is right here with us.

PRAYER: Protective Father, when we feel fear, we will cast our eyes on You and remember Your commands. Help us to fear not. Give us strength. We know we are never alone. We trust You to work in all things for the advancement of Your kingdom. AMEN

DON'T FORGET!

# ON EAGLE'S WINGS

SCRIPTURES: Exodus 19:4; Isaiah 40:31

WRITER: Exodus—Moses; Isaiah—Isaiah

Exodus 19:4 'You have seen what I did to the Egyptians. You know how I carried you on eagles' wings and brought you to myself.'

Isaiah 40:31 'But those who trust in the Lord will find new strength. They will soar high on wings like eagles. They will run and not grow weary. They will walk and not faint.'

On eagles' wings addresses those that need strength and are weary. Have you ever thought that you could handle something alone? You did not need any help and afterwards, you felt beat down. That is why Isaiah 40:31 is so important. The scripture says that those who trust in the Lord will find new strength. So, what is 'new strength?' It is what you need when your tank is empty. When you cannot go any further on your own merits. It is the time when things are rough and you need help quick because you have exhausted everything you have in your toolbox to make it happen. Then, you call on God and ask, 'Please help me God.' This is the hope that you needed and the Creator of the world supplies your every need.

I love how majestic eagles are and their design being strong all the way from their talons that are used for game and their food as well as their eyesight to be able to zero in on its prey. We as humans need also to be able to zero in on the sin in our life and to be able to avoid those pitfalls of life. We will get there when we soar like eagles and those beautiful wings spread out and that is similar to us placing everything on the shoulders of Jesus and allowing Him to work in us.

PRAYER: Most Gracious Lord, thank You for helping us to spread our wings like eagles and to trust in You to fly out of the nest of life and rely on You. AMEN

DON'T FORGET!

# WEARINESS IS CALLING

SCRIPTURE: Isaiah 43:1-3, 22

WRITER: Isaiah

DEFINITION: weariness—to be physically or mentally exhausted by hard work, exertion, strain

Isaiah 43:1-3, 22 'Do not be afraid, for I have ransomed you. I have called you by name; you are mine. When you go through deep waters, I will be with you. When you go through rivers of difficulty, you will not drown. When you walk through the fire of oppression, you will not be burned up; the flames will not consume you. For I am the Lord, your God. 22)But dear family of Jacob, you refuse to ask for my help. You have grown tired of me, O Israel.'

Yes, we all grow tired and weary at different times in our life. First of all, life is hard. You get tired and you begin to feel further out in the deep more now than ever. What comes next? More stretching, more challenges and sometimes more than you ever dreamed.

Weary....Yes, yes God, we are. We are tired you say. Uncertain with too many things to do and not enough time to do them. Sick....This is awful and you want us to be here on earth? Why, why would he tell Israel that they weren't weary for Him? He answers this way, 'Because we can walk this together. I am with you. I will be your strength. I will help you today. There is power in weakness.'

Weariness forces us to look outside ourselves for strength. Weariness forces us to hold tight to faith, hope and trust. Weariness gives us no choice but to believe that God is holding you up. Weariness brings us to a place of full surrender, humbleness and neediness that we would not otherwise know. He desires our whole selves to be pushed to the limits for the cause of the gospel. He wants warriors in His Kingdom. Are you willing to be weary for God today?     'CMS'

PRAYER: Almighty Lord and Savior, thank You for weariness and the fact that Your grace is sufficient for us all. Thank You that Your power is made perfect in weakness. AMEN

DON'T FORGET!

# THE STEPPING STONES OF LIFE

SCRIPTURES: James 5:10; Colossians 1:11; Romans 12:12

WRITERS: James—James; Colossians—Paul; Romans—Paul

James 5:10 'For examples of patience in suffering, dear brothers and sisters, look at the prophets who spoke in the name of the Lord. We give great honor to those who endure under suffering.'

Colossians 1:11 'We also pray that you will be strengthened with all his glorious power so you will have all the endurance and patience you need. May you be filled with joy, always thanking the Father.'

Romans 12:12 'Rejoice in our confident hope. Be patient in trouble, and keep on praying. When God's people are in need, be ready to help them. Always be eager to practice hospitality.'

We all face many pathways in our lives. So many roads to travel and each stepping stone for us is an opportunity to do a number of things to glorify God and truly touch a lot of peoples lives. Some of those stepping stones that we touch are as follows: trust, attitude, Christlikeness, honor, character, difficulty, grace, love, forgiveness, accomplishment, friendship, kindness, mercy, endurance, trouble and joy just to name a few. No doubt, you will have your own list to compile and ponder over after you think for a while.

Obviously, there are so many important decisions to make each day in our life. Decisions of work, relationships, family and spiritual decisions. We are told that we will have suffering and that we will need patience to handle those situations. Paul also shares with us that we will experience trouble yet we are to remain confident and to rejoice. There is only one way to do that in life and understand it and that is through personal relationship with Jesus Christ. I know for sure that your walk will mean more to you in the years to come if the stepping stones of life are with Him each day.

PRAYER: Most Gracious Lord, thank You for marking our steps

and keeping us safe along the way. There are many potholes, slippery slopes and destructive pit falls that we need Your protection from in our lives. AMEN

DON'T FORGET!

# ARE YOU LIVING?

SCRIPTURES: Psalm 69:32; Ecclesiastes 9:9; John 14:19; Titus 2:12

WRITERS: Psalm 69—King David; Ecclesiastes—King Solomon; John—Apostle John; Titus—Apostle Paul

Psalm 69:32 'The humble will see their God at work and be glad. Let all who seek God's help be encouraged.'

Ecclesiastes 9:9 'Live happily with the woman you love through all the meaningless days of life that God has given you under the sun. The wife God gives you is your reward for all your earthly toil. Whatever you do, do well.

John 14:19 'Soon the world will no longer see me, but you will see me. Since I live, you will also live.'

Titus 2:12 'And we are instructed to turn from godless living and sinful pleasures. We should live this evil world with wisdom, righteousness and devotion to God.'

How are we supposed to live? How do we spend our days? God wants us to live free of guilt and to be very happy. This will only happen if we are truly committed to God. Do we have days where things in a relationship go sideways and we are wondering which way the arrow is pointing? Who wronged who and how long will it really take for someone to come forward, take the blame, confess your sin and accept Jesus' forgiving grace?

I believe one of the ways that we have trouble is that trouble breeds more of itself and then our ability to get out of it and truly live becomes more difficult. What we need is God's amazing, rescuing, forgiving grace.

Scriptures that support living are visible for us if we just dig deep enough.

- John 14:19 – Christ is our source
- John 11:25-26 – Speaks about length of time/forever
- I Thessalonians 5:10 – Christs' purpose for our lives

- Titus 2:12 – Manner in which to live
- II Timothy 3:12 – Price to be paid

Ultimately, we all want to live a godly life and we have to understand that we will suffer persecution at some point in our Christian walk. Live for Christ today.

PRAYER: Almighty Father, thank You Lord for Your love for us and the life that You bless us with daily. May we glorify You in all we do. AMEN

DON'T FORGET!

# JOHN 3:16 PROMISES

SCRIPTURE: John 3:16, 17

WRITER: John

John 3:16, 17 'For this is how God loved the world; He gave his one and only Son, so that everyone who believes in Him will not perish but have eternal life. God sent his Son into the world not to judge the world, but to save the world through Him.'

I am sometimes hesitant to quote other people's work but sometimes I do come across promises that trigger a thought that takes me back to a promise as that of John 3:16. The quote is as follows:

> For love paid a debt I did not owe,
>
> To provide a plan of salvation for you to know.
>
> I stretched my hands out all the way,
>
> To remind you how much I love you every day.
>
> Today place your trust in me,
>
> And I will forgive your sins for all eternity.
>
> So now when life is too much to bear,
>
> Look at my hand and see how much I care,
>
> Go and live your life for me,
>
> And I will prepare your mansion,
>
> Where soon we will be.
>
> Love, Jesus
>
> Source – Stars for Eternity.com
>
> copyright 2020

Romans 5:8 quotes 'But God commendeth his love toward us, in that, while we were yet sinners, Christ died for us.' John 15:13 'Greater love had no man than this, that a man lay down his life for his friends.'

Jesus Christ died for you and me, to save us from our sins. Have you ever thought you would lay down your life for someone you love? My answer is yes, I would. Someone that you love dearly that you give your all to is worth that commitment. Christ did that for us. That is true love.

PRAYER: Lord God, thank You for sacrificing Your Son, Jesus for my life. I love You! AMEN

DON'T FORGET!

# HEY GOD!

SCRIPTURE: Romans 5:3-4

WRITER: Paul

Me: Hey, God

God: Hello…

Me: I'm falling apart. Can you put me back together?

God: I would rather not.

Me: Why?

God: Because you aren't a puzzle.

Me: What about all the pieces of my life that are falling down onto the ground?

God: Let them stay there for a while. They fell off for a reason. Take some time and decide if you need any of those pieces back.

Me: You don't understand! I'm breaking down!

God: No – you don't understand. You are breaking through. What you are feeling are just growing pains. You are shedding the things and the people in your life that are holding you back. You aren't falling apart. You are falling into place. Relax. Take some deep breaths and allow those things you don't need any more to fall off of you. Quit holding on to the pieces that don't fit you anymore. Let them go.

Me: Once I start doing that, what will be left of me?

God: Only the very best pieces of you.

Me: I'm scared of changing.

God: I keep telling you – You aren't changing! You are becoming!

Anonymous

We all want to be becoming in our life. Sometimes it is not easy to change what things look like because they have looked that way for so long. Let the Master shed the pieces that you don't need to become who HE really wants you to be.

PRAYER: Dear God, thank You for change. Thank You for taking off what does not need to be present. We want to become more like You. AMEN

### DON'T FORGET!

# BEARING ONE
# ANOTHERS BURDENS

SCRIPTURE: Galatians 6:1-5

WRITER: Galatians—Paul

Galations 6:1-5 'Dear Brothers and Sisters, if another believer is overcome by some sin, you who are godly should gently and humbly help that person back onto the right path. And be careful not to fall into the same temptation yourself. Share each other's burdens, and in this way obey the law of Christ. If you think you are too important to help someone, you are only fooling yourself. You are not that important. Pay careful attention to your own work, for then you will get the satisfaction of a job well done, and you won't ever need to compare yourself to anyone else. For we are each responsible for our own conduct.'

Paul tells us to restore one who is caught (NIV) or overtaken (KJV) in a sin and to do so gently and cautiously. However, this is not the case of the one described in the previous chapter 5:19-21. There we see Paul listing fifteen specific sins such as sexual immorality, impurity, lustful pleasures, idolatry, sorcery, hostility, quarreling, jealousy, outbursts of anger, selfish ambition, dissension, division, envy, drunkenness, wild parties, and other sins like these. Paul is saying people who participate in a practice of a lifestyle of sin will not inherit the Kingdom of God.

Instead, Galatians 6:1 describes someone who has been walking the path of God and was overtaken in a sin. Paul says to restore this person. The mystery is that He gives no instruction or clues on how to do so. My friend shared with me that he was doing work for a retired Southern Baptist preacher and this preacher shared about a friend who had been through the described situation of a person falling and needing help to be restored, without a blink of an eye he said, 'NO we are Southern Baptist – we shoot our wounded.'

What are your thoughts on restoration and helping bear one another's burden as described here today?

PRAYER: Almighty God in Heaven, thank You for Your love for us each day. Thank You for restoration and forgiveness. AMEN

## DON'T FORGET!

# GIFTS OF THE HOLY SPIRIT

SCRIPTURE: I Corinthians 12:10

WRITER: Paul

I Corinthians 12:10 'He gives one person the power to perform miracles, and another the ability to prophesy. He gives someone else the ability to discern whether a message is from the Spirit of God or from another spirit. Still another person is given the ability to speak in unknown languages, while another is given the ability to interpret what is being said.'

There is no greater spiritual growth and insight and hunger for more understanding of God's word than when we are filled with the Holy Spirit. We have seen it before our own eyes that God performs miracles. People were freed from bondage and their lives were changed. God gave a prophetic word through someone who spoke in tongues. Someone else received the meaning of it and the third was touched and encouraged because it was exactly the answer that he had asked God for in his prayers that morning. These things happen when people have open hearts for the Holy Spirit to freely move. This still happens today. We serve an awesome God. Nothing is too difficult for Him.

Yet, we have to acknowledge that we grieve the Holy Spirit when we seek a name for ourselves. Too often this has caused damage and confusion. God desires to be in the center of our lives, but so many put themselves in the center and the Holy Spirit is grieved.

It is crucial and about the gifts of the Holy Spirit, not the gifts to possess for ourselves, for our own glory. Yes, it is wonderful when the Holy Spirit is leading us in these gifts, but the only suitable demeanor is to be humble and full of love for our God. The glory is not about our honor, our name. It is all about God's glory. His name above all names.

'CMS'

PRAYER: Father God, with all my heart, I want to thank You for the Holy Spirit who still works miracles today and leads us in your truth. I bow before You Father, Son and Holy Spirit. To You be the glory of all eternity. AMEN

DON'T FORGET!

# MARKED WITH A SEAL

SCRIPTURES: Ephesians 1:13-14

WRITER: Paul

Ephesians 1:13-14 'And you also were included in Christ when you heard the message of truth, the gospel of your salvation when you believed. You were marked in Him with a seal, the promised Holy Spirit, who is a deposit guaranteeing our inheritance until redemption of those who are God's possession – to the praise of His glory.'

When I think about being marked, I think of a permanent magic marker my Mom always told me to be careful with because it was not coming off. She was right, once it was on there, you are done. I also think about a couple of scars that I have on my forearm and right above my kneecap. Those places are marked.

When we believe that our Lord Jesus died for our sins, we know that He loves us. In marriage, the new bride will bear the surname of her new groom. If we are not married, we will have a surname so people know to which family we belong. In a spiritual sense, this is also true: When we love the Lord, people will see it. People recognize it. The Holy Spirit will begin to work in you. He is known for inspiring, guiding and encouraging believers. We are marked in Him with a seal in Christ and He promises that the Holy Spirit will inspire and guide us who are believers.

Think about your life today. Are you marked by the Holy Spirit? Have you made a commitment to follow Christ and are enjoying that life each day or are you uncommitted?

PRAYER: Lord God, I pray that You would reveal Your ways through Your Word and Your spirit today. AMEN

DON'T FORGET!

# WHERE ARE WE GOING?

SCRIPTURE: Psalm 20:4

WRITER: David

DEFINITION: roadmap—direction in which one is going

Psalm 20:4 'May he grant your heart's desires and make all your plans succeed.'

Planning is great and is also a very essential part of planning a trip, a destination, a vacation or just off to church or work. We need to know the direction in which we are going or we will just be lost and defeated feeling we all need a plan and goals for our lives. We have to remember that sometimes God has other plans that are even better not only for His purpose, but for our own lives. We have to be open to taking a new path or exploring new direction. That nudge you feel or that small voice you hear could be God nudging you along. Take the fear out of that question, where is my life going? Make it exciting pondering of the possibilities when you ask yourself instead, where is my life going next? Some turns will be mistakes but learn from each one. Don't get loaded down in guilt. Some paths will break your heart in the moment but strengthen it for years to come.

I guess with all of the new technology in our vehicles these days, we rely on navigation and an inner computer system that gets us from point A to point B. However, if things shut down and don't work, we shift over to our smart phone to have a backup way of getting someplace. I remember stopping at a gas station many times to ask for directions after having looked at the old paper maps. Those seem to be a thing of the past now. Bottom line, keep moving and keep God close!

PRAYER: Dear Lord, thank You for being the compass in our lives that we need. You always provide the right direction for everything we need to do. AMEN

DON'T FORGET!

# WHO IS GRACE?

SCRIPTURE: Ephesians 2:8; I John 1:9

WRITERS: Ephesians—Paul; I John—John the Apostle

Ephesians 2:8 'For by grace you have been saved through faith. And this is not of your own doing; it is a gift from God.'

I John 1:9 'But if we confess our sins to God, He will keep His promises and do what is right; He will forgive us our sins and purify us from all our wrongdoings.'

Grace is a person (really?). In our lives we are not always the best person. Sometimes we haven't walked in faith. Haven't always known grace. If God were looking at you right now, what do you think He would say? I instantly thought about all of the sins I've committed, all of the people I've hurt, all of those moments where I couldn't believe I just did or said 'that.'

When posed that question, what was your first thought? Some say to themselves, 'God is waiting for me to get better. He's waiting for me to clean up my act BEFORE He loves me.' Not true. It will never be. God is watching us right now with all of our sin, flaws, failures, secrets about us that we hide from other people, and He's smiling. He is looking at us saying, 'I love you. You are mine. I am not mad at you. I am not disappointed in you. I want to be with you. I forgive you. I will never give up on you.'

How can it be that we fail God a hundred times, waivered in our faith and trust and have run from Him more times that we can count, and still, He chooses us, He fights for us, He chases us down in our darkness and reaches out His hand. We ask, 'How can it be that God still loves me?'

That's what grace is…grace is a person. His name is Jesus, and we can rest assured that Jesus did everything necessary for us to be right in God's eyes. No one is too broken for grace. Jesus perfected it. It is finished!

God is the only one that can love everything about us that we think we are not. The moment we confess our sins and ask for forgiveness, God forgives us. Now we must do our part and leave the guilt behind.

PRAYER: Most Gracious Lord, thank You for Your grace that covers our lives. We love You and praise You for all you do. AMEN

DON'T FORGET!

# TOTAL TRUST

SCRIPTURE: Acts 5:12,18

WRITER: Luke

DEFINITION: trust—assured reliance on the character, ability, strength, or truth of someone or something; hope

Acts 5:12, 18 'The apostles were performing many miracles, signs and wonders among the people. And all the believers were meeting regularly at the Temple in the area known as Solomon's Colonnade. They arrested the apostles and put them in the public jail.'

Here are the facts concerning the apostles and just exactly how they kept their trust during some rough times:

SETTING: Jerusalem—the city was small and only covered a third of a mile in each direction

SADDUCEES: filled with jealousy

TIMELINE: 80-90 days since Jesus had been crucified

EVENTS: a movement is taking place/Peter and John—doors locked, guards standing, they are in the temple preaching and we know 10-20% of the population had made decisions for Christ

FEAR: the apostles were only afraid of being stoned. They were being found worthy in the flogging and humiliation.

It is always about us trusting in God. Allowing the Holy Spirit to work in us. Then, mighty things will happen. We will undergo persecution and our proper response should be to rejoice.

What does God expect of us?

➤ Love the Lord your God with all of your heart, soul and mind.
➤ Love your neighbor.
➤ We must love ourselves so we can then love our neighbors.

PRAYER: Almighty God, help us to always have total trust in You. Through the tough times, good times, high days and low days. Always looking to You. AMEN

DON'T FORGET!

# BETTER THAN BEFORE

SCRIPTURES: Luke 20:18; I Corinthians 11:24

WRITERS: Luke—Luke; I Corinthians—Paul

Luke 20:18 'Everyone who stumbles over the stone will be broken to pieces, and it will crush anyone it falls on.'

I Corinthians 11:24 'And gave thanks to God for it. Then broke it in pieces and said, 'This is My body, which is given for you. Do this in remembrance of Me.'

Christianity Today speaks of a writer Makoto Fujimura who wrote a book 'Art and Faith.' His book describes a centuries old art form known as 'Kintsugi.' Ceramic bowls, broken into pieces, are joined back together and remade – but not as they were before. Gleaming gold is set into the seams between the shards. The resulting pieces are unique and more complex, more beautiful, and more valuable than they were before.

As I read the paragraph of this story describing broken pieces, I think of Jesus and how his body was beaten, broken and bruised. This also happens to us as we live our life and we make harsh mistakes that breaks other people's spirit but, in the end, we will be better than before. Remember, the spirit of God can bring unity out of division and love out of enmity. He can make us anew, not as we were before but as we were meant to be, ever more like Christ.

PRAYER: Almighty God, thank You for your Holy Spirit and making us better than before. Also, thank You for putting the pieces back together in our lives when we are broken. AMEN

DON'T FORGET!

# SPIRITUAL RENEWAL

SCRIPTURES: Psalm 23:3; Ephesians 4:23-24; I John 1:5

WRITERS: Psalm—David; Ephesians—Paul; I John—John the Apostle

DEFINITION: renew—to restore freshness, vigor, or perfection; to make new spiritually

Psalm 23:3 'He renews my strength. He guides me along right paths, bringing honor to His Name.

Ephesians 4:23-24 'Instead, let the Spirit renew your thoughts and attitudes. Put on your new nature, created to be like God-truly righteous and holy.'

I John 1:5 'This is the message we heard from Jesus and now declare to you. God is light, and there is no darkness in Him at all.'

I was involved in a property rehab project a couple of years ago and I noticed the following about this project—tons of mildew, green slimy bricks, facia boards looking rotten, overgrown flower beds and the likes. Basically, just a run-down place that had not received attention and personal care for a very long time.

Work began to repair the facia boards, power washing of the brick and doorways, weeding of flower beds, hedges trimmed and digging up of shrubs that needed room for others to grow were removed. Before long, a new amazing look came into play and the renewal of something that looked like it was headed for trash became a treasure. The value quickly changed. The yard was also now manicured and now, a new beginning for the property and the neighbors no doubt appreciated it as well.

There is a great parallel between this example and how we need sometimes to have a spiritual renewal in our own lives. The weeds in our lives are represented by sin in many varieties. Yet, it is still sin. The facia boards that are rotten and the buildup of algae is indicative of just immoral decay on our part. Then, a renewal happens because confession causes us to see things how they really are, and in doing so, we begin to confess and address things that have long needed to be confessed and addressed.

PRAYER: Heavenly Father, help us to spend more time in honest self-assessment, confession and repentance. AMEN

DON'T FORGET!

# TIME TO MEDITATE

SCRIPTURE: Romans 5:8-9

WRITER: Paul

DEFINITION: meditate—to contemplate, reflect, or ponder

Romans 5:8-9 'But God showed his great love for us by sending Christ to die for us while we were still sinners. And since we have been made right in God's sight by the blood of Jesus Christ, He will certainly save us from God's condemnation.'

Remember the last time you got in a hot mess? Then you were searching for a nice way as well as an easy way to get out? It seems that we are always looking for a quick fix with the least amount of resistance. Why not meditate....

Sometimes we look at situations and minimize how critical they are yet we want to turn our heads and hope that it will fix itself. Along with that sometimes comes physical pain and we also hope that will go away. Why not meditate....

We all have the same twenty-four hours in a day and if we really put that on paper as to where our times goes, we will quickly find out that it is in every area of our life than where we really need to be. Parking tickets two days in a row, career expectations on the side line, debt is increasing and our time reading the Bible and prayer time with God is on an as needed basis. Why not meditate....

Mark out a time each month in which you can plan a time to meditate on the cross of Jesus Christ. It is a perfect slow down to really consider all that our relationship to Christ really is each day. Why not meditate....

We all know the reason in which we need such a carved-out time is because of sin. Sin occurred in the world just as it was created. Sin separates us from God. Sin's highway is destruction and we cannot buy our way out of it. It truly is a terminal disease. Why not meditate....

Jesus Christ gave his life as an act of suffering, death as well as a resurrection. It was all necessary in God's plan for the world. There was no other way to reverse what sin had done to the world.

Take time to meditate on forgiveness, reconciliation and the new life that Jesus Christ offers and then be thankful for His love.

PRAYER: Most Gracious Lord, help us to meditate often and give thanks for the great things You have done for us. AMEN

DON'T FORGET!

# PRICELESS

SCRIPTURES: Ruth 3:11; Romans 5:4

WRITER: Samuel

DEFINITION: character—moral excellence and firmness; main or essential nature

Ruth 3:11 'Now don't worry about a thing, my daughter. I will do what is necessary for everyone in town knows you are a virtuous woman.'

Romans 5:4 'And endurance develops strength of character, and character strengthens our confident hope of salvation.'

I recall some time ago plenty of athletes that were and are sponsored by certain companies and especially credit card companies. I will not name the company but the slogan is today's title. I want you to take a trip with me today back to when you were growing up, taking family trips during the summer, having holiday get togethers with family and even exciting times of success for us as individuals. You would step back and say, 'that was a priceless time or even a priceless moment.'

Life changing courage is what we learn from the story of Ruth and where she ends up rather than where she began. For Ruth, she searched out an opportunity to work in the grain fields and pick up dropped grain in order to survive. Ruth's love for her mother-in-law and her faith in a foreign God, led her out of safety and community into a new life not only isolated but also dangerous. Ruth wanted to be part of God's plan and through being faithful, she was redeemed by Boaz and married him and also was blessed with a son. Ruth began with sorrow but ended with joy. Ruth begins with death but ends not only with life but with a son, Obed, who ultimately is to have 9 grandsons, including David, Israel's greatest king. This is a priceless string of events that take place in Ruth's life that impacted the lives of others.

We have to remember that sometimes in life that we have to endure certain events and those events in life will build character that is needed to glorify God and his Kingdom.

PRAYER: Almighty God, thank You Lord for endurance, trials and challenges along the way in life. It makes us depend on You and place our full trust each day. AMEN

DON'T FORGET!

# HOLY

SCRIPTURES: Leviticus 19:2; Leviticus 20:7; Ephesians 4:24

WRITERS: Leviticus—Moses; Ephesians—Paul

DEFINITION: holy—consecrated or set aside for sacred use; standing apart from sin and evil; characteristic of God, especially the third person of the Trinity

Leviticus 19:2 'Give the following instructions to the entire community of Israel. You must be holy because I, the Lord your God, am holy.'

Leviticus 20:7 'So set yourselves apart to be holy, for I am the Lord your God. Keep all my decrees by putting them into practice, for I am the Lord who makes you holy.'

Ephesians 4:24 'Put on your new nature, created to be like God – truly righteous and holy!

We are all called to be holy in this life on earth. We are supposed to be set apart, keeping God's commandments and seeking to live a life that will build others up for the Glory of God.

When we think about how the word 'Holy' stands alone, we always think of God. No one else, none other, only God. Then we study the scriptures and it is very clear the instructions that are given to us to follow and I guess just due to sin in our lives and around us, we miss the mark.

Moses shares in Leviticus early on that we are to be set apart, that does not mean better than others, simply separate on different level of commitment to our Lord to truly follow Him and then the kicker is to put them into practice. Practice in my book is something that is done over and over again until it becomes habit. I remember in college playing basketball and practicing my free throws, shot a hundred each day, six days a week and increased the percentage of success. This is the same with striving for holiness. Put on your new nature today and stive to be righteous and holy in a good way giving glory to God.

PRAYER: Most Gracious Lord, we recognize and praise Your Holy name. Thank You for all You do for us in our lives. AMEN

DON'T FORGET!

# PRAYER OF POWER

SCRIPTURE: Psalm 69:13-17

WRITER: David

DEFINITION: prayer—conversation with God – in praise, thanksgiving, or intercession

Psalm 69:13-17 'But I keep praying to you, Lord, hoping this time you will show me favor. In your unfailing love, O God, answer my prayer with your sure salvation. Rescue me from the mire, do not let me sink, deliver me from those who hate me, from the deep waters. Do not let the flood waters engulf me or the depths swallow me up or the pit close its mouth over me. Answer me, O Lord! Out of the goodness of your love; in your great mercy turn to me. Do not hide your face from your servant; answer me quickly, for I am in trouble.'

Prayer is powerful. Prayer is quiet time, one on one, you and God. Prayer is a step back from the daily grind to evaluate where one really is in their daily walk. Prayer provides a deeper walk because it is that special time that we strive to seek answers and direction. Prayer is pursuit of the ONE who saved us. Prayer is obedience to the One who gave His all for us. Prayer is grace and mercy that is provided on a daily basis if we are seeking Christ. Prayer is anytime, day or night, crisis or not, healthy or sick, the Lord is always protecting us in everything we do. Prayer is special because we get to approach Almighty God knowing and trusting that He hears our petitions, our thanksgiving and our heart. Prayer proves the one true connection that matters the most in life. Prayer is power because of God's goodness and His love for us no matter what we are confronted with.

Pause, take time and pray to the One who loves you more than anyone in this world. He created the world and He created you. A Prayer of thanksgiving to Him for His power is all you need.

PRAYER: Dear God, thank You Lord, for prayer and the ability to have conversation and communication with the One who loves us most. AMEN

DON'T FORGET!

# COURAGE TO DO HIS WORK

SCRIPTURE: Mark 16:1-4

WRITER: Mark

DEFINITION: courage—mental or moral strength, brave

Mark 16:1-4 'Saturday evening when the Sabbath ended, Mary Magdalene, Mary the Mother of James, and Salome went out and purchased burial spices so they could anoint Jesus' body. Very early on Sunday morning, just at sunrise, they went to the tomb. On the way they were asking each other, 'Who will roll away the stone for us from the entrance to the tomb?' But as they arrived, they looked up and say that stone, which was very large, had already been rolled aside.'

When I think of courage, I think of a lot of people and their stories to overcome. But, the story of the stone being rolled away is a great example of faith and love. Mary Magdalene, Mary and Salome are no doubt broken hearted having witnessed the death of Jesus. They have purchased some burial spices to anoint the body of Jesus and honor Him as well. However, they are already thinking about the issue that faces them and that is the 'very large' stone will need to be removed for them to have access to Jesus' body.

Literally hours ago, the events that had taken place were Judas betraying Jesus, The Last Supper, Peter's predicted denial, Jesus and his disciples going off to pray at Gethsemane, Peter to the courtyard, Pilate releasing Barabbas, Pilate turning over Jesus to the Roman soldiers, Jesus being beaten, spit on, mocked, Simon carrying the cross for Jesus to Golgotha, Jesus nailed to the cross, curtain in the temple split, death of Jesus.

Joseph of Arimathea approaches Pilate for Jesus' body. He takes the body down from the cross, wraps it in linen he purchases and laid Jesus in a borrowed tomb. Then rolls a very large stone to cover the carved out burial tomb. Mary Magdalene, Mary, Mother of Joseph experienced what happened and yet also along with Joseph had the courage to honor and bless their Lord.

PRAYER: Almighty God, help us to always have the courage that we need to go the extra mile for You. Help us to always show up regardless of things going on in our life. AMEN

DON'T FORGET!

# HIS BENEFITS

SCRIPTURE: Psalm 103:2-5

WRITER: David

Psalm 103:2-5 (NKJV) 'Bless the Lord, O my soul, and forget not all His benefits: Who forgives all your iniquities, Who heals all your diseases, Who redeems your life from destruction, Who crowns you with loving kindness and tender mercies, Who satisfies your mouth with good things, so that your youth is renewed like eagle's.'

Congratulations on your new job. Your resume sent to the human resources manager got approved and sent to the zone manager who approved moving forward to interview you locally and give you the job. Your benefits package will give you two weeks paid vacation, ten sick days, two personal days, an average salary plus bonuses if you perform at certain markers, a retirement plan, a medical insurance plan with a high deductible and cost sharing measures to also help benefit the company. We have all heard this mumbo-jumbo and guess what? It is just a job and believe or not, you will not stay with this company very long since they are always on the lookout for another you with a bit more talent and younger, if they can get it. The average number of job changes in one's lifetime is ten to fifteen different times. Ouch…..

Let's speak about benefits from God that really matter and last a lifetime. Also, you don't have to make changes, just one commitment to follow Christ and the following are headed your way: Peace, joy, love, kindness, forgiveness, mercy, humility, humbleness, longsuffering, goodness, faithfulness, gentleness, mercy, faith, confidence, encouragement, courage, honor, hope, patience and compassion. Lifestyle features such as physical health, family, home, fun family activities, friends, and freedom to travel are also great benefits from God.

I don't have to remind you that we all feel empty, alone and on the outs sometimes. That is because self-righteousness, pride, jealousy, selfish ambition and envy can destroy our souls.

A daily commitment of choosing to bless the Lord and to consider how God's love really is there for us gives us the best gifts.

PRAYER: Most Gracious Father, thank You for the benefits that You bless us with each day of our lives. AMEN

DON'T FORGET!

# ARE YOU GOING TO QUIT?

SCRIPTURES: II Timothy 2:3; Philippians 1:29-30

WRITERS: II Timothy—Paul; Philippians—Paul

DEFINITION: suffering—the state or experience of one that suffers

Trouble—a state, condition, or cause of distress, annoyance, difficulty, or inconvenience

II Timothy 2:3 'Endure suffering along with me, as a good soldier of Christ Jesus.

Philippians 1:29-30 'For you have been given not only the privilege of trusting in Christ but also the privilege of suffering for Him. We are in this struggle together. You have been my struggle in the past, and you know that I am still in the midst of it.'

When I think about the word 'quit,' it makes my stomach turn and literally everything from within me to say no. I am not going to quit. We see many examples in the Bible about adversity, overcoming obstacles, trials, tribulation, challenges, troubles and pitfalls. The question today is how will we deal with issues and bigger than that, 'Are you going to quit' or stick it out and overcome?

Beth Moore quotes the following about quitting, 'Much of the war against the devil is about whether you will quit.'

You go grocery shopping and you have picked up necessities for meals, some additional items that were not needed but wanted and then just a bunch of random junk items. You get to the cashier and guess what, your debit card or credit card is declined. Do you quit or do you fix the situation?

You stop at the convenience store and you just want to get a fifty-nine-cent drink with ice. You come back out and notice that someone was texting on their phone and overshot the parking spot and rammed into the side of your vehicle.

We could share example after example of events that go on that can push us to want to quit in life. However, God's word clearly states that we will have struggles, trials and the like but, when troubles hit, take it as an opportunity to grow and to expand our abilities to succeed. So, never give up and don't quit.

PRAYER: Almighty Redeemer, thank You Lord for all you do for us on a daily basis. Help us to always keep our head in the game and to always persevere. Quitting is not an option. AMEN

DON'T FORGET!

# COMMIT TO THE JOURNEY

SCRIPTURES: Colossians 3:23-24; Ephesians 2:10; Jeremiah 29:11

WRITERS: Colossians—Paul; Ephesians—Paul; Jeremiah—Jeremiah

Colossians 3:23-24 'Work willingly at whatever you do, as though you were working for the Lord rather than for people. Remember that the Lord will give you an inheritance as your reward, and that the Master you are serving is Christ.'

Ephesians 2:10 'For we are God's masterpiece. He has created us anew in Christ Jesus so we can do the good things He planned for us long ago.'

Jeremiah 29:11 'For I know the plans I have for you saith the Lord. They are plans for good and not for disaster, to give you a future and a hope.'

I love the word commit. It means that someone is 'all in.' Webster's dictionary definition is 'to do' or 'to perform.' How committed are you to the journey? I have some one liners that I like and I try to put as many of them into action as I am able:

- Go to work and do your job and have a strong work ethic
- You can do more than you think you can
- We don't have problems ahead of us, we have opportunities
- You have to expect things of yourself before you can do them
- No matter what happens today good or bad, you have to show up tomorrow and do it again to the best of your ability
- Knowing where you want to end up is the key to the journey
- You only get out of something what you put into it
- The difference between ordinary and extraordinary is the little extra

How is your walk with Christ today? Are you where you really need to be and if not, are you ready to change? Let me give you encouragement to commit to the journey and do not try to go it alone.

PRAYER: Almighty God, thank You for Your love and the plans that You have to prosper us and bless us for now and in the future. AMEN

DON'T FORGET!

# AT ALL COST, YOU
# HAVE TO BE THERE

SCRIPTURES: Philippians 4:7; Hosea 10:12

WRITER: Paul

Philippians 4:7 'Then you will experience God's peace, which exceeds anything we can understand. His peace will guard your hearts and minds as you live in Christ Jesus.'

I was recently reading a new book titled 'It's Not Your Turn' with a picture of a stop light on the cover. When I saw the advertisement, it made me think about my current situation in prison. I am in the early stage of my sentence seeing people that have served their time being called out and preparing them for re-entry into society. It's not my turn at this time. Then I started reading the book and enjoying some very nice stories that touched my heart. As I as reading one particular story, it pricked my heart on something that we all need to be aware of each day.

When we think about just how important life is and how short that it can be when things like accidents, pandemics, and health situations can all turn life from a longevity to something much shorter. So, you ask, where am I going with this story. At all costs, whatever you have to do, don't miss heaven. You have to be there when this world finishes and Jesus calls us home. Perhaps you say well, I still have things that I want to do in my life and I don't want to be rushed into thinking that I might miss something. Again, stop long enough to concentrate on how much God has blessed our lives and how important it really is.

Hosea 10:12 says, 'Plant the good seeds of righteousness, and you will harvest a crop of love. Plow up the hard ground of your hearts, for now is the time to seek the Lord, that He may come and shower righteousness upon you.'

So....don't miss the life of salvation and the ability to follow the One who gave His life for us.

Matthew 24:36 says, 'However, no one knows the day or the hour when these things will happen, not even the angels in heaven or the Son himself. Only the Father knows.' At all cost, you have to be there so don't miss it!

PRAYER: Father God, help us not to miss You or anything about Your love for us. AMEN

## DON'T FORGET!

# FORGIVENESS, RECONCILIATION, CHANGE

SCRIPTURES: Hebrews 9:14; II Corinthians 3:18

WRITERS: Hebrews—Unknown; II Corinthians—Paul

DEFINITION: forgiveness—acquitted or pardon of sins

> reconciliation—to restore to friendship or harmony, especially between God and humans

> change—to make different or transform; to shift, exchange or transfer

Hebrews 9:14 'Just think how much more the blood of Christ will purify our consciences from all sinful deeds so that we can worship the living God. For by the power of the eternal spirit, Christ offered himself to God as a perfect sacrifice for our sins.'

II Corinthians 3:18 'So all of us who have had the veil removed can see and reflect the glory of the Lord. And the Lord—who is the Spirit—make us more and more like him as we are changed into his glorious image.'

I guess that I would have to say that at the place in my life where I am today that I am probably the best example of forgiveness, reconciliation, and change simply due to my current circumstances. I am serving a prison sentence for having done wrong in society and harming individuals financially. I recall at my sentencing having the opportunity to speak to the judge, attorneys, as well as the victims affected. I had thought about what God would place on my heart as I addressed each one of them on literally the day that would affect my future, my loved ones, my family, my friends, my church and onlookers that had been following my case. On my Zoom hearing, I apologized from the bottom of my heart to all those affected by my actions. I then gave my word to the judge that it would never happen again. I asked for forgiveness from those harmed and then I shared that based on being a believer that God had forgiven me.

I then desired to reconcile with those closest to me so I could be restored in my life to be able to look forward and move forward. I have done that with God's help and direction. Today, I am most thankful for forgiveness, reconciliation and change.

PRAYER: Almighty God, thank You for forgiveness, love, mercy and grace. We can only be transformed by allowing You into our life for a personal daily walk. AMEN

DON'T FORGET!

# FREEDOM IN CHRIST

SCRIPTURES: Psalm 119:45; Galatians 2:4; Ephesians 1:7

WRITERS: Psalm—David; Galatians—Paul; Ephesians—Paul

DEFINITION: freedom—liberation from slavery, restraint, or the power of another

Psalm 119:45 'I will walk in freedom, for I have devoted myself to your commandments.'

Galatians 2:4 'Even that question came up only because of some so-called believers there – false ones, really – who were secretly brought in. They sneaked in to spy on us and take away the freedom we have in Christ Jesus.'

Ephesians 1:7 'He is so rich in kindness and grace that he purchased our freedom with the blood of His Son and forgave our sins.'

Because of Jesus,

> We are enough…
> We are secure…
> We are the salt of the earth.
> We are cared for…
> We are seen…
> We are forgiven.
> We are free…
> We have hope.
> God is love and that means we are loved.
> God is peace, and His peace lives in us.
> God is enough, and we are filled with His enoughness.
> God is who He says He is, and He made us to be His beloved.

Anonymous

In Christ, we walk in freedom. We devote ourselves to His commandments. He purchased our freedom with the blood of Jesus and forgives our sins.

PRAYER: Almighty God, thank You for the freedom we have through Your Son, Jesus Christ. AMEN

DON'T FORGET!

# CHURCH IS HARD
## John Waldron

- Church is hard for the person walking through the doors, afraid of judgement.
- Church is hard for the prodigal soul returning home, broken, and battered by the world.
- Church is hard for the girl who looks like she has it all together, but doesn't.
- Church is hard for the couple who fought the entire ride to service.
- Church is hard for the single mom, surrounded by couples holding hands, and seemingly perfect families.
- Church is hard for the widow or widower with no invitation to lunch after service.
- Church is hard for the person singing worship songs overwhelmed by the weight of the lyrics.
- Church is hard for the wife who longs to be led by a righteous man.
- Church is hard for the single woman and the single man, praying God brings them a mate.
- Church is hard for sinners.
- Church is hard for me.

It's hard because on the outside it all looks shiny and perfect, Sunday best in behavior and dress. However, under those layers, you find a body of imperfect people, carnal souls, and selfish motives.

But here is the beauty of the church....

- Church isn't a building, mentality or expectation.
- Church is a body.
- Church is a group of sinners saved by grace, living in fellowship as saints.
- Church is a body of believers bound as brothers and sisters by eternal love.
- Church is a holy ground where sinners stand as equals before the Throne of Grace.
- Church is a converging of confrontation and invitation.

Where sin is confronted and hearts are invited to seek restoration.
- Church is a lesson in faith and trust.
- Church is a family. A family coming together, setting aside differences, forgetting past mistakes, rejoicing in the smallest of victories.

Remember, He has NEVER failed to meet me there.

PRAYER: Lord God, we fully believe in all You do and all You are. Continue to guide us in all we do. AMEN

## DON'T FORGET!

# HAVE YOU BEEN
# RADICALLY CHANGED?

SCRIPTURES: John 1:18; Colossians 1:17

WRITERS: John—John; Colossians—Paul

John 1:18 'No one has ever seen God. But the unique One, who is Himself God, is near to the Father's heart. He has revealed God to us.'

Colossians 1:17 'He existed before anything else, and He holds all creation together.'

Knowing Jesus personally radically changes your life. Knowing about Him does not do much good unless you are experiencing Him personally. To know Jesus personally, one must abide with Him, live in His presence, hear His whisper, and understand what brings Him pleasure and how He desires to work with you, in you and through you.

Jesus has a plan for each of us if we will simply surrender our all to Him and begin to make a radical change.

Think back in your life to a time when you had things going on in your life and noticed day after day that you did not like what was mounting up in your life. Bad choices, wrong attitudes, tarnished friendships along with other things that really took you away from the commitment that you needed to make as well as to keep to live a life for Christ.

When you think about the word 'radical,' it gives you the opportunity to quickly think outside the box and to get to a new level in life that exceeds anything that you have experienced ever before.

Perhaps there are people that you have been meaning to share Christ with and for whatever reason, it has not happened. Maybe it is a situation where you have wronged someone and you need to make it right with them. These are good examples that we can take a radical approach and go for it and begin making the impact that we are capable of doing.

PRAYER: Heavenly Father, thank You for the radical approach You took to give Your life for a sinful world. We are not deserving but we are appreciative. AMEN

DON'T FORGET!

# WHO IS GOD TO YOU?

SCRIPTURES: John 1:1; John 14:6

WRITER: John

John 1:1 'In the beginning the Word already existed. The Word was with God, and the Word was God.'

John 14:6 'Jesus told him, 'I am the Way, the Truth, and the Life. No one can come to the Father except through Me.'

This is not a test question, but it is the most important question to answer when one considers a personal relationship with Jesus. For me, I think about everything God has done for me in my life and the blessings He has bestowed upon me and my family.

Jesus is the most unique individual in the history of the world. He deserves the highest place in our heart and in our life. When you commit all you have to Him, your one-on-one relationship will catapult to new levels. Stress levels will be lower, favor on your life will be higher and then through the touch of the Holy Spirit, you will little by little impact those around you.

So, who is God to you? Is he someone way off in outer space that you know is around only to acknowledge His existence or is there an intimate relationship that you are seeking so you can develop a daily walk? God is always there to give us strength, comfort, direction and love for all of our needs.

Forgiveness, mercy, grace, steadfastness, faithfulness, humility, kindness, foundation, savior, advocate are just a few of the adjectives that describes who God is to me. My Savior, my Lord, my Redeemer, my Comforter, my Father in whom I am very thankful for each second of the day.

PRAYER: Lord God, 160 miles from my home, in a position of uncertainty in prison and being in a new environment, I find You, Your guiding spirit and Your love. Thank You. AMEN

DON'T FORGET!

# HOPE

SCRIPTURES: Romans 15:13; Psalm 42:5; Proverbs 13:12

WRITERS: Romans—Paul; Psalm—Solomon; Proverbs—Paul

DEFINITION: hope—confident trust with the expectation of fulfillment.'

Romans 15:13 'I pray that God, the source of hope, will fill you completely with joy and peace because you trust in Him. Then you will overflow with confident hope through the power of the Holy Spirit.'

Psalm 42:5 'Why am I discouraged? Why is my heart so sad? I will put my hope in God! I will praise him again – my Savior and my God!'

Proverbs 13:12 'Hope deferred makes the heart sick, but a dream fulfilled is a tree of life.'

Not everything in life is pleasant. HOPE is not a passing feeling but an active force. HOPE is not based on feelings, but on the potential of better things to come. There is a future! Focus on nutrition, hydration, rest, exercise, fellowship, and the mind/soul to cultivate HOPE. HOPE stands against suffering and exploitation. Pain is not permanent, but it gives us time for growth and maturity. Pain loses in the end! HOPE lives through pain. Pain reminds us that we are alive, it gives us the opportunity to comfort others. HOPE is a choice. To choose despair assumes a foreordained outcome. Wisdom chooses HOPE because the future cannot be fully determined. HOPE is essential for life. HOPE and fear cannot occupy the same space. Invite HOPE to stay!

My Dad for many years has shared with me the 'Open Windows' devotional. He would highlight some of the topics that he felt I should read and apply to my life. I am reminded of HOPE when I see an Open Windows. A belief in opportunity, the ability to experience a change, something new. HOPE is so important and integral to life each day because it gives a person something to look forward to in the future. For us, that is a side by side walk with Jesus.

PRAYER: Most Gracious Lord, thank You for the hope that You give us each day in you. It is all we need and we thank You. AMEN

DON'T FORGET!

# WHAT IF?

SCRIPTURE: I Corinthians 9:24-27

WRITER: Paul

I Corinthians 9:24-27 'Don't you realize that in a race everyone runs, but only one person gets the prize? So run to win! All athletes are disciplined in their training. They do it to win a prize that will fade away, but we do it for an eternal prize. So, I run with purpose in every step. I am no just shadowboxing. I discipline my body like an athlete, training it to do what it should. Otherwise, I fear that after preaching to others I myself might be disqualified.'

- What if God couldn't take the time to bless us today because we couldn't take time to thank Him yesterday?
- What if God decided to stop leading us tomorrow because we didn't follow Him today?
- What if we never saw another flower bloom because we grumbled when God sent the rain?
- What if God didn't walk with us today because we failed to listen to His message?
- What if God didn't send his only begotten Son because He wanted us to prepare to pay the price of sin?
- What if God stopped loving and caring for us because we failed to love and care for others?
- What if God would not hear us today because we would not list to Him yesterday?
- What if God answered our prayers the way we answered His call to service?
- What if God met our needs the way we give Him our lives?
- What if we failed to pass along His message?

There are many 'what ifs' in life. Don't miss out on how your life changes when you choose Jesus.

PRAYER: Heavenly Father, thank You for the 'what ifs' that you give us in life. The ability to think, to reason, to ponder, to trust. We love You. AMEN

DON'T FORGET!

# PRAYER TO PERSEVERE

SCRIPTURES: Luke 18:7; I Timothy 6:11-12

WRITERS: Luke—Luke; I Timothy—Paul

DEFINITION: perseverance—to continue in a course of action even in the face of difficulty or with little or no prospect of success

Luke 18:17 'Even he rendered a just decision in the end.'

I Timothy 6:11-12 'But you, Timothy, are a man of God; so, run from all these evil things. Pursue righteousness and a godly life, along with faith, love, perseverance, and gentleness. Fight the good fight for the true faith. Hold tightly to the eternal life to which God has called you, which you have declared so well before many witnesses.'

God intervenes. He listens. He always hears our prayers. He doesn't overlook someone who prays! This part of scripture about prayer is consciously put here. The chapter is talking about the return of Christ and the way people live right before his coming. A time of decline. In the following chapter, we read that Jesus is blessing the children and He also says we need to have faith like children. In between those chapters we read our text about the necessity of prayer and perseverance.

We may see a lot of misery around us, or even in our own life we can experience hardship. Sometimes God allows things to happen we don't understand. And yet, we must stay confident! Don't stop praying…persevere. But how? It's really simple, pray from our heart. There is no need for beautiful words. One word is enough, just like a child would do! After all, we are His children.

PRAYER: Most Gracious Heavenly Father, thank You for challenges in life that drive us to perseverance. It helps us to always look to You. AMEN

## DON'T FORGET!

# AUDACIOUS FAITH

SCRIPTURES: Hebrews 11:6; II Corinthians 9:2

WRITERS: Hebrews—unknown; II Corinthians—Paul

DEFINITION: audacious—daring, bold, insolent

Hebrews 11:6 'And it is impossible to please God without faith. Anyone who wants to come to him must believe that God exists and that He rewards those who sincerely seek Him.'

II Corinthians 9:2 'For I know how eager you are to help, and I have been boasting to the churches in Macedonia that you in Greece were ready to send an offering a year ago. In fact, it was your enthusiasm that stirred up many of the Macedonian believers to begin giving.'

I can honestly share with you that God has truly blessed with 'Audacious Faith' the devotions from Oakdale project. I am nearing seven months with literally a handful of writings left to go. Through my first seven months in federal prison, one might ask, 'How has it been for you there?' To live on a compound of nearly 2,000 inmates. Yet day to day I am around 100 other men who have or are serving from 22 years down to sentences of less than a year. I have seen a lot of things, heard a lot of things and experienced a lot of things. I have felt many emotions for myself as well as seeing emotions from grown men that are like me, away from loved ones, family and friends. You have to know that without an audacious faith, one would not be able to make it. This not an easy experience by any stretch of the imagination. But I also know that I am here for a specific reason.

I am here at the Oakdale Federal Prison Camp to impact and shape the lives of those men that God has called me to live with, work with, serve with until my sentence has been completed. I prayed to God before I came here that he would pave the way before me. I did not pray that it would be easy because I knew that would not be the case for me. I did something wrong; I am sorry for what I did and I have been forgiven by the ONE who died on the cross for me. I am thankful for grace, mercy and love that I am shown each and every day. Audacious faith makes things easier for me on a daily basis.

PRAYER: Almighty Father, thank You for faith in You and love from You that makes life worth living and sharing. AMEN

DON'T FORGET!

# THE DON'T FORGETS
# OF YOUR LIFE

SCRIPTURES: I Corinthians 10:12-13; Galatians 5:22-23

WRITERS: I Corinthians—Paul; Galatians—Paul

DEFINITION: don't forget—something that you do not want to ever forget that has had an influence in and on your life.

I Corinthians 10:12-13 'If you think you are standing strong, be careful not to fall. The temptations in your life are no different from what others experience. And God is faithful. He will not allow the temptation to be more than you can stand.'

Galatians 5:22-23 'But the Holy Spirit produces this kind of fruit in our lives: love, joy, peace, patience, kindness, goodness, faithfulness, gentleness, ad self-control. There is no law against these things.'

I had an awesome opportunity eleven years ago to author my first book, 'The Don't Forgets of Life.' Today, this writing is about the Don't Forgets of Your Life.' We all have things that happen in our life. A prompting from the Holy Spirit, a God moment, a God wink, just something out of the norm and one can only step back and recognize it was of God. That is a don't forget. Perhaps it is a relationship with a spouse, a new friendship that you were not expecting or even a special coincidence or event that just happens to take your breath away.

I want to challenge you as I am winding down the 'Devotions from Oakdale' and think about the many don't forgets that God has blessed you with in your life. Answered prayers in one's life is a must to recognize a special don't forget especially when you are not expecting something.

I can say without a doubt that I am truly blessed to be where I am in my life and I am super excited with the possibilities of the journey that God has for me. Think about your Don't Forgets today.

PRAYER: Lord God, thank You for all of the special moments that You continue to bestow upon me. I am a very blessed man. AMEN

DON'T FORGET!

# BOLDNESS

SCRIPTURES: Philippians 1:20; I Chronicles 17:25; Hebrews 4:16

WRITERS: Philippians—Paul; I Chronicles—Ezra; Hebrews—unknown

DEFINITION: boldness—fearless before danger; self-assured, confident, prominent, a daring spirit

Philippians 1:20 'For I fully expect and hope that I will never be ashamed, but that I will continue to be bold for Christ, as I have been in the past.'

I Chronicles 17:25 'Oh my God, I have been bold enough to pray to You because You have revealed to your servant that You will build a house for him-a dynasty of Kings.'

Hebrews 4:16 'So let us come boldly to the throne of our gracious God. There we will receive His mercy, and we will find grace to help us when we need it most.'

'I can do it!' 'You can make it happen!' 'Take the step of faith to believe it can take place' These are but a few statements that have been said that exhibit boldness. Boldness screams confidence in one's life and speaks of one's ability to believe that a specific situation can be accomplished.

Think about your life right now and the certain scenarios where you need to step forward with an attitude of boldness. Perhaps you have lived a life where your self-esteem is not at the level you would prefer it to be. Today can be your day. All you have to do is believe, expect, hope, pray, and have faith that you can live a life of boldness.

We have to be bold to ask and have faith. We have to be bold to believe in ourselves. We have to be bold enough to regularly activate our faith by asking God for big 'don't forget' outcomes. We have to be bold in the stand that we take for Christ every day.

Lastly, we have to have the boldness to choose right from wrong and stay away from sin. Be bold today in Christ!

PRAYER: Most Gracious Lord, thank You for Your love, Your kindness, Your touch in our lives each day. May we have the boldness to always share about You with others. AMEN

DON'T FORGET!

# NO PLAN 'B'

SCRIPTURES: Psalm 90:17; Jeremiah 29:11; Hebrews 11:6

WRITERS: Psalm—David; Jeremiah—Jeremiah; Hebrews—unknown

DEFINITION: plan 'b'—an alternative, a fallback position; an easier way to perhaps do life if the real thing fails

Psalm 90:17 'And may the Lord our God show us his approval and make our efforts successful. Yes, make our efforts successful! (NLT)

Jeremiah 29:11 'For I know the plans I have for you, declares the Lord. They are plans to prosper you and not to harm you, plans to give you hope and a future.' (NIV)

Hebrews 11:6 'And it is impossible to please God without faith. Anyone who wants to come to Him must believe that God exists and that He rewards those who sincerely seek Him.'

We have all heard it before in our lifetime. Once we explain a situation or a plan to someone like a family member or a friend, they ask, so, what is your 'Plan B' if it doesn't work?

God's word clearly states that 'without faith it is impossible to please God.' So, here is a quick question to get your mind going today. Are you in spiritual survival mode? Have you eased off into spiritual mediocrity? Maybe the 'faith' thing has just not worked well for you so far?

Remember, faith is a force that gets you to the next level. It is a better way, a higher calling and a more intimate connection with the One who loves us the most.

Recently, I read through a car magazine that showed off all of the navigational systems, touch screens and voice recognized activators and it was pretty amazing to see how technology continues to progress. God's GPS system in our lives is similar. God knows our direction and He knows which way in life we need to go. Sometimes God leads us to a dead end so we can see Him show up to be there for us. We need to always be expectant in our faith, our trust and in our personal relationship with Him. Then, we need no 'Plan B' with God. He is the only way and He is our plan through Jesus our Lord and Savior.

PRAYER: Heavenly Father, thank You that we are not in need of a 'Plan B' with You in our life. There are plenty of things, stuff, and obstacles that can get in the way but You are the only one that matters. AMEN

DON'T FORGET!

# HE IS OUR ADVOCATE

SCRIPTURES: I John 2:1; John 15:26; Philippians 2:8

WRITERS: I John—John; John—John; Philippians—Paul

DEFINITION: advocate—one who pleads the cause of another; someone that helps

I John 2:1 'My dear children, I am writing this to you so that you will not sin. But if anyone does sin, we have an advocate who pleads our case before the Father. He is Jesus Christ, the one who is truly righteous.'

John 15:26 'But I will send the Advocate-the Spirit of Truth. He will come to you from the Father and will testify all about Me.'

Philippians 2:8 'He humbled Himself by becoming obedient to the point of death-even to death on a cross.'

I remember being introduced into an advocacy program when I was in the financial services business. One particular man had designed an instructional overview of advocacy and how someone would refer you and they would be an advocate for you. Jesus Christ is our advocate in that He represents us each day before God. When we sin, we are guilty of a wrong against God. We enter a plea, therefore confessing, I am guilty. Jesus speaks on our behalf, pleading our case through His blood that was shed for us on the cross.

It is the advocacy of Jesus that makes us whole. He offers Himself to receive our penalty and He took the punishment for our sins. As soon as we can understand what Jesus has done for us, then we can allow for His influence of his love upon our lives.

When you can make some time, sit and ponder just exactly how great of an advocate Jesus has been for you in your life. We all cross over the line and sin and then we get entangled in situations that we are not good at getting out of and still understand what just happened. Jesus knows our heart, our timing of mistakes, yet He still steps in to preserve our relationship with the Father.

How is your relationship with Christ Jesus, our advocate?

PRAYER: Gracious Heavenly Father, thank You Father for Jesus being my advocate each and every day. AMEN

DON'T FORGET!

# WHAT'S HAPPENING?

SCRIPTURES: Deuteronomy 31:6; Psalm 37:4

WRITERS: Deuteronomy—Moses; Psalm—David

Deuteronomy 31:6 'So be strong and courageous? Do not be afraid and do not panic before them. For the Lord Your God will personally go ahead of you. He will neither fail you nor abandon you.'

Psalm 37:4 'Take delight in the Lord, and He will give you your heart's desire.'

How do you spend your time and what is it like where you are?

I have to tell you that I have been surrounded by God's presence years before my arrival at Oakdale. Upon arriving at Oakdale, God's hand was and is protecting me every step I make, every thought I think, every action that takes place along with His perfect timing from the men that He has put in my life as well as the friendships that have grown from each one of them. As for my time, I work 8 hours a day doing what I love to do and that is serving people, magnifying the name of Jesus and striving to impact the men around me for God's Kingdom.

We all live demanding lives to some degree and that is why I am going to challenge you to step away from your fast paced life and answer a few questions. List three of the most important things that have ever happened to you. Next, list your most important struggle that you have ever faced and then share how you overcame that struggle. Last, share about the most wonderful gift that you have ever been given.

As you go through this short exercise, think of the things that you need to let go of as well as the things that are holding on to you. Hopefully, this will free you to seek Jesus more fully and to celebrate what He has done for you. So....what's happening with you in your life? Be strong and courageous and take delight in the Lord!

PRAYER: Thank You for making things happen in our lives each and every day that moves us towards You. May we always be mindful of all You do. AMEN

DON'T FORGET

# 'SPIRITUAL WAR' –
# THE STUMBLING BLOCKS

SCRIPTURE: Ezekiel 14:1-5

WRITER: Ezekiel

DEFINITIONS: stumbling blocks—anything or anyone that leads you to desire to do something that is wrong in the eyes of God (sin)

Idols—any person, place, or thing that exercises control over thoughts and desires of your heart that only God should have

Ezekiel 14:1-5 'Then some of the leaders of Israel visited me, and while they were sitting with me, this message came to me from the Lord: 'Son of Man, these leaders have set up idols in their hearts. They have embraced things that will make them fall into sin. Why should I listen to their requests? Tell them, 'This is what the Sovereign Lord says: The people of Israel have set up idols in their hearts and fallen into sins, and then they go to a prophet asking for a message. So I, the Lord, will give them the kind of answer their great idolatry deserves. I will do this to capture the minds and hearts of all My people who have turned from Me to worship their detestable idols.'

We are all faced with some form of spiritual warfare on a daily basis. The reason, our daily battle with sin. It is what makes friendships strained, marriages face difficulty, as well as parenting our children. Spiritual war is also about materialism, gotta have more stuff, gotta do what the next-door neighbor does along with things that just seem to trip us up. Just look around you, you will see it right in front of you. Our kids and grandkids are being exposed to so many things at such an early age that it is frightening to say the least. Again, spiritual warfare.

You may say, 'I don't experience those kinds of things that you are talking about and I sure don't have any idols in my life. Your neighborhood 24-hour gym can become an idol for you. If it exercises control over you, then it is an idol. Perhaps you are spending time away from your family at business functions and dinners. Where is your spouse? Business has become your idol. Vehicles, money, more, more and more stuff can begin to take over. Materialism has become your idol.

God is saying that whatever is taking over your heart will without a doubt control your behavior. Also, whatever captures your mind, your thoughts and then initiates direction, that leads to idolatry. What are the desires of your heart?

Are you spiritually safe? Strive today for a deeper relationship with the One who loves you and died for you. That person is Jesus Christ!

PRAYER: Heavenly Father, thank You Lord for showing us the stumbling blocks that are in our life today. May we veer away and draw closer to You. AMEN

DON'T FORGET!

# ON A DIFFERENT LEVEL

SCRIPTURE: Luke 6:27-31

WRITER: Luke

DEFINITION: compassion—sympathy, usually granted because of unusual or distressing circumstances

Luke 6:27-31 'But to you who are willing to listen, I say, love you enemies! Do good to those who hate you. Bless those who curse you. Pray for those who hurt you. If someone slaps you on one cheek, offer the other cheek also. If someone demands your coat, offer your shirt also. Give to anyone who asks; and when things are also taken away from you, don't try to get them back. Do to others as you would like them to do to you.'

Listen, lover, do good, bless, pray, offer and give. These are words described in our text today that calls us to a different level. The so called 'golden rule' of life is not always easy to follow through on when unusual circumstances happen to us and around us. When we see the phrase speaking of being slapped on the cheek, it is really an insult. Jesus says for us to take the insults even though what we really want to do is throw it back at them. We have it inside of us to quickly strike back with our tongue. That is not what we are called to do.

Jesus calls us to pray for those that hurt us and cause us to stumble.

The act of showing compassion on our part is to not belittle or run others down. We are to make them feel important, loved and cared for. Why? Because they matter. We have to remember that it is easy to love those who are like us. We also must love those who make our lives difficult. I can attest to the opportunities that have been before me from my indictment all the way through my sentencing. I understand how compassion is needed for everyone. Even when we are mistreated and things feel difficult, we are still to pray for those who wrong us and treat us in challenging ways. Take a stand to do the right thing and lift those around you to a different level.

PRAYER: Almighty God, thank You for Your compassion. Thank You for all circumstances that we are faced with so we can always look to You for our answers.

DON'T FORGET!

# CREATE RIPPLE EFFECTS

SCRIPTURE: Luke 6:35-38

WRITER: Luke

Luke 6:35-28 'Love your enemies! Do good to them. Lend to them without expecting to be repaid. Then your reward from heaven will be very great, and you will truly be acting as children of the Most High, for He is kind to those who are unthankful and wicked. You must be compassionate, just as your Father is compassionate. Do not judge others, and you will not be judged. Do not condemn others, or it will come back against you. Forgive others, and you will be forgiven. Give, and you will receive. Your gift will return to you in full-pressed down, shaken together to make room for more, running over, and poured into your lap. The amount you give will determine the amount you get back.'

I remember specifically a trip with my Paw Paw and Mee Mee when we drove to Colorado and were on a river doing some rainbow trout fishing. Before we began to fish, my Paw Paw picked up a couple of flat rocks. The river was as smooth as glass. He slung a rock and it skimmed on the water making the most beautiful ripple effect and then the rock dropped beneath the water. He then handed me a rock and told me to take a turn. Oh my, how cool was that! Rock after rock, ripples small and large. What a great weekend spending time with him and learning basic rock skipping.

Our Christian walk is very similar to the rock example being tossed on the top of the water. People cross us, they wrong us. We are not to judge or condemn. We forgive and then we share Christ with them through our actions.

Are you creating ripple effects in the lives of others? It is not as hard as you think it is. A simple smile, a kind word, a nice gesture can create effects that convert over to a new friend, a new Christian believer, all because of the actions you display. Be aware that every action just as that of tossing a rock can have a ripple effect that will come back to you. Try it today!

PRAYER: Dear God, thank You for Paw Paws and Mee Mees of this world that have poured into our lives that are still creating ripple effects in the lives of our own children and grandchildren. AMEN

DON'T FORGET!

# PAY MERCY FORWARD

SCRIPTURE: Psalm 86:15; Romans 9:15; James 3:17-18

WRITER: Psalm 86—David; Romans—Paul; James—James

DEFINITION: mercy—a blessing that is an act of divine favor or compassion; withholding of the punishment or judgment our sins deserve

Psalm 86:15 'But You, O Lord, are a God of compassion and mercy, slow to anger.'

Romans 9:15 'For God said to Moses, 'I will show mercy to anyone I choose, and I will show compassion to anyone I choose.' So it is God who decides to show mercy. We can neither choose it nor work for it.'

James 3:17-18 'But the wisdom from above is first of all pure. It is also peace loving, gentle at all times, and willing to yield to others. It is full of mercy and the fruit of good deeds. It shows no favoritism and is always sincere. And those who are peacemakers will plant seeds of peace and reap a harvest of righteousness.'

I always love the holidays and what it brings to individuals who are looking to impact others. Paying things forward is always neat because people are not expecting something nice someone does to lift their feelings, emotions and their spirit.

I have a few challenges for you today beginning with some ideas on how to pay mercy forward. Pay for someone behind you in a fast-food line. Surprise them! Leave an extra tip for your server when they are not expecting it. It is the little things in life that always make a huge difference. The unexpected phone call when someone has lost a loved one, a visitor that drops in just to say hello and to let you know they care. These are acts of paying mercy forward.

You can never go wrong sharing compassion with those around you. We can all use a divine blessing, favor and mercy in our lives. Life is always full of challenges, peaks, valleys and accomplishments. The real question is how things can be shared in life with others so they know that we are genuine and that we honestly care about them.

Always remember to pay all things forward to give honor and glory to God.

PRAYER: Most Gracious Father, thank You for mercy, compassion and love that You freely give us each and every day. AMEN

DON'T FORGET

# THE DON'T FORGETS
# OF OAKDALE

SCRIPTURES: Hebrews 11:1; Ephesians 1:13-14; Ephesians 3:19

WRITERS: Hebrews—unknown; Ephesians—Paul

Hebrews 11:1 'Faith shows the reality of what we hope for, it is the evidence of things we cannot see.'

Ephesians 1:13-14 'And now you Gentiles have also heard the truth, the Good News that God saves you. And when you believed in Christ, He identified you has His own by giving you the Holy Spirit, whom He promised long ago. The Spirit is God's guarantee that He will give us the inheritance He promised and that He has purchased us to be His own people. He did this so we would praise and glorify Him.'

Ephesians 3:19 'May you experience the love of Christ, though it is too great to understand fully. Then you will be made complete with all the fullness of life and power that comes from God.'

What you hold in your hands is the final devotion titled 'The Don't Forgets of Oakdale.' This journey to write 40-day devotional booklets has turned into a 365-day devotional. There have been a few anonymous writings along the way but each of the titles have come by the way of the Holy Spirit and his promptings on what to share. This process began with my oldest daughter recommending that I write some devotions while being in prison. One, to pass the time, another to inspire and lastly, to watch how God could put pen to paper to impact many readers around the world.

I am very thankful for the devoted loved ones that have been involved in this process on a daily basis to make this happen with me.

I am reminded daily that I have been sealed by the precious blood of Jesus. Our Heavenly Father wrote the contract for us, sent His Son to pay for our sins. He also put a seal of ownership on each of us, branded us with the Holy Spirit to show His ownership and the contract does not require our signature. It is a unilateral contract that simply states that we only have to believe.

My greatest prayer and desire in writing the devotions from Oakdale has been to share the gospel of Jesus Christ in an understanding fashion. To clearly depict that the only way to make it in this life is through a personal relationship with Jesus as our Lord and Savior. Also, I strive to place scripture along with daily readings that will give you, the reader, a desire to dig deeper. To build your self-esteem so you would believe in God's word and trust in Him. My heart is so touched and moved for you taking time daily to invest in yourself through His Word and encouragement.

May God bless you and give you the desires of His heart.

DON'T FORGET!

GREG SMITH....

# ABOUT THE AUTHOR

Gregory A. Smith is married to Cheri Smith. He is a graduate of Seminary Extension of the Southern Baptist Convention with a diplomas in Ministries/Pastoral Education and in Theological Foundations. A public speaker and author who loves to be around people and impact their lives for good.

Greg served in the financial services industry for 28 years and had 3,000 relationships prior to serving a prison sentence at Oakdale Federal Correctional Institute from January 2021 to December 2023.

Greg is the proud father of three beautiful daughters. He is also PawPaw to seven wonderful grandchildren.

Greg and Cheri reside in Shreveport, Louisiana where they are both speakers with their 501 ©(3) Non-Profit – 49 Ministries Foundation along with Magnificent Marriage, LLC where they will lead married couples at weekend marriage conferences.

# HAVE YOU BEEN BLESSED
# BY READING THIS BOOK?

Please help others receive these words by donating
to 49 Ministries. We are a registered 501 © (3)
not for profit organization in the United States
and all donations are tax deductible.

We are a small organization with a big mission.
Your donation makes all the difference. Monthly
or one-time donations are gratefully accepted.

OFFICE IN THE UNITED STATES

49 Ministries Foundation
2154 Silverwood Drive
Shreveport, Louisiana 71118
Contact us at
318-470-2254
or
df49ministries@att.net

To purchase this book please visit Amazon

# NOTES

# NOTES

# NOTES

# NOTES

# *Salvation*

## God's Plan of Salvation for Your Life

Do you feel stuck in life? Don't have the answers and just do not know what would happen if you died today? The answer is simple. Trust God and ask Jesus Christ into your heart today. Then, go share with someone in a Bible believing, Bible teaching church, that you have committed your heart to God. That community of believers will point you in the right direction in learning about daily prayer time and daily Bible Study.

*Romans 6:23 "For the wages of sin is death, but the free gift of God is eternal life through Christ Jesus."*
*(Turn away from sin and face Christ)*

*Romans 8:28 "And we know that God causes everything to work together for the good of those who love the Lord, and are called according to His purpose."*
*(Love the Lord with your heart)*

*Romans 5:8 "But God showed His great love for us by sending Christ to die for us while we were still sinners."*
*(God sent His son Jesus to die on the cross)*

*Romans 8:1 "So now, there is no condemnation for those who belong to Christ Jesus." (Belong to Him)*

*Romans 10:9-10 "If you openly declare that Jesus is Lord and believe in your heart that God raised him from the dead, you will be saved." For it is by believing in your heart that you are made right with God, and it is openly declaring your faith that you have been saved. (Public Profession)*